Robert Hovenden

The Register Booke of Christninges, Marriages, and Burialls

Within the Precinct of the Cathedrall and Metropoliticall Church of Christe

Robert Hovenden

The Register Booke of Christninges, Marriages, and Burialls
Within the Precinct of the Cathedrall and Metropoliticall Church of Christe

ISBN/EAN: 9783337132903

Printed in Europe, USA, Canada, Australia, Japan

Cover: Foto ©Lupo / pixelio.de

More available books at **www.hansebooks.com**

The
Register Booke
OF
Christninges, Marriages, and Burialls
WITHIN THE PRECINCT OF THE
Cathedrall and Metropoliticall Church of Christe of Canterburie.

EDITED BY

ROBERT HOVENDEN.

LONDON:

1878.

PREFACE.

Of the Register Books of Canterbury Cathedral containing entries of Christenings and Burials, subsequent to 1812, and of Marriages subsequent to 1756, it is needless to offer any remarks, they being of the usual printed forms in accordance with the several Acts of Parliament; but of the remaining books, all manuscripts, it may be well to place on record the following notes.

The earliest register is a vellum book, containing the entries of christenings from the year 1564, marriages from 1583, and burials from 1571, in each case terminating with the year 1687. In the second book, also of vellum, are the christenings and marriages commencing with 1687, and the burials with 1688, each ending in 1733. In the third book, also of vellum, the entries commence with 1733, the marriages terminating, with the exception of ten special entries, in 1756; the christenings and burials in 1812. With the exception of the marriages, these three books constitute the Register proper of the Cathedral, recording an uninterrupted series to 1812. In addition to these three manuscript books, there is another vellum book entitled "The Register Booke of Burialls within the Precincts of the Cathedrall and Metropoliticall Church of Christ In Canterbury according to the direction of a late Act of Parliament for burying in Woollen," the first entry in which is dated September 5th, 1678, the entries being continued regularly until October 21, 1722, when a blank page occurs, the next being 29th November, 1725. After this date the book appears to have been kept irregularly until the 18th October 1798, the date of the last entry; in one instance a space of four years occurs without any burial being registered. Although these entries are duplicates of the burial register for the same period, they contain in addition the date when the certificate was produced to the Cathedral Authorities, certifying that the burial had been made in woollen in accordance with the law. Several instances are recorded of burials otherwise than in woollen, the amount of fine paid for the breach of the Act of Parliament, and to whom it was paid.

At the time the transcript was made for the printer the manuscripts here enumerated comprised the contents of the Register Chest, and as they presented a continuous record, no others were expected; but when the present volume was two-thirds printed, mention was made of another book—an index—that should be in existence, although not in the chest. The Reverend Sacrist undertook the necessary inquiries, and a little investigation produced the Index, a manuscript such as is seldom found in parish register chests. It consists of a tradesman's long folio account book of some 350 leaves, ruled with money columns, the second page being headed "An Alphabetical Account of the Registers for Baptisms, Burials, and Marriages in the Cathedral of Christ Church, Canterbury, copied from several books kept in an Iron Chest in the Vestry. May 29th, 1846. W. Bennett, Sacrist." It is what its title professes it to be, namely, an alphabetical transcript of the Registers, so that upon turning to the christenings under letter A will be found all the entries of names commencing with that letter, arranged in chronological order from the beginning of the Register to 1846. The christenings are transcribed on one side of the leaf only, the opposite page being reserved for occasional notes; the marriages and burials occupy both sides, filling the book. The first, third, and fifth pages contain notes from "Burn on Parish Registers," and observations upon the Registers themselves. Thus, under date of 1620, will be found: "about this time the mother's name is seldom mentioned;" "that Mr. is added to the Xtian name;" 1638, "ff used instead of F;" 1641, "Frances indifferently used for a male or female name;" "Clacay, a singular name;" "Sackbutier, query what?" 1663, "Prebend improperly for Prebendary." This manuscript has been restored to its proper place in the chest, where it is desirable it should ever remain, in close companionship with the Registers themselves, and as a memorial to the Reverend compiler, to whom is due the hearty thanks of all those who have to make searches.

Although the Registers of Christenings commence as early as 1564, it is very doubtful whether they are a perfect record prior to 1597, the date of the Canon by which it was ordered that the paper registers should be transcribed on parchment. The entries to this date convey an impression that they have been registered from memory, or oral information; not transcribed from an older book. For instance, the first four entries of the Christenings, covering a period of eight years, relate to the Pownoll family. In like manner, the first entries in the Marriages and Burials relate to the same family. Nor can the first seven entries in the present Burial Register, extending over a period of twenty-six years, be taken as a complete record of all the interments in that period, the older plans of the Cathedral shewing that in addition to the interior of the building, the Chapter House, the Cloysters, and the Cloyster-yard, the present open space south of the Cathedral, and perhaps some of the ground now enclosed as gardens to the Canons' residences, was formerly used as a cemetery. This is confirmed by the burial of Ann Constance, August 28, 1665, and by the two following burials, she being "Buryd in the south side of the Church where not any before by the space of forty yeares at the least have bin buried." In the Lady Chapel is a stone recording the burial of Dean Rogers, who died May 19th, 1597. Somner, in his 'Antiquities of Canterbury' (edition 1640, p. 184), mentions that monuments existed to William Lovelace and Anne his wife, 1576; of Dobs, an Alderman 1580; and Lady Crook, 1579. If the evidence of these inscriptions inside the building can be relied upon, assuming that Somner is correct, and that the dates represent burials; and also assuming that the desires to be buried within the Cathedral expressed in the wills of inhabitants of Canterbury who died between 1571 and 1597 were fulfilled, it is then certain that a number of interments took place during this period of which no record exists in the present Register.

It is difficult to believe that no earlier records than 1597 existed. Their absence may be accounted for by the too frequent cause that they were lost. Assuming this to be the case, it is strange that the present books contain no note to that effect; on the other hand, as the Cathedral was, and still is, extra-parochial, it is within probability that no earlier register did exist, and that all entries of christenings, marriages, and burials within the Cathedral and its precincts were made in the Register Books of the various parishes in which the persons resided. For instance, in the adjoining parish of St. Alphage there are several entries of burials, both in the Cathedral and its adjoining Churchyard, the earliest being "the xxij daye of M'che 1558 was buryed Will'm Stephens in Christ Church yearde."

Although there are many entries in the Registers of St. Alphage of burials of persons who died of the plague, it is remarkable that there is not a single entry in the Cathedral Registers in which the word Plague, or the equally well known letter P, occurs.

With the exception of the marriages, the entries relate principally to the clergy and their families who resided within the precincts; but during the latter years the precincts include some places of business adjoining the Cathedral buildings; many entries consequently record the trades of the various persons named. In the first half of the eighteenth century, the Cathedral was evidently the favourite resort for marriages of the inhabitants of the eastern part of the county, and the Registers are interesting in giving the locality of a number of Kentish yeoman families.

In transcribing the original for the press, the dates in all cases have been modernized, and for uniformity placed at the commencement of each entry. In all other respects the spelling and style have been as closely adhered to as the type will admit; no attempt has been made to interfere even with palpable errors or contractions of the original scribe. Thus, at page 115 will be found an entry: 1620. June 22. The Lady Thornx (or Thornix). This is as nearly as the name can be read, it being evidently a contraction for Thornehurst. In every such case it has been left for the genealogist to place his own construction upon the entry.

On behalf of the Members of the Harleian Society, I have to acknowledge the courtesy of the Dean and Chapter for permission to print these interesting Registers, and for the facilities so kindly extended to me while passing them through the press; and I am particularly indebted to the Reverend Frederick Rouch, the Sacrist, for his hearty assistance during the time the originals were in his custody.

R. HOVENDEN.

CROYDON,

November, 1878.

The Registers

OF

Canterbury Cathedral.

CHRISTENINGS.

Year.	Month.	Day.	Names.
1564	December	3	Abdias, the sonne of Robert Pownoll
1567	April	26	Barnabas, the sonne of Robert Pownoll
1569	June	1	Ezechiell, the sonne of Robert Pownoll
1572	February	10	Posthumus, the sonne of Robert Pownoll
1580	November	6	Elizabeth, the daughter of John Winter
1581	February	5	Nicolas, the sonne of Nicolas Simpson
1582	October	28	Elizabeth, the daughter of Richard Colfe
1583	February	17	Joane, the daughter of Nicolas Simpson
1583	July*	7	William, the sonne of John Winter
1584	November	18	Catherin, the daughter of John Winter
1589*	April	2	Anne, the daughter of Thomas Boys
1587	March	5	Elizabeth, the daughter of Will'm Walsall
1587	August	13	Isaack, the sonne of Richarde Colfe
1588	August	25	Roger, the sonne of John Winter
1589	December	25	Jacob, the sonne of Richard Colfe
1590	May	3	John, the sonne of Thomas Boys
1590	January	18	Joseph, the sonne of Richard Colfe
1592	October	29	Elizabeth, the daughter of Richard Colfe
1590*	August	23	Margaret, the daughter of Will'm Walsall
1592	October	26	John, the sonne of William Walsall
1593	June	10	Thomas, the sonne of Thomas Boys
1593	November	18	John, the sonne of John Wynter
1594	July	7	Frauncis, the daughter of Thomas Boys
1594	March	21	Elizabeth, the daughter of Will'm Walsall
1595	February	29	Richard, the sonne of Thomas Boys
1596	March	9	Richard, the sonne of Richard Colfe
1596*	April	4	Frauncis, the daughter of Will'm Walsall
1597	July	10	Elizabeth, the daughter of Thomas Boys
1598	October	1	Anne, the daughter of Richard Colfe
1598	November	19	Peter, the sonne of Thomas Boys
1598	November	19	Hope, the daughter of John Mainwaringe
1597*	December	4	Martin, the sonne of Martin Fotherbye

* So in the original.

Year.	Month.	Day.	Names.
1598	November	10	John, the sonne of Martin Fotherbye
1599	October	21	Margaret, the daughter of John Mainwaringe
1599	December	16	Anne, the daughter of Rufus Roger
1599	December	21	Edwarde, the sonne of Thomas Boys
1599	December	27	Anne, the daughter of Goldwell Roger
1599	The last day of February		Ciceley, the daughter of Martin Fotherbye
1599	March	2	Anne, the daughter of Adam Longworth
1600	June	22	John, the sonne / Elizabeth, the daughter } of John Miller
1600	February	6	William, the sonne of Will'm Walsall
1601	April	16	Neuile, the sonne of Edwarde Whitegraue
1601	May	17	Marie, the daughter of Rufus Roger
1601	May	24	William, the sonne of Adam Longworth
1601	May	24	Mabell, the daughter of Charles Fotherbye
1601	June	5	Afra, the daughter of William Warriner
1601	June	28	Cicelie, the daughter of George Marson
1601	November	1	Elenor, the daughter of Arthure Cocke
1601	November	1	Hope, the daughter of Richarde Birde
1601	November	29	Marie, the daughter of Martin Fotherbye
1601	January	3	Margreatt, the daughter of Thomas Calldom
1601	March	2	Bengiamin, the sonne of Richard Colfe
1602	April	12	Being Easter daye, Ann, ye daughter of Edward Whitgraue
1602	June	20	John, the sonn of John Maneringe
1602	August	15	Susana, daughter of Mr Thomas Boyce
1602	September	8	Anne, the daughter of Mr Golldwell Rogeres
1603	July	15	Margreat, the daughter of Mr. Masssters
1603	September	12	Peter, the sonne of Mr Richard Bird
1603	October	2	Hurselaw, the daugter of Mr Ewell
1603	October	21	Charlles, the ssonn of Mr Martayn ffotheresby
1603	December	9	John, the sonn of Mr Collf
1603	December	9	Jann, the daughter of M^r haman of the beshores pallas
1603	January	25	Thomas, the sonn of Edward Whitgraue
1603	January	27	Pelludia, the daugter of Mr Adam Langworth
1604	August	31	John, the sonne of Rufus Roger
1604	January	27	George, the sonne of Mr Doctor Clarke
1604	March	5	Cislye, the daughter of Mr Masters one of the wor' prebendaries
1604	March	6	Ralfe, the sonne of Mr Colfe one of the wor' prebendaries
1605	April	5	John, the sonne of Adam Langworth
1605	August	28	Pelludia, the Daughter of Mr. Birde one of ye wor' prebendaries
1605	February	23	James, the sonne of Mr Doctor Clarke
1605	February	23	Nicolas, the sonne of Mr Nicolas Sympson
1605	March	2	Frances, the sonne of Mr Marson
1605	March	11	Martine, the sonne of Mr Masters one of the wor' prebendaries
1606	April	3	Ralfe, the sonne of Mr Rufus Roger
1606	April	13	Marye, the daughter of William Wariner
1606	June	29	Marget, the daughter of John Miller
1606	July	5	Frances, the sonne of Mr Addam Langwoorth
1606	August	25	Pelludia, the daughter of Thomas Caldam
1606	January	4	Adrian, the Sonne of Mr Dee
1606	February	22	Lea, the daughter of James Nicoles
1607	April	7	Charles, the sonne of Mr Masters one of the worshipfull prebendaries

Year.	Month.	Day.	Names.
1607	June	21	Elizabeth, the daughter of William Wariner
1607	July	12	Anne, the daughter of Mr Frances Roger
1607	September	27	John, the Sonne of Mr. George Marson
1607	November	22	Elizabeth, the Daughter of Mr. Addam Langworth
1608	March	27	George, the sonne of Mr Masters one of the worshipfull prebendaries
1608	May	15	Thomas, the sonne of Mr. Leader
1608	September	13	Elizabeth, the daughter of Mr Rufus Roger
1608	February	26	William, the sonn of Doctor Clarke
1609	May	25	Thomas, the sonne of Mr Masters one of the worshipfull prebendaries
1609	October	29	Margaret, the daughter of Mr Marson
1609	November	26	Thomas, the sonne of Doctor fothersbye one of the worshipfull Prebendaries
1609	January	4	John, the sonne of Goodman Shotwater
1609	January	18	Frances, the sonne of Mr Nicolas Simpsone
1610	July	24	Kenburrow, the daughter of Doctor Masters one of the worshipfull prebendaryes
1610	October	8	Richard and Marye, ye sonne and daughter of Doctor fothersbye, one of the worshipfull Prebendaries
1610	December	27	William, the sonne of William Sawkins, borne at paddoc
1611	April	7	Roger, the sonne of William Warriner
1611	April	21	Marye, the daughter of Doctor Clarke
1611	April	28	Katheren, the daughter of Mr Nicholas Sympsonne
1611	August	4	Thomas, the sonne of Mr Nicolas Parker
1611	September	27	Jone, the daughter of Doctor Masters
1612	April	5	Phebe, the daughter of Mr Marson
1612	May	12	William, the Sonne of William Warriner
1612	June	4	Margaret, the daughter of Mr Nicholas Sympson
1612	August	21	Ellenor, the Daughter of Mr Nicholas Parker
1612	September	12	Thomas, the sonne of Thomas Calda'
1612	October	28	Beniaben, the sonne of Doctor Master
1613	June	20	Ann, the Daughter of Mr Hanken
1613	September	26	Peludia, the Daughter of Richard ffilcockes
1613	September	28	William, the sonne of Doctor Clarke
1613	December	2	Anne, the daughter of Doctor Masters
1613	December	26	Debora, daughter of Mr Nicholas Sympson
1614	April	24	Being Easter daye, Elzabeth, the daughter of Mr Doctor Fothersbye
1614	May	27	Elzabeth, the Daughter of Sir John Wilde Knight
1614	June	7	Valentine, the Sonne of Mr Nycholas Parker
1614	July	19	Margaret, the daughter of Willia' Warriner
1614	September	28	William, the sonne of Mr Browne
1614	October	30	Aphora, the daughter of Mr Merrewether
1614	November	28	John Shepherd
1614	November	28	Tunstall Scott, Sonn of Mr William Scott, the Sonn in lawe to the worsheipfvll Mr Tunstall, prebendary of this church
1614	December	15	Catheren Tenterden, daughter of Mr John Tenterden, kinesman to mr do. huntt, one of the worshipfull prebends of our churche
1615	December	11*	Anna, the daughter of Richard Fylocck
1615	April	13	Peter Tebball, Sonn of William Tebball
1615	May	15	Dudly Jackson, Sonn of Mr Doctor Jacksonn
1615	July	20	Mary warriner, daughter of Mr Mathew warriner pety canon
1615	August	27	Charlles Simpsonn, sonn of Mr Doctor Simpsonn

* So in the original.

Year.	Month.	Day.	Names.
1615	February	20	George Kingsle[y],* sonn of Mr Kingsle[y]* one of the worshipfull Prebendaries of this Church
1616	June	30	John, the sonn of Mr Barton
1616	July	14	John, the sonn of Mr Ludde
1616	August	29	Elizabeth, the daughter of Doctor Jacson one of the worshipfull Prebendaries
1616	August	29	John, the sonn of Mr Nicholas Sympson
1616	March	21	Sarai, the daughter of Rowland Vahan, Laye Clarke
1617	April	13	Damaris, the daughter of Doctor Masters
1617	May	4	John, the sonne of Roger Simpson
1617	May	29	Damaris, the daughter of Doctor Kingesle[y]
1617	June	18	Richard, the sonne of William Tybball of the paddock
1617	July	27	Richard, the sonne of Mr Warrinar
1617	August	12	Thomas, the sonne of Mr Nicholas Simpson
1617	December	7	Cysly, the daughter of Mr Robart Moyle
1617	December	21	Kathern, the daughter of Richard Filcock
1617	January	6	Bridget, the daughter of Mr Ludde
1617	January	24	John, the sonne of Doctor Clarke
1618	July	13	Joseph, the sonne of Mr Burrows
1618	July	29	Jayne, the Daughter of Doctor Masters
1618	July	30	Edward, the sonn of Michaell Boyle
1618	November	30	John Simpson, sonne of Doctor Simpson
1618	February	21	Anne, the daughter of Mr Fleet
1618	February	28	Elisabeth, the daughter of Richard Filcock
1619	April	28	Elisabeth Moyle, the daughter of Mr Robert Moyle
1619	May	9	Marie Tebball, the daughter of William Tebball
1619	July	14	Katherine Man, the daughter of Mr Man
1619	August	22	Elisabeth Lamb, the daughter of Mr James Lambe
1619	October	18	George Jackson, the sonne of Dr Jackson
1619	October	21	John Warriner, the sonne of Mr Warriner
1619	November	13	Katherine Clark, the daughter of Doctor Clarke
1619	December	5	Marie Boyle, the daughter of Michaell Boyle
1619	December	16	Dudley Wiles, the sonne of Sir John Wiles
1619	December	17	Nicholas Simpson, the sonne of Mr Roger Simpson
1619	March	5	Samford Ludd, ye sonne of Mr Ludd
1620	April	2	Katherine Kingsley, ye daughter of Doctor Kingsley
1620	April	13	Elisabeth Drayton, ye daughter of Mr Drayton
1620	May	3	Elisabeth Ager, ye daughter of Sir Anthony Ager
1620	May	11	Thomas Beuin, ye sonne of Mr Beuin
1620	October	14	Mary, ye daughter of Mr Player
1620	October	15	Nicholas Simpson, ye sonne of Docter Simpson
1620	October	19	Margaret Lucan, ye daughter of Mr Lucan
1620	November	19	John Lambe, the sonne of Mr [James]† Lambe
1620	March	16	Edmund, the sonn of William Woolton
1621	April	17	John, the sonn of William Tibball
1621	May	9	Elizabeth, the daughter of Doctor Kingsle
1621	September	6	John, the sonn of Mr Horton Drayton
1621	September	14	Alexander, the sonn of Rowland Vaham, Laye Clarke
1621	September	18	John, the sonn of John Barnarde, Laye Clark
1621	October	26	William, the sonn of Mr Player
1621	October	27	Thomas, the sonne of Sr Thomas Periam, Knight
1621	February	7	James, the sonne of Mr James Lambe
1621	February	18	Robart, the sonne of Matthew Washington
1621	March	7	Jerremye, the soonne of Henrye Sellers

* The letter "y" has been added in a later hand.
† James is written in a later hand.

Year.	Month.	Day.	Names.
1622	April	11	Marye, the daughter of Richard Filcocke
1622	May	10	William, the sonn of Mr Slatter
1622	May	20	William, the sonne of Doctor Kingsley Archdeco' of Canter:
1622	June	1	Robart, the sonne of Mr Lucann
1622	November	24	William, the sonn of William Woolton
1622	January	5	Marye, the daughter of Mr Horton Drayton
1622	February	21	Thomas, the sonn of Isacke Rainard
1622	March	4	Nicholas, the sonne of Doctor Simpson
1623	April	27	John, the sonne of Philemon Pownoll
1623	May	15	George, the sonne of Sirre William Barnes, Knight
1623	May	16	Elizabeth, the daughter of Mr John Colte
1623	June	15	Anne, the daughter of William Aurcher
1623	July	23	Phebe, the Daughter of Mr Robart Moyle
1623	August	8	Daniell, the sonne of William Tybball
1623	August	19	Susan, the Daughter of Mr John Ludde
1623	September	7	Edwinn, the sonne of Mr Edwin Auger
1623	October	18	John, the sonn of John Miller
1623	December	13	Mary, the daughter of Sr John Proud, Knight
1623	December	24	Edwinn, the sonne of Mr Lucann
1623	January	6	Willia', the sonne of Thomas Terre
1623	January	20	Angell, the daughter of Doctor Kingeslе[y]* Archdecon of Cant'
1623	March	10	Jayne, the daughter of Mr William Hamman
1623	March	12	Grace, the daughter of Mathew Washenden
1623	March	16	Damaris, the daughter of Mr Player
1623	March	21	William, the sonne of Mr James Lambe
1624	April	5	John, the sonne of Mr William Jaruis
1624	April	20	Frances, the daughter of Mr John Euerdath
1624	June	12	Jone, the daughter of Richard Filcock
1624	June	24	Thomas, the sonne of Doctor Challener
1624	July	22	William, the sonn of Isacke Raynard
1624	July	26	Sydne, the sonne of Sirre William Barnes, Knight
1624	September	30	John, the sonne of Mr John Coult
1624	October	14	Cyslye, the daughter of Mr Walter Mansell
1624	November	28	John, the sonn of Mr Sam'uell Rauen
1624	December	9	Elizabeth, the daughter of Mr John Ludde
1625	April	3	Swifte, the sonne of Thomas Witherden
1625	April	19	Prissilla, the daughter of Willia' Parker
1625	May	29	Alexsander, the sonn of Mr Horton Draiton—and Kinge Charles cac' to Can' the last of Maye to meete quene Marye
1625	June	2	Charles, the sonn of Doctor Kingeslе[y] Archdecon of Cant'
1625	June	20	Marye, the daughter of Doctor Sympson
1625	July	14	Kathern, the daughter of Mr James Clark
1625	August	4	Henry, the sonn of Mr John Lucann
1625	October	3	John, the sonne of Mr John Paine
1625	January	22	Isaacke, the sonne of Isacke Raynara
1625	January	29	Elizabeth, the daughter of Thomas Terre
1625	February	3	William, the sonn of John Joyce
1625	February	19	Mary, the daughter of Mr James Lambe
1626	April	5	Charles, the sonne of Doctor Saye
1626	April	6	Thomas, the sonne of John Euerer
1626	April	30	Sara, the daughter of Peter Goodhew
1626	July	2	Thomas, the sonne of Mr Thomas Ingham, Esquire
1626	July	23	William, the sonn of William Archer

* The "y" in a later hand.

Year.	Month.	Day.	Names.
1626	September	22	William, the sonne of Mr Doctor Kingeslye, Archdecon of Canterbury
1626	November	17	Izack, the sonn of Doctor Bargar, Deane of this Church
1626	December	3	Marye, the daughter of Mr Rouen
1626	March	4	Marye, the daughter of Peeter Swinford
1626	March	11	frances, the daughter of Mr William Watts
1627	April	3	Ham'on, the sonn of Richard Struggle
1627	April	11	Thomas, the sonne of William Parker
1627	April	24	Edwarde, the sonne of Thomas Witherden
1627	July	1	Hester, the daughter of Horton Drayton
1627	July	18	Phebe, the daughter of Mr Walter Mansett
1627	August	20	William, the sonn of Peeter Symon
1627	October	3	Frances, the daughter of Doctor Simpeson
1627	November	25	Marye, the daughter of Thomas Jaruis
1627	March	23	Thomas, the sonn of Isacke Rainard
1628	March	25	Susane, the daughter of Matthew Weste
1628	March	30	Robart, the sonn of Doctor Barger, Deane of this Church in his chapple
1628	June	29	Thomas, the sonne of Doctor Kingeslye, Archdecon of Canterbury
1628	July	4	Thomas, the sonne of John Joyce
1628	July	27	Katheren, the Daughter of John Eueret
1628	October	23	Alexsander, the son' of Mr James Lambe
1628	January	12	Peter, ye son'e of Peter Swinforde
1628	February	8	Isaack, ye son'e of Mr Horton Drayton
1629	April	6	John, ye son'e of William Archer
1629	May	17	Samuell, ye son'e of Samuell Rauen, Vsher of ye freeschoole
1629	May	31	Mary, ye daughter of Dor Bargraue, Deane of this church
1629	June	9	Elizabeth, ye daughter of Isaacke Rainard
1629	July	19	Thomas, ye son'e of Thomas Crumpton, gentleman
1629	November	18	Thomas, ye son'e of Thomas Jarvis
1630	April	15	Edwarde, ye son'e of William Tonstall, one of ye Lay Clarkes of this Church
1630	May	30	Susanna, ye daughter of Mr Anthony Marshall
1630	June	1	Henry, ye son'e of Mr John Euerarde was bapti.
1630	June	20	Sara and Dorathy, ye daughters of Do. Kingsly, Archdeacon of Canterbury
1630	October	12	Anne, ye daughter of Thomas Gilbarte
1630	October	21	William, ye son'e of Isaacke Rainarde
1630	November	5	Dorothy, ye daughter of Mr William Watts of London
1630	March	9	Mary, ye daughter of John Joyce
1631	March	30	Francis, ye daughter of Joseph Harte
1631	May	15	Martha, ye daughter of Peter Swinforde
1631	July	21	William, ye son'e of William Tunstall, one of ye lay Clarkes of this Church
1631	August	22	James, ye son'e of Mr Causabone one of ye worll Prebends of this church
1631	September	6	Anne, ye daughter of Dor Kingsly, one of ye wrll Prebends of this church
1631	September	11	Anne, ye daughter of Mr Horton Drayton, Auditor of this Church
1631	September	18	Margaret, ye daughter of William Archer
1631	October	23	Thomas, ye sone of Thomas Jaruis
1631	November	24	Katherin, ye daughter of Mr William Brockman
1631	January	8	Hester, ye daughter of Mr William Jordan, one of ye Peticanons of this Church
1632	April	22	William, ye son'e of John Somner

Year.	Month.	Day.	Names.
1632	July	26	Hellen, ye daughter of John Bix
1632	October	13	Mary, ye daughter of Do^r Kingsly, one of ye wor^{ll} Prebends of this Church
1632	December	23	Hester, ye daughter of Do^r Bargroue, Deane of this Church
1632	March	7	John, ye son'e of Thomas Denn
1632	March	14	John, ye son'e of William Tunstall
1633	April	28	Horton, ye sone of Mr Horton Drayton
1633	June	2	Elizabeth, ye daughter of Peter Swinforde
1633	August	16	Anne, ye daughter of John Bayly, one of the Lay clarkes of this Church
1633	September	1	Francis, ye daughter of William Dale
1633	December	12	Thomas, ye son'e of Mr John Marson, Peticanon
1634	April	7	Isaack, ye son'e of Mr Causabone, one of the Prebends of this Church
1634	April	24	Robarte, ye son'e of John Somner
1634	June	22	Anne, ye daughter of Mr William Wats
1634	July	27	Dorathy, ye daughter of John Bix
1634	August	17	William, ye sone of Mr William Jordan, one of ye Petticanons of this Church
1634	August	21	Thomas, ye sone of John Vincent, one of ye Lay Clarkes of this Church
1634	October	5	Mary, ye daughter of Mr Thomas Cater, Minister
1634	October	20	Mary, ye daughter of Doctor Peake, one of the worshipfull Prebends of this Church
1634	January	2	Thomas Tonstall, ye sonne of William Tonstall
1634	January	18	Damaris, ye daughter of Mr Ham'on Leucknor
1634	January	27	Susan'a, ye daughter of Peter Swinford
1634	February	20	Frances, ye sonne of Mr James Lambe
1634	March	11	Eliasbeth, ye daughter of Isaack Bargraue, Deane of Xst Church Cant.
1635	June	7	Mary, ye daughter of William Dale
1635	June	18	Hester, ye daughter of Mr Horton Drayton
1635	July	26	Jane, ye daughter of John Vincent, Lay clearke
1635	October	14	Thomas Bayly, ye sonne of Mr John Bayly, Lay Clercke
1635	November	2	Jane Pising, ye daughter of Mr William Pising, Layclercke
1635	December	15	James Rayner, Sonne of Isaack Rayner
1635	January	21	Katherine Beames, daughter of John Beames
1635	January	31	Charles Gibbons, Sonne of Mr Richard Gibbons, Lay Clark
1636	June	2	Gouldinge Bickes, Sonne of Mr Bickes, gent.
1636	June	28	George Somner, Sonne of John Somner
1636	July	24	John Causabone, Sonne of Mr Causabone, one of the wor^{ll} Prebendaries of this Church
1636	August	9	Charles Stooks, Sonne of Mr John Stokes
1636	August	18	John Skilton, Sonne of Robart Skilton
1636	December	1	Mary, ye daughter of Mr William Tonstall, Peticanon of this Church
1636	December	12	Martha, ye daughter of Do. Peake, one of ye wor^{ll} Prebends of this Church
1636	December	23	Anne, ye daughter of Do. Bleshenden, one of ye wor^{ll} Prebends of this Church
1636	December	28	Henry, ye son'e of Do. Bargraue, Deane of this Church, being sick was baptized at home ye 28th day of December, and brought to Church ye 8th day of Janu', and according to order receiued into ye congregation
1636	February	20	Margaret, ye daughter of Mr Lambe, one of ye Peticanons of this Church, was baptized ye 20th day of February

Year.	Month.	Day.	Names.
1637	March	25	Elizabeth, ye daughter of Richarde Kennarde, one of ye Substitutes of this Church
1637	June	26	Margaret, ye daughter of John Vincent, one of the lay Clarkes of this Churche
1637	September	23	Susanna, ye daughter of William Pisinge, one of ye Lay Clarkes of this Church
1637	October	27	John, ye sone of John Shorter
1637	January	10	Elizabeth Peake, daughter of Dr Peake, one of the wor^ll Prebendaries of this Church
1637	January	21	Elizabeth Gibbones, daughter of Mr Richard Gibbons, Lay Clarke
1638	April	29	William Drayton, Sonne of Mr Horton Drayton
1638	June	10	Mary, the daughter of John Ludlow, beinge very weake and sicke was Baptized at home, the 10th day of June, and brought to Church the 6 of July and receiued into the Congregation accordinge to order
1638	July	25	Thomas, the Sonne of James Hudsone
1638	August	21	Jane Anslow, daughter of ffrances Anslow
1638	August	24	Mary Vencent, daughter of John Vencent one of the Law (*sic*) clarks of this Church
1638	September	9	William Painter, Sonne of Christopher Painter
1638	December	16	John, ye sone of Mr Tunstall one of the peticanons
1638	January	19	Margaret, ye daughter of Richarde Gibbons, one of the lay Clarkes of this Church, being sick was bap. at home ye 19th day of January and brought to Church ye 20th of Janu' and according to order receiued into ye congregation
1639	May	14	Sybella, ye daughter of Mr Bayly, one of the Petticanons
1639	July	25	Isaack, ye sone of Mr Lambe, one of ye Peticanons of this church
1639	August	27	Thomas ye sone of Mr William Jordan, one of ye Peticanons of this church
1639	September	8	William, ye sone of John Shorter
1639	September	10	Whorton, ye sone of Richard Kennard
1639	October	27	Elizabeth, ye daughter of Mr John* Robartes, in Sr John Fothersby his house
1639	January	7	Mary, ye Daughter of Dr Blechenden, one of the Prebends of this Church
1639	February	21	Katherin, ye Daughter of Mr Christopher Berry, living in Mr Doctor Fruery (?) house
1639	February	22	Thomas, ye son of Merick Causabone, one of our Prebends, and Francis his wife, was baptized ye 22nd of February in his owne house, beinge weake And receyued into the Congregation ye 8th day of March
1639	March	19	William, ye son of William Dawe and Barbara his wife
1640	April	10	John, ye son of John Somner and Susanna his wife
1640	May	7	Johnamaria, ye son of Frances Ansloe and Clare his wife
1640	May	17	Leonard, ye son of Richard Gibbons, Laye Clarke, and Margarett his wife
1640	June	25	Margarett, ye Daughter of Mr John Bayliss one of the Petticannons, and Katherin his wife
1640	June	28	Judith, ye Daughter of Mr William Tonstall, one of ye Petticannons, and Margery his wife

* Interlined in the original.

Year.	Month.	Day.	Names.
1640	July	16	Frances, ye Daughter of Mr Horton Drayton, Auditor of Christ-church, and Freeman of the Citty of Canterberry, and Mary his wife
1640	August	13	Ann, ye daughter of Mr John Vincent, Lay-Clarke, was baptized at his owne house, being very weake, ye 13th of August and brought to ye Church ye next day, and according to order receyued into ye Congregation
1640	September	29	Robert, ye son of Robert Cumberland and Margaret his wife
1640*	December	10	William, the son'e of William and Francis Edfforth
1640*	December	14	Christopher, the son'e of Edward and Elizab. Mills
1640*	January	31	An'e, the daughter of Robert and Ellen Jynkinson
1640*	February	12	Elizabeth, the daughter of Dr Thom: Paske, Prebend of this Church, and An'e his wife
1640*	February	26	Edward, the son'e of Beniamin and Rebecka Jones
1640*	March	12	Thomas, the son'e of Dr Thom: Blechenden, Prebend of this Church, and Margaret his wife
1641*	June	3	Anthony, the son'e of John and Elizabeth Shorter
1641	July	4	Nicholas, the son'e of Henry White, Gentleman, and Margret his wife
1641	July	8	Susan, the daught. to Christopher and Clare Paynter
1641	August	8	Thomas, the son'e of Richard and Margaret Gibbons
1641	August	19	John, the son'e of Richard Wilkinson, Gentleman, and Francis his wife
1641	September	1	William, the son'e of William and Susan Pising
1641	September	20	An'a, the daughter of Christopher and An'a Berry
1641	September	27	Isaak, the son'e of Dr Merick Casaubon, Prebend of this Church, and Francis his wife
1641	October	21	Katharine, the Daughter of Mr Mathew Hadd, Esquier, and Margaret his wife
1641	November	18	William, the son'e of Mr George Kingsley and An' his wife
1641	December	5	An', the daughter of Mr William Jordan, Pettycanon of this Church, and Dorothy his wife
1641	December	19	Clacay, the daughter of Frances Ansloe, one of the †Sackbutiers of this Church, and Clacay his wife
1641‡	(January?)	15	Thomas, the son'e of Dr Humphry Peake, Prebend of this Church, and Mary his wife
1641‡	(January?)	25	Phebe, the daughter of Mr Henry Palmer, Esquier, and An' his wife
1641‡	(January?)	26	Phebe, the daughter of Daniel Bollen, Pettycanon of this Church, and Phebe his wife
1641	February	6	Peregrin, the son'e of Richard and Elizabeth Benson
1641	February	13	Francis, the son'e of John Vincent, Laye Clarke, and Mary his wife
1641	February	20	John, the Son'e of John and Edeath Ludlow
1642§	May	15	An', the daughter of Mr James Lamb, Pettic., and Susan his wife
1642	June	4	An', the daughter of Mr John and Lewey Boys
1642	July	24	Mary, the daughter of Dr Thomas Paske, Prebend of this Church, and An' his wife
1642	December	4	Margaret, the daughter of Dr Thom: Blechenden, Prebend of this Church, and Margaret his wife

* These entries have been overwritten at a more recent date.
† Sambucarius, one who plays on the sackbut.
‡ The month is not filled up in the original.
§ Overwritten and interlined in the original.

Year.	Month.	Day.	Names.
1642*	January	19	Susan, the Daughter of Robert and Ellen Jenkinson
1642*	March	3	Katharine, the daughter of Mr John Bayly, one of the Peticanons of this Church, and Ka: his wife
1643*	March	1 (?)	William, ye son of Mr Daniele Bollen, one of ye Peticannons of this Church, and Phebe (?) his wife
1643	March	30	Augustin Pising, the sone of William Pising, one of the Laye Clarkes
1643	June	5	Richard, the son'e of Richard Wilkenson, Esquier
1643	June	19	Nicholas, the son'e of Richard Kinard, Laye Clarke, and Mary his wife
1643	July	8	Ardnall, the son'e of Mr Mathew Hadd, Esquir, and Margaret his wife
1643	July	9	Mathew, the son'e of Richard Warrinar and Sarah his wife
1643	October	17	Dorathey, the Daughter of Mr William Jurdan and Dorathey his wife
1643	January	18	An'e, ye daughter of John Ludlow and Edith
1643	January	19	John Vincent, sone of John Vincent and Mary his wife
1644	June	27	Adry Masters, ye daughter of Mr Robert Masters
1644	October	13	Mary Gibbons, ye daughter of Mr Richard Gib:
1644	November	2	Rebecka Hadds, ye daughter of Mr Mathew Hadds
1644	December	4	Margaret Pising, ye daughter of William
1644	February	9	Lad Shorter, ye sonne of John
1645	May	29	John Jenkinson, ye sonne of Robert
1645	December	20	Robert Spratling, ye sonne of Mr Robert Spratling
1645	January	6	Elisabeth Masters, ye daughter of Mr Robert Masters
1645	January	22	Susanna Shorter, ye daughter of John Shorter
1645	March	9	Bartholomew, ye sonne of Mr James Lambe
1645	March	16	Anne, ye daughter of Michaell Richardson
1645	March	23	Anne Goffe, ye daughter of Mr John Goff
1646	July	12	Margery, ye daughter of Edward Cater and Ben'itt
1646	December	14	Rachaell Bowman, daughter of Walter
1646	January	8	Penelope Masters, ye daughter of Mr Robert Masters
1647	May	19	Jonathan Best, ye sonne of Jonathan
1647	October	9	Elisabeth, daughter of Michaell Richardson
1647	February	18	William, ye sonne of Mr Robert Masters
1648	March	30	Edward, sonne of Philip Monke
1648	April	27	Gualter Knight, ye sonne of Mr Gaulter
1648	March	24	Elisabeth Browne, ye daughter of Mr Edward Browne
1649	September	7	Mary Richardson, ye daughter of Michaell Rich:
1649	November	18	George Buckley, ye sonne of George
1649	November	26	Francis, ye daughter of Francis Ansloe
1649	December	29	Anne Cheney, ye daughter of Mr Richard Cheney
1650	January	30	Elisabeth Cheney, ye daughter of Mr Richard Cheney
1652	May	30	William Harrison, ye sonne of Henery
1652	January	18	John Boyce, ye sonne of Mr John Boyce
1652	February	25	John Best, sonne of Jonathan
1653	April	26	Adam, the son of Mr Robert Sprackling
1654	July	11	Mary Boyce, ye daughter of Mr John Boyce
1654	September	28	George Kingsly, ye sonne of Mr William Kingsly
1654	January	11	John Cheney, ye sonne of Mr Richard Cheney
1655	December	8	Robert, ye sonne of Mr Daniell Cucko
1655	March	5	Anna Peake, ye daughter of Mr Thomas Peake
1655†	January	17	Damaris Kingsly, ye daughter of Mr William Kingsly

* Overwritten in the original.
† So in the original.

Year.	Month.	Day.	Names.
1656	May	25	Ann Lott, daughter of John and Ann
1656	July	14	Elizabeth Hey, the daughter of Jeremy and Ann
1656*			Elizabeth Durance, the daughter of John and Mary borne July 14
1656*			Richard Croyden, sonne of Robert and Elizabeth, borne July 23
1656	September	8	William, sonne of Jonathan Best and Rebec.
1656	October	26	Susan, the daughter of John Denew and Mary, borne the 10th
1656	September*	23	Rachell Crux, the daughter of John and Bennit
1656	December	26	Richard Harrison, sonn of Richard and Ann
1656	February	28	Paule, sonne of Mr Paule Barret and Mary
1656*			Aphra, the daughter of John Jacob and Francis, borne March 22
1657*			Junior Naze, the sonne of Robert Naze, borne July 16
1657	July	16	John Loth, sonne of John and Ann, borne June 29
1657*			Thomas, the sonne of Thomas Greene and Francis, borne July 6
1657	September	3	William Browne, the sonne of William and Alice
1657	September	22	William Boyce, ye sonn of Mr John Boys
1657	September	29	Mary Broadnex, ye daughter of Mr Wm Broadnex and Mary
1657	October	3	ffrancis, ye sonn of Jonathan Best and Rebecka
1657	October	8	ffrancis Bathon, daughter of John and Grace
1657	November	8	Elizabeth, daughter of James Church
1657	January	9	Hester, the daughter of Mr Robert Bargraue
1657	January	14	Samuell Dauis, the sonne of William and Sarah
1657*			Josiah, sonne of Gregory Bigeon and Katherine, borne March 19
1658	May	16	Mary Harrison, daughter of Henry
1658	July	29	Margarett, the daughter of John [Reuther or] Renther and Margarett
1658*			Jane Jacob, the daughter of Mr John Jacob and Francis, borne July 29
1658	August	10	William Cucko, ye sonne of Daniell & Elizabeth
1658	October	3	Richard, sonn of John D. New & Mary
1658	October	4	Henry Foach, sonn of Henry and Susan
1658	November	12	Francis Condor, the sonne of ffrancis and Jane
1658	November	23	Ellenor Turner, the daughter of Thomas and Elizabeth
1658	February	16	Sarah Wiggins, daughter of Henry and Abigall
1658	March	2	Damorice Boyce, the daughter of Mr John Boyce
1658	March	2	Susana Burton, daughter of John Burton
1658	March	18	John, the sonn of Thomas Bayley
1659	April	4	Mary Nayre, ye daughter of Wm and Mary
1659	May	1	Rebecca Best, ye daughter of Jonathan and Rebecca
1659	July	10	Elizabeth Harrison, ye daughter of Henry and Elizabeth
1659	August	10	Thomas Denn, the sonn of William
1659	September	28	Thomas Cucko, ye sonn of Thomas
1659	November	11	Jane Russell, the daughter of James
1659*			Renouata Durance, ye daughter of John, borne Nov. 14
1659	December	26	Elizabeth Dauis, daughter of William, borne Decr 25, bap. 26
1659*			John Jacob, sonne of John borne, Feb. 21
1660	August	14	Isaac, the sonn of Mr Robert Bargraue
1660	September	6	James, the sonne of James Church
1660	September	11	Barbara, ye daughter of Mr William Somner
1660	October	14	Mary Nazie, ye daughter of Robert Nazie

* So in the original.

Year.	Month.	Day.	Names.
1660	November	1	Mary, the daughter of John Burton
1660	November	2	Margarett Price, the daughter of John Price
1660	November	18	John Bathorne, the sonn of John Bathorne
1660	December	23*	Thomas Harrison, the sonn of Henry
1660	November	18	Judith, the daughter of Thomas Banfeild and Mildred
1660	December	19	Mary, the daughter of William and Mary Naire
1660	January	11	Susan Best, the daughter of Jonathan and Rebecca
1660	February	15	Richard Russell, sonn of James
1660*			Thomas Jacob, sonn of John and Francis, borne Feb. 17
1660	March	1	Charles Peake, the sonn of Mr Thomas and Katherine
1660	March	12	Elizabeth Cucko, ye daughter of Daniel and Elizabeth
1660	March	20	William, son of Mr Lawence Rooke
1661	April	13	Anthony, the sonn of Mr Henry Decaringe
1661	June	11	Charles Chilton, ye sonn of Daniel
1661	July	6	Debora, the daughter of Edward Randolph and Jane
1661	August	10	Charles, the sonn of Mr William Kingsley and Margaret
1661	November	3	William, ye Sonne of Mr William Somner, Auditor of Christ Church, Canterbury, and Barbara his wife
1661	November	10	Judith, ye daughter of Andrew Weare and Frances his wife
1661	January	5	Walter ye sonne of Francis Conners and Jane his wife
1662	June	3	Ann, ye daughter of Thomas Fray and Dorothy his wife
1662	June	29	Elizabeth, daughter of William plom'er, one of the vesturers of the church, and Elizabeth his wife
1662	July	4	Katherin, ye daughter of Mr Richard Langham, one of the Minor Cannons of this Church, and Francis his wife
1662	July	16	Elisabeth ye daughter of William Nayer and Mary his wife
1662	July	20	Joseph, ye son of Jonathan Best and Rebecca his wife
1662	September	21	Ann, the daughter of Edward Woodfall and Jane his wife
1662	November	21	Thomas, the son of Henry Harrison and Elisabeth his wife
1662	November	26	Mary and Martha, ye twins of Mr Decro
1662	December	9	Ann, ye Daughter of Thomas Banfeild and Mildred his wife
1662	December	15	Ann, ye daughter of Captayne William Kingsly and Margaret his wife, was baptised at his house
1662	December	27	Richard, ye son of John Bathan and Grace his wife
1662	January	22	William, ye son of William Dauis and Sarah his wife
1663	May	15	Elisabeth, ye Daughter of William Pising ye younger, Lay Clarke of this Church, and Alice his wife
1663	June	18	Catherine, ye daughter of Dr Edward Willford and Elisabeth his wife
1663	July	7	Thomas, ye son of Mr Richard Langham, one of ye Minor Cannons of this Church, and Frances his wife
1663	July	16	Frances, ye daughter of Mr Thomas Gibbs, Organist, and Mary his wife
1663	August	13	William, ye son of Mr Thomas Fray and Dorothy his wife
1663	August	13	John, the son of Stephen Moss and Tomasin his wife
1663	August	16	Frances, ye son of Mr William Somner, Auditor of this Church, and Barbary his wife
1663	September	3	Andrew, ye son of Andrew Ware and Frances his wife
1663	October	8	Sophia, ye daughter of Dr John Aucher, a Prebend of this Church, and Susanna his wife, was the first that was baptised in the new Font
1663	November	9	Michaell, ye son of James Russell and Mary his wife
1663	February	19	Elizabeth, ye daughter of Daniell Chilton and Sarah his wife

* So in the original.

Year.	Month.	Day.	Names.
1664	April	20	Jane, ye Daughter of ffrancis Conder and Jane his wife, was baptised Aprill 20th, being Easter day
1664	July	14	John, ye son of Robert Howell and Ann his wife
1664	August	15	Katherine, ye Base Born Child of Jone Stephens, servant to ye Reverend Deane, was baptised in her chamber
1664	November	15	ffraunces and Anne, ye Twins of William Plomer, one of ye Vesturers of this Church, and Elizabeth his wife, were Baptised at home
1664	January	12	Ann, ye Daughter of Mr William Pising ye Junior and Alice his wife
1664	February	14	Edward, ye son of Mr Richard Langham, a minor Cannon of this Church, and Frances his wife
1664	February	14	John, ye son of Thomas Banfeild and Mildred his wife
1665	May	16	Edwin, ye son of Sr Richard Sands and ye Lady Mary his wife
1665	June	4	Elisabeth Frances Best, ye Daughter of Mr Jonathan Best and Rebecca his wife
1665	July	16	Andrew, ye son of Andrew Ware and Frances his wife
			Two imperfect entries of the baptisms of Margaret Chilton and Charles Cholmeley are here cancelled and entered below
1665	January	21	Mary, ye daughter of Mr Edmund Burges, one of y^e minor Canons, and Francis his wife
1665	February	9	Margaret, the daughter of Daniel and Sarah Chilton
1665	March	1	Charles, y^e son of Richard and Joanna Cholmely
1665	March	19	Richard, the son of Doctor Edward Wilford and Elizabeth his wife, was baptized March the 19th, 166$\frac{5}{6}$.
1666	July	1	John, y^e son of M^r* William and Barbara Sumner
1666	August	30	Gabriel, the son of William and Joane Richards
1666	August	30	Susanna, y^e daughter of Doctor John Aucher and Susanna his wife
1666	August	26†	John, the son of Francis and Jane Conniers
1666	September	5	Edward, y^e son of William and Sarah Davis
1666	September	16	Dennis, the son of Andrew and Francis Ware
1666	October	13	Sarah, the daughter of William and Sarah Nayer, *alias* Ayer
1666	November	7	Sarah, the daughter of Robert and Mary Sampson
1666	November	24	William, the son of Lawrence and Mary Holman
1666	December	7	Bridget, the Daughter of John Bathan and Grace his wife
1666	December	30	William, the son of William Plom'er, one of the Vesterers of this Church, and Elizabeth his wife
1666	January	30	Rebecca, ye Daughter of Thomas Banfeild and Mildred his wife
1667	April	3	Elisabeth, the Daughter of Mr Edward Ingham and Sarah his wife
1667	July	14	Elisha Robert the Son of Robert Ewen and Catherine his wife aged about eight years
1667	August	8	Edward, the son of Mr Edmond Burges one of the Minor Cannons, and Frances his wife
1667	August	11	Mary, the Daughter of William Pising the younger and Alice his wife, lay-clarke
1667	August	25	John, the son of Mr John Denne and Mary his wife
1667	September	26	John, the son of Mr Henry Foach and Susanna his wife
1667	December	29	Thomas, ye son of William Nayer (*alias* Ayer) and Sarah his wife
1667	January	3	Rebecca, ye daughter of Andrew Ware and Frances his wife

* "M^r" is interlined in a later hand.

† So in the original.

Year.	Month.	Day.	Names.
1667	January	12	Elizabeth Mary, being of the age of 18 years and upward (daughter to John Allen and Emm his wife, of the parish of St Donston's, both of them being probaptists), was Baptised the 12th day of January
1667	February	23	Hannah, ye daughter of Ann Birch, a way going woman, who was deliuered in the Body of Christ Church, Canterbury
1667	March	8	Mathew, ye son of Mr Edward Hadds and Catherin his wife
1668	April	13	John, ye son of Dr John Aucher, Prebend of this Church, and Susanna his wife
1668	April	16	Margaret, the daughter of Mr Richard Langham, a Minor Cannon of this Church, and Frances his wife
1668	April	30	Elisabeth, ye daughter of Mr William Kingsly the younger and Priscilla his wife, was baptised at home by Mr Alday
1668	February	5	Margaret, the daughter of Francis Conder and Jane his wife
1668	February	21	Katherine, ye daughter of Mr Edward Hadd and Katherine his wife
1669	May	7	John, ye Son of Robert & Mary Sampson
1669	May	21	Mary, ye daughter of Mr John Denew & Mary his wife
1669	June	21	William, ye son of Mr William and Priscilla Kingsley
1669	August	15	Sarah, ye daughter of William and Sarah Nayer (*alias* Ayer)
1669	September	16	Mary, the Daughter of Dr John Castillian, Prebend of this Church, and Margaret his wife
1669	October	8	Anne, ye Daughter of Simon Attaway & ffrances his wife
1669	October	20	John, ye Son of Mr Edmund Burges, a Minor Canon of this Church
1669	December	11	Ann, ye Daughter of John Wanstall and Margaret his wife, was baptised in Mr Hadds his house
1669	December	13	John, ye son of Thomas Banfeild, one of ye Lay Clarks, and Mildred his wife
1669	January	30	Hannah Fisenden, (the Daughter of Robert Fisenden and Mary his wife,) of the age of seauenteen yeares, was baptised by Dr Castillion, one of the Prebends of Christ Church, Canterbury
1670	April	17	George, the son of Andrew Scott and Mildred his wife, liuing in the Bishopps Pallace
1670	April	29	Elisabeth, ye daughter of George Essex and Elisabeth his wife, aged about 23 yeares, was baptised by Mr Robinson, one of the Minor Cannons of Christ Church, Canterbury
1670	May	14	Annabella, ye Daughter of William Edgford and Annabella his wife
1670	May	25	Ann, ye Daughter of Mr William Kingsly and Priscilla his wife
1670	June	29	Elisabeth, ye Daughter of Henery Perkins and Elisabeth his wife
1670	September	19	Hester, ye daughter of Mathew Raggath and Jane his wife
1670	October	26	John, ye son of John Ward, a Tayler, and Amy his wife
1670	November	18	Edward, ye son of Mr Edward Hadds and Katherine his wife (*born ye 12th day, ante?*)*
1670	November	22	Sarah, ye Daughter of Mr Edward Ingham and Sarah his wife

* Interlined in different ink.

Year.	Month.	Day.	Names.
1670	January	6	Andrew, ye sonne of Andrew and Dennis Bruce
1670	March	20	Joseph, ye sonne of ffrancis and Jane Couder
1671	April	20	Richard, ye sonne of Mr Edmund Burges, A Minor Canon of this Church, and ffrances his wife
1671	September	27	William, ye sonne of Mr William Pysing, Junr, & Alice his wife
1671	September	29	Thomas, ye Son of Mr William Kingsly, of this p'cincts, and Priscilla his wife
1671	November	2	Thomas, ye Son of Dr John Castillian, Prebend of this Church, and Margaret his wife
167½	January	14	Francis, ye son of William Edgeford and Annabella his wife
167½	January	27	Thomas, ye Son of Tho. Bamfeild, of the Lay Clerkes of this Church, and Mildred his wife
1672	February	4	John, the son of Robert Sampson, one of ye Singingmen of this Church
1672	February	16	William and John, Twins, sons of John Kirke and Elizabeth his wife
1672	June	2	Anthony, ye son of Robert Ansley, in ye Bishops Pallace
1672	October	26	Thomas, the sonne of Edward and Sarah Engeham, borne and christened ye 26 day of October 1672
1672	October	26	George, ye son of Mr William Kingsley and Priscilla his wife
1672	December	8	Thomas, ye son of Andrew Bruce and Dennis his wife
1672	December	15	Margaret, the Daughter of Mr Edmond Burges, a Minor Cannon of this Church, and Frances his wife
1672	January	28	Margaret ye daughter of Mr Edward Hadds and Catharine his wife
1673	March	25	Elisabeth, ye Daughter of William Edgeford and Anabella his wife
1673	April	24	Elisabeth, ye Daughter of Daniell Wood, one of the Vesterers of the Church, and Elisabeth his wife
1673	August	9	John, ye son of Frances Conder and Jane his wife
1673	December	1	Mary, ye Daughter of Robert and Mary Sampson, Lay Clerke, of this Precincts
1673	February	13	Frances, ye Daughter of John and Mary Lewsly, of this Precincts
1673	March	20	William, ye Son of Thomas Turner and Ester his wife
1673	March	23	William, ye Son of William Edgeford and Anabella his wife
1674	March	27	William, ye Son of Tho. Bamfeild, A Lay Clerke, and Mildred his wife
1674	April	8	John, ye Son of Mr William Pysing, Junr, A Ley Clerke, and Alice his wife
1674	April	9	Mary, ye Daughter of Mr Arthur Key, A sixe Preacher of this Church, and Elizabeth his wife
1674	May	4	Elizabeth, ye Daughter of Andrew and Dennis Bruce
1674	May	25	Mary, ye Daughter of William Canon, of this Precincts
1674	July	23	Susanna, ye Daughter of Mr Edmund Burges, a Minor Canon of this Church, and ffrances his wife
1674	August	9	Thomas, ye Son of John Kirke, of this P'cincts, and Elizabeth his wife
1674	September	19	Anthony, ye Son of Mr William Kingsley, of this precincts, and Priscilla his wife
1674	February	21	William, ye son of John Lewsly and Mary his wife
1675	March	29	Saray, ye Daughter of James Williams and Sarah his wife
1675	April	20	Michall Daniell, ye son of Thomas Banfeild and Mildred his wife
1675	May	23	Robert, ye son of Mr Henry Hughs, a Minor Cannon of this

Year.	Month.	Day.	Names.
			Church, and Catherine his wife, was Baptised the 23th day of May being Whitsunday
1675	August	1	Barbarah, ye Daughter of Mr Arthur Key, one of the six preachers, and Elisabeth his wife
1675	August	7	Thomas, ye son of Mr John Langham, Minor Cannon of this Church, and Ursula his wife
1675	February	17	Daniell, ye son of Daniell Wood
1675	March	19	Peter, the Son of Peter Scrivner and Sarah his wife
1676	April	16	Joseph, the Son of Andrew Bruce and Dennis his wife
1676	April	16	Elizabeth, the daughter of Robert Sampson and Mary his wife
1676	June	12	Thomas Kennon, son of William Kennon and Mary his wife
1676	July	20	Thomas, the Son of John Kirke and Elizabeth his wife
1676	October	11	Phœbe, the daughter of Mr William Kingsley and Priscilla his wife
1676	December	3	John, the Son of Mr John Langham and Ursula his wife
1676	December	13	Thomas, ye son of Mr Thomas Hayes, late Curate att Iekham, & Hester his wife
1676	January	22	Anne, the Daughter of Mr Edward Hadds & Katherine his wife
1676	January	23	Simon, ye sonn of Mr Henry Hughes, Minor Canon of Christ Church, & Katherine his wife
1676	February	13	John ye Son of Mr John Gostling Minor Canon of Christ Church and Elizabeth his wife
1676	February	21	Frances, ye Daughter of William Pysing, Lay Clark, & Alice his wife
1676	March	1	Elizabeth, ye Daughter of Mr Arthur Key, Six Preacher of Christ Church, & Elizabeth his wife
1677	May	8	William, ye Son of Thomas Bamfield, Lay Clerk, & Mildred his wife
1677	July	12	John, ye son of John Lewsley & Mary his wife
1677	August	20	John, ye Son of John Williams and Sarah his wife
1677	December	9	Sarah Spillet, Daughter of Henry & Jone Spillet, of Woodchurch (aged 21 years), was by ye industry of Mr John Sargenson persuaded to leaue her Anabaptist . . . ets & to become member of ye church & was by him Baptized att ye Font in Christ Church
1677	December	28	Sarah, Daughter of Peter Screven
1677	December	29	Fotherby, son of Mr Will. & Priscilla Kingsley
1677	February	5	Robert, sonne of Daniell Wood, Vesterer
1678	May	1	Rebecka, Daughtr of Edward Kiblwhite
1678	May	9	George, ye Son of Mr John Cullen
1678	June	15	Anne, ye Daughter of Daniel & Anne Pickard
1678	June	30	William, ye Son of Thomas Bamfield
1678	July	16	Elizabeth, ye Daughter of John Kirke
1678	December	1	Elizabeth, ye Daughter of Mr John Gosling, Minor Canon
1678	December	18	Francis, son of Thomas Hill and Mary his wife
1679	March	30	Grace, daughter of Mr Edward Hadds and Katherine his wife
1679	April	22	Thomas, Son of Peter Scrivener and Sarah his wife
1679	May	2	Thomas, Son of Sr Robert Faunce, Knt, and Elizabeth his wife
1679	May	30	Daniell, Son of Mr Daniell Picard and Ann his wife
1679	June	9	Elizabeth, daughter of Mr William Kingsley and Priscilla his wife
1679	June	23	Thomas, Son of Thomas Caue and Mary his wife

Year.	Month.	Day.	Names.
1679	July	3	John, son of Mr Robert Wren, Organist of this Church, and . . . his wife
1679	July	24	Aldy, son of Mr John Sargenson, Minor Canon of this Church, and Mary his wife
1679	July	31(?)	Joseph, Son of Thomas Banfield, lay Clerk, and Mildred his wife
1679	August	14	Robert, son of Mr Arthur Key, one of ye Six preachers of this Church, & Eliz. his wife
1679	August	25	Eliz., daughter of Tho. Friend & Margaret his wife
1679	November	28	Michaell, son of Mr John Cullen, Usher of the Kings Schoole, and Ann his wife
1679	November	29	William, son of Mr Edward Ingham, of the Bishops Pallace, & Sarah his wife
167$\frac{8}{9}$	January	19	Lucy, y^{e} Daughter of Mr Paul Lukin & Grace his wife
1679	March	15	Edward, y^{e} Son of Edward Kibblewhite & Elizabeth his wife
1680	May	5	Hester, y^{e} daughter of Daniel Piccard & Anne his wife
1680	May	28	James, y^{e} son of John Williams & Sarah his wife
1680	June	28	Edward, y^{e} Son of Mr William Kingsley & Priscilla his wife
1680	August	1	Thomas, the Son of John Lewsley & Mary his wife
1680	September	26	John, ye Son of Mr Jacob Janeway & Frances his wife
			☞ Jo. Friend should have been placed here.
1680	January	2	Charles, son of Thomas Hills & Mary his wife
1680	January	20	Rebecka, daughter of Mr Edward Hadds and Katherine his wife
1680	October	9	John, son of Thomas & Margarett Frend
			☞ This was misplaced by forgetfulnesse.
1680	February	2	Thomas, Son of Mr John Sargenson, Minor Canon of this Church, & Mary his wife
1680	March	8	Jane, daughter of Mr Anthony Horsmonden and Jane his wife, was borne the 16th day of ffebruary and baptized the 8th day of March
1680	March	14	William, Son of Thomas Banfield and Mildred his wife
1680	March	23	Thomas, Son of Mr John Gostling, Minor Canon of this Church, and Elizabeth his wife
1681	April	7	Silas, Son of Mr Tho. Johnson, Minor Canon of this Church, and Ann his wife
1681	October	11	George, Son of Mr George Upton, of the Bishops pallace, and Elizabeth his wife
1681	February	12	Duke, son of Robert Fance, K^{nt}, & Elizabeth his wife
1681	March	23	Charles, ye Son of Thomas Hills & Mary his wife
1682	April	2	Anne, daughter of Dr Key, one of ye six preachers of this Church, & of Elizabeth his wife
1682	April	16	Thomas, Son of Mr Thomas Johnson, Minor Canon of this Church, & Anne his wife
1682	April	30	George Wraith, of St Peters parish (educated by his Anabaptiz'd Parents) at ye age of 21 yeers was baptized & confirmed by ye Reverend Father in God Wm Lord Bishop of Peterborough in his Episcopal Visitation
1682	June	21	Elizabeth, daughter of Ed. Kiblewhite & Elizabeth his wife
1682	June	21	Richard Wall, ye son of George Wall and Rebecca his wife
1682	May *	16	Mary, daughter of Mr John Sargenson and Mary his wife
1682	July	7	John, ye son of Mr John Gostling & 2nd son of y^{t} name, Minor-Canon of this Church, & of Elizabeth his wife
1682	August	4	James, ye Son of Mr Jacob Janeway & Francis his wife

* So in the original.

Year.	Month.	Day.	Names.
1682	August	12	Francis, ye Daughter of Mr William Kingsley & Priscilla his wife
1682	August	14	Ursula, ye daughter of Mr Anthony Horsmonden & Jane his wife
1682	September	28	Charles, ye Son of Mr Robert Wren, Organist of this Church, and Anne his wife
1682	October	24	Maurice, ye son of Maurice Horner & Susan his wife
1682	October	?	Martin, the Son of Mr George Upton, of the Bishops Pallace, and Elizabeth his wife
1682	November	26	Mary, ye daughter of Thomas & Margarett Friend
1682	November	30	Ann, ye daughter of Thomas Harrison and Ellinor his wife
1682	December	...	Silvester, the daughter of Mr Thomas Marsh and Frances his wife
1682	February	22	Mary, the daughter of Mr Rowswell, Curate at Chartham, and Mary his wife
1682	March	22	Richard, the son of Henry Cullen and Elizabeth his wife
1683	August	2	Edward, the son of Thomas Banfield and Mildred his wife
1683	August	16	Katherine, daughter of Mr John Gostling, Minor Canon of this Church, and of Elizabeth his wife
1683	November	18	Charles, son of Thomas Hills and Mary his wife
1683	November	27	Mary, daughter of James Williams and Sarah his wife
1683	February	14	John, ye son of Maurice & Susan Horn'
1683	February	26	Elizabeth ye Daughter of Thomas Harris and Eleanor his wife
1683	March	6	Margaret, ye Daughter of Dr Key, (one of ye 6 preachers of this Ch., and Elizabeth his wife
1683	March	10	Mary, ye Daughter of Mr Charles Kilburn & Mary his wife
1684	July	11	Mary, ye Daughter of Mr John Gostling (Minor Canon of this Church), and Elizabeth his wife
1684	July	29	Mary, ye Daughter of Mr Jacob Janeway and Frances his wife
1684	December	7	Thomas and Ann, son and daughter of Mr Thomas Johnson, Minor Canon of this Church, and Ann his wife
1684	February	7	James, the son of Thomas Banfield and Mildred his wife
1684	February	17	Elizabeth, daughter of Mr Robert Wren, Organist of this Church and Ann his wife
1684	March	3	Ann, the daughter of Edward Kiblewhite & Eliz. his wife
1684	March	8	Elizabeth, daughter of Mr Charles Dodd, one of the Vesterers of this Church, and Ann his wife
1685	May	3	Thomas, son of Thomas and Margarett ffriend
1685	August	5	John, the son of William and Mary Smith, borne in the street without Waddells gate
1685	September	4	Elizabeth, daughter of Mr Jacob Janeway and Mary his wife
1685	September	20	John, son of Christopher Goatly and Elizabeth his wife
$168\frac{5}{6}$	January	10	Edward, y^e^ son'e of Maurice Horner and Susan his wife
$168\frac{5}{6}$	January	11	Priscilla, y^e^ daughter of Mr Tho. Johnson, Minor Canon of y^s^ Church, & An'e his wife
1686	May	11	Mary, y^e^ daughter of Mr Charles Dod, one of y^e^ Vesterars of y^s^ Church, and An'e his wife
1686	May	14	Mary, y^e^ daughter of Mr James Williams and Sarah his wife
1686	July	24	Lewis, ye son' of Mr Charles Kilburn (Min' Canon and Præcentor of y^s^ Cathedral), and Mary his wife
1686	October	26	Mary, ye daughter of Herbert Randolph, Esq., & Mary his wife
1686	December	27	Margaret, the Daughter of Henry and Elizabeth Cullen his wife
1687	April	10	Margaret, the Daughter of Thomas and Margarett Friend
1687	April	29	Elizabeth, the Daughter of Robert and Mary Buckewell
1687	September	15	Jacob, the sone of Mr Jacob Janeway and Frances his wife

Year.	Month.	Day.	Names.
1687	October	27	Mary, the Daughter of Edward Kibblewhite and Eliz. his wife
1687	October	30	Elizabeth, the Daughter of John Church and Margaret his wife
			Charles Kilburne, Sacrist.

THE END OF THE CHRISTENINGS IN THE FIRST BOOK.

1687	December	20	James, son of Charles Dod, one of the Vesterers of this Church, and Mary his wife
1687	February	20	Rebecca, daughter of Morris Horner and Susan his wife
1688	March	29	Tufton, Daughter of the Reverend Dr James Jefferys, one of the Prebendarys of this Church
1688	May	31	Ellinor, daughter of Simon Wakefeild and Ann his wife
1688	June	3	Sarah Hadlow, born of Anabaptis Parents and Sixteen years of Age—Whitsunday
1688	August	2	Henry, Son of Henry Lee, Esq., and Dorothy his wife, was borne July 23rd, and baptized August 2nd
1688	November	23	Elizabeth, the daughter of Herbert Randolph, Esqr, and Mary his wife, borne and baptized 23rd day November
			Tho. Johnson, Sac^{t}
1688	November	28	Mary, Daughter of John Clark & Anne his wife
$168\frac{8}{9}$	January	6	Richard, son of John Fowl & Mary his wife
$168\frac{8}{9}$	January	8	Anne, Daughter of Robert Buckwell & Mary his wife
1689	March	28	Susanna, Daughter of Stephen and Susan'a Bunce
1689	March	30	Elizabeth, Daughter of Mr Richard Johnson & Eliz. his wife
1689	August	19	Edward, Son of Edward & Elizabeth Kibblewhite
1689	August	22	John, Son of y^{e} Reverend Dr James Jefferys & Margaret his wife
1689	November	19	Susanna, Daughter of Maurice Horner & Susanna his wife
$168\frac{9}{90}$	January	24	Mary, Daughter of John & Annabella Bates
$168\frac{9}{90}$	February	3	Elizabeth, Daughter of John Cullen, of y^{e} Paddock, & Elizabeth his wife
1690	March	28	Jane & Diana, Daughters of Charles Dod and Mary his wife
1690	May	30	Francis, Daughter of Mr Jacob Janeway & Frances his wife
1690	June	2	John, Son of Herbert Randolph, Esqr, & Mary his wife
1690	July	22	Thomas, Son of Thomas & Margaret ffriend
1690	July	23	Anne, daughter of Robert Scudder & Mildred his wife
			S. D'Evereux, Sacrist
1690	January	3	George, son of Mr Robt Wren, Organist of this Church, and Ann his wife
1690	March	1	Gilbert, Son of Gilbert Burrough and Marget his wife
1690	March	10	Marg^{t}, Daughter of Robert & Mary Buckwell
1691	May	22	Thomas, Sone of Mr James White and Grace his wife
1691	October	2	Herbert, son of Herbert Randolph, Esq., & Mary his wife
1691	October	25	Mary, Daughter of Ed^{w}. and Mary Burges
1691	November	4	Martha Balldock, about forty years old
			Charles Kilburn, Sacrist
1691	December	11	William, Son of Joseph Crowther, Clerke, and Grace his wife
1691	December	14	Sarah, Daughter of Thomas Clarke and Ann his wife
1691	February	1	John Broxeye, about forty years of Age
1691	February	16	Margarett, daughter of Edward Kibblewhite & Elizabeth his wife

Year.	Month,	Day.	Names.
1691	March	3	Elizabeth, daughter of Mr Peter Gleane and Jane his wife
1692	April	5	Elizabeth, daughter of Vincent Ladde and Ann his wife, borne 22^{d} day of March
1692	July	2	Thomas, Son of Mr Gilbert Burrough
1692	July	19	Ann, ye Daughter of Jacob Janeway & ffrances his wife
1692	September	1	Margaret, Daughter of Herbert Randolph, Esq., and Mary his wife
1692	November	6	Jacob, the Son of Robert Buckwell and Mary his wife
			Tho. Johnson, Sacrist
1692	December	7	Daniel, the Son of William Cuckow and Elizab. his wife
1692	January	8	Ann, the Daughter of Mr Anthony Belke, Auditor of this Church, and Elizabeth his wife
1693	April	9	Susan, the Daughter of Morris and Susanah Horner. Borne April 4th
1693	April	23	George, Son of Thomas and Margaret Friend
1693	May	9	Vincent, sone of Vincent and Ann Ladd, borne Apr' 23
1693	February	14	Herbert, Son of Herbert Randolph, Esqr, Recorder of ye City of Canterbury, & Mary his wife
1693	March	18	Edward, Son of Edward and Mary Burges
1694	May	24	Ann, Daughter of Samuel Mills, Esq., and Ann his wife
1694	July	26	Sarah, Daughter of Mr Jacob Janeway and Frances his wife
1694	August	17	William, Son of Mr Gilbert Burrough and Margaret his wife
1694	October	2	Mary, Daughter of Thomas Maurice, Drummer in Coll. Coot's Reg^{t}, and Elizabeth his wife
			S. D'Evereux, Sacrist
1694	December	23	Peter, Son of Maurice Horner & Susan his wife, borne 16th December
1694	February	10	William, Son of Valentine Austen and Ann his wife
1694	March	5	John, Son of Edward Kibblewhite and Elizabeth his wife
1694	March	7	Ann, Daughter of Herbert Randolph, Esq., and Mary his wife
1694	March	24	John, son of John Carter & Martha his wife, borne within the precincts of the Arch Bishops Pallace on the 19th day of ffebruary
1695	March	30	John, son of Robert Buckwell and Elizabeth his wife
1695	May	2	John, Son of Mr Thomas Battely and Ann his wife, borne 26th day of Aprill
1695	June	5	Elizabeth, Daughter of Anthony Belke, Auditor of this Church, and Elizabeth his wife, borne May the 30th
1695	June	6	Christopher, Son of Samuel Mills, Esq., and Mary his wife
1695	June	11	Anna Maria, Daughter of William Courthope, Esq., and Amy his wife
1695	July	18	John, son of Mr Edmund Hardresse & Jane his wife
1695	August	29	Thomas, son of Robert Low and Ann his wife
1695	September	1	Elizabeth, daughter of Mr Robert Cumberland and Elizabeth his wife, borne the 31st day of August
1695	November	21	John, son of Vincent Ladd and Ann his wife
			Tho. Johnson, Sacrist
1695	January	2	Mary, Daughter of Daniell White, Gent., and Anne his wife
1695	January	30	William, son of Mr John Gostling, Minor Canon of this Church, and Dorothy his wife
1695	February	6	Charles, son of Thomas and Margaret Friend
1695	March	10	Margaret, Daughter of Mr Gilbert Burroughs and Margaret his wife
1696	June	4	William-Henry, son of Mr Jacob Janeway and Frances his wife, borne May 26th

Year.	Month.	Day.	Names.
1696	August	23	Thomas, son of Edward & Mary Burges
1696	September	27	Sarah Tall, born of Anabaptist Parents, and Eighteen years old
1696	October	19	George, Son of Herbert Randolph, Esq., and Mary his wife
1696	November	23	Mary, daughter of Samuell Mills Esqr, & Anne his wife
			R. Cumberland, Sacrist
1696	June (*sic*)	16	Jane, the Daughter of Mr Peter Gleane & Jane his wife
			Charles Kilburne, Sacrist
1696	December	9	Charles, the Sone of Mr Charles Elstob, one of the Prebends of Christ Church, and Matylda his wife
1696	March	11	Ann, daughter of Mr Thomas Battely and Ann his wife, borne the 10th day of March
1697	March	28	Robert, sone of Robert Buckwell and Mary his wife
1697	March	28	Elizabeth, daughter of Robert Low and Ann his wife
1697	May	30	Mary, daughter of Maurice Horner and Susan his wife
1697	October	17	Susan, the Daughter of Mr Robert Cumberland and Elizab. his wife
1697	October	28	Elizab. The Daughter of Mr Thomas Atkins and Mary his wife
			Charles Kilburne, Sacrist
1697	November	30	Mary, daughter of Mr Edmund Hardresse and Jane his wife
1697	January	25	Dorothy, daughter of Herbert Randolph, Esq., and Mary his wife
1697	January	29	Christopher, son of Sammuell Mills, Esq., and Ann his wife, born Jan. the 9th
1697	February	6	Phillip, son of Michaell Daniell Banfield & Elizabeth his wife, born within the precincts of the Arch. Bp. Pallace
1697	February	28	Ann, daughter of Mr Gilbert Burroughs and Margarett his wife
1698	April	1	Sarah, daughter of Willia' Courthop, Esq., and Amy his wife
1698	April	19	Michaell, son of Vincent Ladd, of the Arch Bishops Pallace, & Ann his wife
1698	June	5	Mary, daughter of Charles Beeson and Ann his wife
1698	November	11	Hester, daughter of Mr Thomas Battely and Ann his wife
			Tho. Johnson, Sacrist
1699	June	18	Robert & Susanna, Twins of Maurice Horner & Susanna his wife
1699	August	3	Elizabeth, Daughter of Thomas and Margaret Friend
1699	August	7	Sarah, Daughter of Samuel Milles, Esq., & Anne his wife
1699	August	18	Catherine, Daughter of Mr Gilbert Burroughs & Margaret his wife
1699	October	7	Frances, Daughter of Mr Owen Evans, Minor Canon of this Church, and Frances his wife
			Rob. Cumberland, Sacrist
1699	December	5	Richard, son of Michael Banfield & Elizabeth his wife
1700	July	19	Thomas, son of William Stokes & Ann his wife
1700	September	9	Ann, daughter of Mr Robert Cumberland, Minor Canon of this Church, & Elizabeth his wife
			S. D'Evereux, Sact
1700	December	3	Mary, Daughter of Vincent Ladd & Ann
1700	December	9	Mary, Daughter of Mr Thomas Batteley & Ann his wife
1700	December	9	John, son of John Mahew & Elizabeth his wife
1700	January	1	George, son of Mr Jacob Janeway & Frances his wife
1701	June	25	William, son of William Newson and Susanna his wife
1701	July	27	Sarah, Daughter of Maurice Horner & Susanna his wife
1701	September	7	Thomas, son of Herbert Randolph, Esq., and Grace his wife

Year.	Month.	Day.	Names.
1701	October	26	Catherine, Daughter of John Quoif, of ye Padocke, & Catherine his wife
			Robert Cumberland, Sacrist
1701	December	17	Mary, Daughter of Robert Buckwell, Coachman, and Alice his wife
1701	February	20	Elizabeth, Daughter of John Mahew, Porter of this Church, and Elizabeth his wife
			Charles Kilburne, Sacrist
1702	February	25	William, Son of John Mayhew, by Elizabeth his wife
1702	March	2	John, Son of John Pysing, by Bennet his wife
1703	August	6	Damaris, daughter of Mr Robert Cumberland, one of the Minor Canons of this Church, and Elizabeth his wife
1703	August	7	Mary, daughter of Mr Gilbert Parker and Margarett his wife
1703	October	3	Elizabeth, daughter of Maurice Horner & Susanna his wife
1703	October	13	Jane, daughter of Herbert Randolph, Esq., & Grace his wife
1703	November	5	Margarett, daughter of Jacob Janeway & Frances his wife
1703	November	7	Elizabeth, daughter of Samuell Mills, Esq., & Ann his wife
			Tho. Johnson, Sacrist
1704	April	9	Elizabeth, daughter of John Mahew & Elizabeth his wife
1704	April	18	Ann, daughter of Robert Buckwell & Alice his wife
1704	July	14	Bennet, Daughter of John Pysing & Bennet his wife
1704	May *(sic)*	11	Ann, daughter of Sr Francis Head & Margaret his Lady
1704	October	1	Vincent, son of Vincent Ladd & Ann his wife
1704	October	4	Alicia, daughter of Mr James Henstridge & Joyce his wife
1704	October	20	John, son of Herbert Randolph, Esq. & Grace his wife
			James Henstridge, Sacrist.
1704	March	5	Mary, daughter of Mr Robert Cumberland, Minor Canon of this Church, & Eliz: his wife
1705	May	16	Samuel, Son of Samuel Milles, Esq., & Ann his wife
1705	June	28	A male child found at a door in ye Precincts of ye Arch Bishops Palace, ye Parents of it unknown, & named John
1705	July	8	Margaret, Daughter of Maurice Horner & Susanna his wife
1705	October	19	Robert, son of Vincent Ladd & Ann his wife
1705	November	4	Robert, son of John Mahew & Elizabeth his wife
1705	November	8	Mary, Daughter of Mr Thomas Battely & Ann his wife
			Robert Cumberland, Sacrist.
1705	January	3	Simon, Son of ye Revd Mr Simon Hughs & Mary his wife
1706	July	7	Elizabeth & Grace, Daughters of Hubert Randolph, Esqr, & Grace his wife
1706	August	14	Hannah, daughter of Mr Charles Kilburne, Minor Canon of this Church, & Mary his wife
1706	September	29	William, son of John Pysing & Bennet his wife
1706	October	30	Charles, son of Samuel Mills, Esqr, & Ann his wife
			James Henstridge, Sacrist
1706	February	16	Mary, the daughter of John Mahew & Elizab: his (wife)
1707	April	14	Robert, the sone of Mr Robert Cumberland, Minor Canon of this Church, & Elizab. his wife
1707	May	25	Thomas, sone of Vincent Ladd & Ann his wife
1707	July	2	Judeth, Daughter of Herbert Randolph, Esq., & Grace his wife
1707	August	16	Thomas, sone of Tho. Robeson, a souldier in Col. Haines Regiment, & Ann his wife
			Charles Kilburne, Sacrist.

Year.	Month.	Day.	Names.
1707	January	27	Katherine, Daughter of the Rev. Dr Green, Vice Dean of this Church, and Katherine his wife
1707	February	20	Thomas, son of Sammuell Mills, Esqr, & Mary his wife, borne Feb. the 6th
1708	April	6	Margarett & Martha, twin Daughters of John Mahew and Elizabeth his wife, born & baptized April the 6th
1708	May	23	Lancelott, son of Vincent Ladd and Ann his wife
1708	June	9	Ann, daughter of James Rondeau & Elizabeth his wife, born May the 23rd
1708	August	10	Frances daughter of John Pysing and Bennett his wife
1708	August	14	Moutagu, son of the Revd Mr Ralph Blomer, one of the Prebendarys of this Church, and Hester his wife, borne August the first
			Tho. Johnson, Sacrist
1708	December	12	George, Son of Herbert Randolph, Esqr, & Grace his wife
1709	May	5	Catherine, daughter of Samuell Mills, Esqr, & Ann his wife
1709	June	1	Sarah, Daughter of Mr Robt Cumberland, minor Canon of this Church, & Elizabeth his wife
1709	July	7	Ann, Daughter of Vincent Ladd & Ann his wife
1709	July	16	Charlott, Daughter of Dr Tho. Green, Arch Deacon & one of ye Prebendaries of this Church, & Kath. his wife
1709	September	24	Thomas, son of ye Revd Mr Ralph Blomer, one of ye Prebendarys of this Church, and Hester his wife
			Jas. Henstridge, Sacrist
1709	December	16	Joseph, Son of John Pysing & Bennett his wife
1710	May	7	Elizabeth Chambers, borne of Ana Baptist Parents, and Aged about 18 years
1710	May	14	Thomas, son of John Friend & Elizabeth his wife
1710	August	1	James, son of James Rondeau, Gent., & Elizabeth his wife
			Rob. Cumberland, Sacrist
1710	December	27	Dorothy, daughter of Herbert Rondolph, Esq., and Grace his wife
1710	February	9	Thomas, son of the Reuer^{d} Dr Green, Prebend of this Church and Arch Deacon of Canterbury, and Katherine his wife
1710	February	23	Charles, sone of Vincent Ladd & Anne his wife
1711	May	20	Joseph, sone of John Piseing and Bennit his wife
1711	June	7	Katherine, the daughter of Samuell Mills, Esqr, and Ann his wife
			Ch. Kilburne, Sacrist
1711	March	13	Dorothy, daughter of the Reverend Mr Edward Tennison, Præbendary of this Church, and Ann his wife
1712	June	15	Mary, daughter of Nicholas Ladd and Frances his wife
1712	July	7	Charles, son of Herbert Randolph, Esqr, and Grace his wife
1712	August	10	Ann, daughter of John Pysing and Bennett his wife
1712	September	7	William, son of Henry Rigden and Mary his wife
1712	September	21	Charles, son of the Revd Dr Green, Arch Deacon and præbendary of this Church, born September 11
			Tho. Johnson, Sacrist
1713	May	15	Ann, Daughter of Vincent Ladd and Ann his wife
1713	October	15	Francis, ye Son of Herbert Randolph, Esqr, & Grace his wife
1713	October	30	Mary, Daughter of ye Revd Dr Tho. Green, Prebendary of this Ch. & Arch Deacon of Cant., and Catherine his wife
			Ja. Henstridge, Sacrist
1713	December	8	John, son of John Coats & Ann his wife

Year.	Month.	Day.	Names.
1713	March	4	Elizabeth, Daughter of John Brice, of ye Arch Bishops Palace, and Sarah his wife
1713	March	24	Martha, Daughter of Mr Benjamin Mockaree & Martha his wife
1714	August	10	Charles, son of ye Revd Mr Simon Hughes, Rector of Smarden, and Mary his wife
1714	September	16	Ann, Daughter of ye Rever^d Mr John Smith, Master of ye Kings School, and Damaris his wife
1714	September	20	Edward, son of Samuell Milles, Esqr, and Ann his wife
1714	September	21	Isabella, Daughter of Vincent Ladd and Ann his wife
1714	October	7	Ralph, son of ye Reverend Dr Ralph Blomer, Predendary of this Church, and Hesther his wife
1714	November	9	Elizabeth, Daughter of Herbert Randolph, Esqr, & Grace his wife
			Rob. Cumberland, Sacrist
1714	January	21	George, Son of John Pising and Bennit his wife
1714	January	27	William, son of William Smithson and Ann his wife
1714	January	30	Sarah, daughter of the Reuerend Dr Green, Prebendary of this Church and Arch Deacon.
			Ch. Kilburne, Sacrist
1715	February	17	Daniel, son of Mr John Smith, Master of the Kings School, and Damaris his wife, receiued priuate baptism on the seventeenth day of February, and was publickly admitted into the Church on the 6th day of March
1716	July	30	Ann, daughter of Herbert Randolph, Esqr, and of Grace his wife, born the 21st of July
			Tho. Johnson, Sacrist
1717	May	11	Margaretta, daughter of ye Revd Dr Green, Arch Deacon & Prebendary of this Church, & Catherine his wife
1717	May	13	William, Son of Mr John Smith, Master of ye Kings School, & Damaris his wife
1717	May	16	Mary, Daughter of John Pysing & Bennet his wife
1717	August	29	A Child, born in ye Bishops Palace of a wayfaring woman, received private Baptism, & was named John
			James Henstridge, Sacrist
1717	January	1	Lancelot, son of Samuel Head & Elizabeth his wife
1717	March	23	Sarah, Daughter of John Brice, of ye Arch Bishops Palace, & Sarah his wife
1718	May	13	Sarah, Daughter of Stephen Taylor, of ye Arch Bishops Palace, & Mary his wife
1718	July	11	Thomas, son of Edward Keet, one of ye Vesterers, & Mary his wife
			Robt Cumberland, Sacrist
1718	February	20	John, son of Samuel Head and Elizabeth his wife
1718	March	3	Ann, daughter of John & Bennitt Piseing
1719	April	30	Nathaniel, son of Mr George Smith, Master of the Kings Scool, and Hannah his wife
1719	June	1	John, son of John Clarke and Elizabeth his wife
1719	July	12	John, Son of John Friend and Elizab. his wife
1719	August	9	Anna Maria, Daughter of Stephen and Elizabeth Philpott
1719	August	18	Hester, Daughter of Mr William Gostling and Hester his wife, born August ye ninth
1719	September	28	Mary, daught. of George Friend and Elizab. his wife
1719	September	19	Mary, Daughter of ye Revd Mr Simon Hughes, Rector of Smarden, & Mary his wife (borne on ye 11th between 7 & 8 in ye morning)
			Ch. Kilburne, Sacrist

Year.	Month.	Day.	Names.
1719	February	7	John, son of John Brice, Inhabiting within the Precincts of the Arch Bishops Pallace, and Sarah his wife
1719	March	15	Elizabeth, daughter of Edward Keet and Mary his wife
1720	April	11	Ann, daughter of Stephen Taylor, of the Precincts of the Arch Bps Pallace, and Mary his wife
1720	May	10	Ann, daughter of John Pising & Bennett his wife
1720	February	14	Elizabeth, Daughter of George Friend & Eliz. his wife
1721	April	20*	Thomas, ye Son of John Clark & Elizabeth his wife
1721	April	10	Mary, ye Daughter of Stephen Philpot & Elizabeth his wife
1721	June	6	Parry, ye son of John Pysing & Bennett his wife
			Jas. Henstridge. Sacrist
1721	January	20	Howe-Lee, Son of Lee Warner Esqr & Mary his wife was Bap: privately Jan. 20, & Received into ye Church Jan. 27
1721	February	21	Elizabeth, Daughter of John Friend & Elizabeth his wife
1722	April	15	Elizabeth, Daughter of George Friend & Elizabeth his wife
1722	May	18	John, son of Edward Keet & Mary his wife
1722	May	20	Elizabeth, Daughter of ye Reverd Mr William Burroughs, Usher of ye Kings School, & Dorothy his wife
1722	July	28	Squire, son of John Pysing & Bennet his wife
1722	August	5	Thomas, son of John Brice, of ye Archbishops Palace, & Sarah his wife
			Robt Cumberland, Sacrist.
1722	March	12	Susan, daughter of Stephen Taylor & Mary his wife, of ye Archbishops Palace
1723	April	21	Frances, daughter of John Friend and Elizabeth his wife
1723	July	12	Elizabeth, daughter of James & Elizabeth Turner
1723	August	2	Robert, the son of Mary de Noon, a wayfaring woman, was baptized privately at a house in Northgate by ye Deans order
1723	September	1	Edward, Son of Stephen & Elizabeth Filpot
1723	September	15	Margaret, daughter of George Friend & Elizabeth his wife
1723†	November	3	Hanna Greenlond a foundling Child
			John Gostling, Sacrist
1724	August	9	Mary, daughter of John Clerk & Elizabeth his wife
1724†	August	20	Gibbs, son of Stephen Taylor and Mary his wife
1724†	October	13	George, son of James Turner & Elizabeth his wife
1724†	November	16	Mordecai Vesey, son of Major Mordecai Abbott & Isabella his wife
			Simon D'Evereux, Sacrist
1724	‡	18	Ann, daughter of the Revd Dr Blomer, one of the Prebendarys of this Church, and Hester his wife
1724	December	29	Elizabeth, daughter of John and Sarah Brice, of the Precincts of the Bishops Pallace
1725	March	29	John, the son of Wm Gostling, Clerk, & Hester his wife, born March 10th 1724
1725	July	18	Mary, daught. of John and Isabella Buckwell
1725	February	17	Ann, Daughter of William Gostling, Clerke, and Hester his wife, borne Feb. 6th
1726	April	3	Thomas, son of George ffriend and Elizabeth his wife
1726	August	16	James, Son of James Turner & Elizabeth his wife

* This entry and the two following it have been overwritten, and although overwritten the 20th, it is probably an error, and should be the 10th.

† Overwritten.

‡ The month is omitted in the original; query November.

Year.	Month.	Day.	Names.
1726	November	23	Edward, Son of Edward Kite and Mary his wife Tho. Johnson, Sacrist
1726	December	9	Matilda, Daughter of Mr Thomas Hill & Matilda his wife
1726	February	20	William, son of John Clarke & Elizabeth his wife
1726	February	25	Charlott, Daughter of ye Revd Dr William Egerton, Prebendary of this Church, and Ann his wife
1727	April	30	George, Son of George Freind & Elizabeth his wife
1727	May	26	Ann Margarett, Daughter of ye Revd Mr. William Gostling and Hester his wife, born May ye 6th
1727	November	27	Ann, Daughter of Thomas Hill, Gent., & Matilda his wife
1727	February	29	Mary, Daughter of ye Revd Mr Herbert Randolph & Catherine his wife
1728	May	23	William, son of ye Revd Mr William Gostling, Minor Canon, & Hester his wife
1728	July	4	Francis-Gunsly, son of ye Revd Dr William Ayerst, Prebendary of this Church, and Jane his wife
1728	February	2	Margaret, Daughter of George Friend & Elizabeth his wife
1729	May	25	Thomas, son of the Rev. William Gostling and Hester his wife
1729	June	8	Mary, daughter of Edward Keet & Mary his wife
1729	July	2	James, son of John Pysing, junr, & Elizabeth his wife
1730	June	5	William, Son of William Gostling & Hester his wife, born May 23
1730	June	28	Margaret, Daughter of George Friend & Elizabeth his wife
1730	July	14	Thomas, son of the Revd Mr Robert Tyler and Mary his wife, born and privately baptized July ye 14, was received into the Church August the sixth
1730	November	30	John, Son of John Pysing & Elizabeth his wife
1730	February	2	Charles, the Son of Mr Thomas Hill and Matilda his wife
1731	July	29	Sarah, Daughter of Richard Elsey and Mary his wife
1731	November	25	Henry, Son of ye Revd Mr Henry Shove, Recr of St Margaret's, Cant., and Mary his wife
1731	December	13	George, Son of George Lynch, Dr of Physick, and Mary his wife
1731	February	9	Mary, Daughter of William Lewis and Mary his wife
1732	May	30	William, Son of ye Revd Dr William Egerton, Prebendary of this Church, and Ann his wife
1732	June	17	William, son of ye Revd Dr Thomas Gooch, Prebendary of this Church, and Hannah his wife
1732	September	14	Thomas, son of John Phillmore and Alicia his wife
1732	October	12	Harriot, daughter of ye Revd Mr Thomas Clendon, Vicar of Reculver, & Elizabeth his wife
1732	December	3	John, Son of Francis Whitfield & Elizabeth his wife
1732	December	16	Mary, Daughter of ye Revd Mr William Gostling, Minor Canon, and Hesther his wife, born November 23
1732	January	19	Sarah & Mary, Daughters of Richard Neves, of ye Paddock, and Mary his wife
1733	June	3	John, son of John Philpot, of the Archbishops Palace, and Margaret his wife
1733	November	14	Jane, Daughter of George Lynch, Dr of Physick, and Mary his wife

End of the Christenings in the Second Register.

Year.	Month.	Day.	Names.
1733	November	23	Mary, daughter of the Revd Mr Thomas Clendon, Vicar of Reculver, and Elisabeth his wife
1733	January	27	Elisabeth, daughter of John Clark and Mary his wife
1733	February	28	William, Son of the Revd Mr Julius Deeds, Rector of Mongeham, and Dorothy his wife (living in the Archbishops Palace), born Feb. 6
1734	April	28	John, son of Richard Halsey & Mary his wife
1734	June	20	John, son of Francis Whitfield & Elisabeth his wife
1734	July	30	Stephen, Son of Crisp Stephen Hall and Anne Jane Mary his wife
1734	November	9	Roger, Son of Mr Richard Martin, of the Archbishops Palace, and Anne his wife
			William Gostling, Sacrist
1734	February	16	Sophia, Daughter of George Friend and Elizabeth his wife
1735	September	18	Mary, a bastard Child of Mary Mitchelbourn
1735	October	5	Sarah, daughter of John Phillpott & Margarett his wife
			James Henstridge, Sacrist
1735	December	23	William Remnant, Son of the Revd Mr Thomas Clendon, Vicar of Sturry, & Elizabeth his wife
1735	December	29	Elizabeth, Daughter of George Lynch, Dr of Physick, & Mary his wife
1735	January	5	Richard, Son of Mr Richard Martin, of the Arch-Bishops Palace, & Anne his wife
1736	March	27	Ann, Daughter of the Revd Mr. William Gostling, Minor Canon, & Hester his wife, born March 25, 1736, & privately baptized March 27. And brought to Church April 14
1736	May	31	Ann, Daughter of the Revd Mr Richard Monins, Master of the Kings School, & Mary his wife
1736	July	4	Hannah, Daughter of the Revd Mr James Evans, Under-Master of the Kings School, & Hannah his wife
			Tho. Buttonshaw, Sacrist
1736	December	1	Sarah, a Bastard child of Mary Pysing
1737*	June	15	James, ye Son of John Phillmore & Alicia his wife
1736/7	February	28	John Dendy
1736	March	9	Anna Maria Martin, Daughter of Mr Rich. Martin, Gent.
1737	July	28	Frances, Daughter of George Lynch, Dr of Physick, and Mary his wife
†	July	19	Tho. Austin, an adult person
†	August	9	Wm, Son of Rich. & Mary Halsey
†	October	6	James, Son of the Revd Mr James Evans, Under Master of ye Kings School, & Hannah his wife
			Robt Jenkin, Sacrist
1738	October	20	William, Son of Richard & Mary Halsay
†	October	25	Samuel, Son of Samuel & Martha Dendy
			Peter Vallavine, Sacrist
1738	December	1	Mary & Margaret, daughters of George & Eleanor Wilicot, servants to the Revd Dr Geckie
1738	December	26	Ann, daughter of George Lynch, M.D., & Mary his Wife
1738	December	28	Charles, Son of ye Revd Mr James Evans, Under-Master of the Kings School, & Hannah his wife
1738	February	22	Frances, Daughter of the Revd Mr Richard Monins, Master of ye Kings School, and Mary his wife

* So in the original.

† The year omitted in the original.

Year.	Month.	Day.	Names.
1739	August	1	Hester, daughter of the Revd Mr Robt Jenkin, Minor Canon of this Church, & Catharine his wife
			William Broderip, Sacrist
1739	January	23	William, Son of the Revd Mr. William Broderip, Minor Canon of this Church, & Elisabeth his wife (by the Revd Mr Dean)
1740	May	2	Ann, Daughter of John & Alicia Phillmore, by Mr Vallavine
1740	May	28	Eleanor, Daughter of George Woolcott & Eleanor his wife
1740	June	13	Richard, Son of the Revd Mr James Evans, Under Master of the Kings School, & Hannah his wife
1740	June	16	John, Son of James Agar (Servant to the Revd the Dean) and Mary his wife
1740	July	25	Catharine, Daughter of the Revd Mr Robert Jenkin, Minor Canon of this Church, and Catharine his wife (by the Revd Mr Dean)
			William Gostling, Sacrist
1740	December	18	Susan, base borne Daughter of Mary Spry
1740	January	13	John, Son of the Revd Mr William Broderip, a Minor Canon of this Church, & Elizabeth his wife, by the Rev. Mr Dean
1740	January	25	Catherine, the Daughter of the Revd Dr John Lynch, Dean of this Church, & Mary his Wife, by the Honble & Revd Dr Dawnay, Vice-Dean
1740	February	10	John, Son of Henry Despain & Mary his wife
1741	July	30	John, Son of the Revd Mr Richard Monins, Master of the Kings School, & Mary his wife, by ye Revd ye Dean
1741	August	13	Henry, Son of the Revd Mr Robert Jenkins, Minor Canon of this Church, & Catherine his wife
			James Henstridge, Sacrist
1741	December	5	Mary, ye Daughter of Richard & Mary Halsey
1742	March	31	James, ye Son of James & Mary Agar
1742	April	15	James, ye Son of ye Revd Mr Wm Broderip, a Minor Canon of this Ch., & Eliz: his wife
1742	May	28	Susanna, ye Daughter of James & Mary Horne
1742	June	21	Mary, ye Daughter of Mrs Mary Tenison & Dr Thos Tenison, late Prebendary of this Church
1742	July	17	Susanna, ye Daughter of Robert Jenkin, a Minor Canon of ys Church, & Catherine his wife
1742	September	26	George, ye son of George Woolcot and Eleanor his wife
1742	November	17	Hester Elizabeth, ye Daughter of the Revd Dr John Lynch, Dean of this Church, & Mary his wife, by the Rev. Dr Ayerst, Vice Dean
			Robt Jenkin, Sacrist
1742	February	22	Robert, son of the Revd Dr Samuel Stedman, Vice Dean of this Church, and Martha his Wife
			Peter Vallavine Sacrist
*	August	16	Ann, Daughter of John Knowler, Esq., Recorder of the City of Cant., and Mary his wife
1743	September	15	Elizabeth, daughter of ye Revd Mr William Broderip, a Min. Can: of this Church, & Elizabeth his wife
1743	November	24	Richard, Son of Richard & Mary Halsey
			James Henstridge, Sacrist, from Midsummer 1743
1744	June	1	Elizabeth, daughter of the Revd Mr Wm Gourney (under master of the Kings School), & Alicia his wife

* The year omitted in the original; query 1743.

Year.	Month.	Day.	Names.
*	August	7	W^{m}, Son of W^{m} & Eliz. Broderip
*	July	25	Mary, Daughter J^{s} & Mary Agar
*	August	10	Rich^{d}, the Son of Geo: & Elionor Woollcott
			Wm Broderip, Sacrist
1745	April	12	Mary, Daughter of John Knowler, Esq: Recorder of the City of Canterbury, & Mary his wife, baptized April 12; and brought to Church Apr. 22, 1745.
1745	June	2	Margaret, daughter of James Horne & Mary his Wife
1745	August	4	Ann, Daughter of Samuel & Martha Dendy
1745	August	28	James, the Son of James & Martha Butler
			Thomas Lamprey, Sacrist
1745	March	23	Jemima, Daughter of ye Revd Mr Thomas Lamprey, Minor Canon of this Church, & Frances his wife
1746	April	18	Susanna, Daughter of ye Revd Mr Wm Broderip, Min^{r} Canon of this Church, & Elisabeth his wife
1746	July	24	Herbert-Frend, Son of ye Revd Mr Richd Marsh, Minor Canon of this Church, & Elisabeth his wife
1746	August	1	Jane, Daughter of George & Eleanor Woolcot
1746	September	28	James-Smith, Son of James Horne & Mary his wife
			Richard Leightonhouse, Sacrist
1747	August	17	Mary, Daughter of ye Rev. Mr Fran. Gregory, Minor Canon of this Church, & Elisabeth his wife
			Fran. Gregory, Sacrist
1748	April	16	Hannah, Daughter of George & Eleanor Woolcot, baptized April 16th, and brought to Church April 28
1748	May	12	Elizabeth Gunsley, Daughter of ye Revd Mr Robt Ayerst, Minor Canon of this Church, & Frances his wife
1748	November	3	Catharine Petty, Daughter of Gregory & Grace Berners
			Rob. Ayerst, Sacrist
1748	January	7	Charles, son of the Rev. Mr William Broderip and Elizabeth his wife, privately baptized Jan: 7, and brought to Church Jan. 27
1748	March	9	Mary, Daughter of Abraham Butler & Sarah his wife
			Fran: Gregory, Sacrist
1749	January	23	James, son of John Abbot & Alice his wife, of the Archbishops Palace
1749	January	28	Daniel, son of James & Martha Butler
1750	May	4	William, Son of George & Eleanor Woolcott
1750	September	30	William, Son of James & Mary Horne
			Willliam Gostling, Sacrist
1750	February	21	Elizabeth, daughter of John Abbot & Alice his wife, of the Arch Bishops Palace
1751	April	27	Bois, son of the Revd Mr Osmond Beauvoir, Master of the Kings School, & Anne his wife
1751	July	30	Hester, Anne, Mary, Daughters of Richard Pembroke, Grocer, of the Church-Gate (lately dec^{d}), by Mary his wife, were born July 30th and baptized the same day 1751, by Richard Leightonhouse
			Wm Broderip, Sacrist
1752	May	10	Elisabeth, daughter of George & Eleanor Woolcot
1752	August	23	Osmund, Son of the Revd Mr Osmund Beauvoir, (Master of the Kings School), & Ann his wife, by the Revd Mr Tucker
1752	October	17	John, the base born son of Elisabeth Stephens, (late Servant to Dr Ayerst) Th^{o} Lamprey, Sacrist

* The year omitted in the original.

Year.	Month.	Day.	Names.
1753	January	3	James Russel, Son of John & Mary Russell, born at Bugbrook in Northamptonshire, May 17, O: S: 1742, baptized in X^t Church Caut'bury, Jan. 3^d 1753
1753	July	19	George, Son of George & Mary Turner
			Richd Leightonhouse Sac^t
1753	November	30	William, Son of the Revd Mr Osmund Beauvoir, (Master of the Kings School), and Anne his wife, born Octob. 24
1754	January	14	John, Son of the Revd Mr John Airson, (Minor Canon of this Church) and Anne his Wife, born and privately baptized Jan: 14
1754	April	18	Hester Elizabeth, Daughter of John & Rebecca Saffary
1754	August	8	Elizabeth, Daughter of George & Mary Turner
1754	October	31	Ann, the Daughter of the Revd Mr Osmund Beauvoir, (Master of the Kings School) and Ann his wife, born Oct. 7
			Fran. Gregory, Sacrist
1755	April	28	John, Son of the Rev. Mr John Airson, (Minor Canon of this Church) & Ann his wife, born April 13th
1755	May	1	Elizabeth, Daughter of William & Mary Rouse, was privately baptized May 1st & brought to Church May 11th
1755	November	3	William, Son of Mr David Bell (an officer in Lord Ancrams Dragoons) & Dorothy his wife, of the Arch-Bishops palace, born Octob. 7th
1755	November	16	Rebecca, Daughter of John & Rebecca Saffary
1755	November	18	Elizabeth, Daughter of the Revd Mr Osmund Beauvoir, (Master of the Kings School) & Anne his wife, born Oct. 21
			Jh: Airson, Sacrist
1756	April	18	Mary Ann, Daughter of the Revd Mr John Airson (Minor Canon of this Church) and Ann his wife, born April 4th, privately baptized April 18, and received into the congregation May 5
1756	November	2	Hester, Daughter of William Rouse & Mary his Wife
1756	October	13	Jane, Daughter of the Revd Mr John Tucker, Under Master of the King's School, & Jane his wife, was baptized privately Oct. 13, and received into the Congregation Nov. 2^d following
			William Gostling, Sacrist
1756	November	29	Edward, Son of the Revd Mr Francis Gregory, (Minor Canon of this Church), and Elizabeth his wife, born Nov. 26, and privately baptized Nov. 29, was received into the Congregation Dec. 16
1757	May	4	Jane, Daughter of John & Anne Philpot
1757	May	9	Alice, Daughter of John Abbot & Alice his wife (of the Arch-Bishops palace)
1757	March	11	George, the Son of George Philpot & Sarah his wife, (of the Arch-Bishops Palace), by John Airson
1757	May	25	Elizabeth, Daughter of the Revd Mr John Airson, (minor Canon of this Church), & Ann his wife, born May 25, privately baptized the same day, & received into the Congregation June 22
1757	October	2	Robert, Son of Bennett & Catharine Cuthbertson (an officer in Benticks Regiment of Foot) was privately baptized

Year.	Month.	Day.	Names.
1757	October	5	Cholmondeley, Son of the Revd Mr Osmund Beauvoir (master of the Kings School), and Anne his wife
1757	November	14	Anne Frances, daughter of John Fleming (an officer in Manners's Regiment of foot), and Lucy his wife, was privately baptized Nov. 14. And received into ye Congregation Dec. 28
			Wm Broderip, Sacrist
1758	February	11	Ester-Maria, daughter of Samuel Porter (Organist of this Church) and Sarah his wife, was privately baptized Feb. 11, & Received into ye Congregation April 6
1758	March	25	John, Son of ye Revd Mr John Tucker (Under-Master of the Kings School) & of Jane his wife, was privately baptized Mar. 25, & received into the Congregation April 14 following
1758	May	7	Hester, daughter of the Revd Mr Francis Gregory, Minor Canon of this Church, and Elizabeth his wife, was privately baptiz'd May 7, & received into the Congregation ye 30th of May following
1758	July	8	John, Son of John Abbot (of ye Archbishop's Palace) & Alice his wife
1758	August	6	John, son of John & Ann Philpot
1758	October	4	Jane, Daughter of the Revd Mr Osmund Beauvoir, (Master of the Kings School), and Ann his wife, was privately baptiz'd Oct. 4, & received into ye church Oct. 28
			Th^{o} Lamprey, Sacrist
1758	December	29	Catharine, Daught^{r} of Mr William Gostling (Lieutenant of the Royal Regim^{t} of Artillery) & Mary his wife, was born & privately baptiz'd Dec. 29 & rec^{d} into ye Church Jan. 22 1759
1759	June	5	Elisabeth, Daughter of John & Catharine Neame
1759	August	22	John, Son of Adde Read & Sarah his wife
1759	August	13*	William, Son of the Revd Mr John Tucker (Under Master of the Kings Schole) & Jane his wife, was born and privately baptized Aug. 13th: & receiv'd into the Congregation Sep. 7.
			Richd Leightonhouse, Sacrist
1759	November	30	Matilda, Daughter of the Revd Mr John Airson, Minor Canon of this Church, and Anne his wife
1760	February	3	John, Son of the Revd Mr Osmund Beauvoir (Master of the Kings School), and Ann his wife, was born Jan. 28, baptiz'd privately Feb. 3rd, and receiv'd into the Church March 1st
1760	March	6	Francis, Son of the Revd Mr Francis Gregory (Minor Canon of this Church) and Elizabeth his Wife, was privately baptiz'd March 6, and receiv'd into the Congregation April 9
1760	April	13	Thomas, son of John & Ann Philpot
1760	April	26	Alice-Elizabeth, Daughter of John and Alice Abbot (of the Archbishops Palace)
1760	May	27	John, base born Son of Ann Taylor
			Fran. Gregory, Sacrist
1760	November	18	Elizabeth, Daughter of the Revd Mr John Tucker (Under Master of the Kings School) and Jane his wife, was born & privately baptized November 18th, & received into the Congregation Dec. 11

* So in the original.

Year.	Month.	Day.	Names.
1761	January	1	Martin, son of the Revd Mr John Benson (One of the Six Preachers of this Church), & Susanna his wife, was privately baptiz'd January 1st, & received into the Congregation January 23rd
1761	March	31	Ann, Daughter of John & Catherine Neame
1761	February	14*	Isabella, Daughter of the Revd Mr Osmund Beauvoir (Master of the Kings School) & Ann his wife, born Jan. 18th
			J. Airson, Sacrist
1762	February	10	Hannah-Mary, Daughter of John Philpot and Ann his wife
1762	March	25	Sarah-Priscilla, Daughter of Samuel Porter (Organist of this Church) & Sarah his wife
1762	April	4	Rebecca-Ann, Daughter of William Rouse & Mary his wife
1762	August	24	Jenkin Middleton, Son of Captain Jenkin Reding & Sarah his wife
			J. Goodwin, Curate of Lyd
1762	August	4*	Alice Dorothy, Daughter of the Rev. Mr John Tucker (Under Master of the Kings School) & Jane his wife, was born & privately baptized August 4th, and received into the Congregation Aug. 26th
1762	October	26	Charles, Son of John Abbot (of the Archbishops Palace) and Alice his wife
			William Gostling, Sacrist
1763	February	7	Sarah, Daughter of Adde Reed and Sarah his wife
1763	July	16	Henry, Son of Captain Henry Knight and Catherine his wife, was baptized by me Wm Tatton, Preb: of Cant.
			Will. Broderip, Sacrist
1763	October	27	Edward Carlos, Son of the Revd Mr Francis Gregory & Elizabeth his wife, born & privately baptized Oct. 27, & receiv'd into ye Congregation Nov. 25
1763	December	11	Sarah Elizabeth, Daughter of the Revd Mr John Duncombe (Rector of St Andrews) & Susanna his wife, was privately baptized Dec. 11, & receiv'd into the Congregation Dec. 27
1764	January	20	Stephen, Son of the Revd Mr John Tucker (Under-Master of the Kings Schole) & Jane his wife, was born and privately Baptiz'd Jan^{ry} 20, & rec^{d} into the Congregation Feb. 17
1764	January	31	Elizabeth Anne, Daughter of the Revd Mr Thomas Freeman (Minor Canon of this Church) & Margaret his wife, was privately baptized Jany 31st, & received into the Congregation February 22
1764	June	8	Elizabeth, Daughter of Thomas Scammell & Elizabeth his wife
1764	September	3	Robert, Son of Henry Knight, Esq., & Catharine his wife, was born (in the Archbishop's Palace) Aug. 24
1764	October	30	Catharine Charlotte, Daughter of John & Catharine Neame
1764	November	3	Charles, Son of Edward & Hester-Elizabeth Thurlow
			Richard Leightonhouse, Sacrist
1765	March	13	Mary, Daughter of Thomas & Mary Leutton
1765	April	20	Anna-Maria, Daughter of the Rev. Mr John Duncombe (Rector of St Andrews) and Susanna his wife
1765	March	28	William, Son of the Rev. Mr Francis Gregory (Minor Canon of this Church) & Elizabeth his wife, was privately baptized March 28, and received into the Congregation on 22 Ap^{ril}

* So in the original.

Year.	Month.	Day.	Names.
1765	August	29	Mary, Daughter of the Rev. Mr William Taswell (Minor Canon of this Church) and Hannah his wife
1765	September	10	Samuel, Son of Mr Samuel Porter (Organist of this Church), and Sarah his wife
1765	November	5	Thomas, Son of Isaac & Sarah Sladden
			Fran. Gregory, Sacrist
1766	February	18	William Henry, Son of Henry Knight Esq., & Catharine his Wife
1766	March	20	Edward, Son of Edward & Elizabeth Smith, of the Archbishops Palace
1766	April	6	William, Son of the Revd Mr John Tucker (under master of the Kings School) & Jane his wife, was privately baptized April 6th, & received into the Congregation May 2nd
1766	May	15	Sarah, Daughter of John Philpot & Ann his wife
1766	October	9	Elizabeth, Daughter of the Revd Mr William Taswell, Minor Canon of this Church, & Hannah his wife
1766	October	11	John & Henry, Sons of the Rev. Francis Gregory, Minor Canon of this Church, & Elizabeth his wife, were privately baptiz'd Oct. 11th, & received into the Congregation Nov. 6th
			John Airson, Sacrist
1767	January	19	Hannah, Daught^{r} of John & Alice Abbot
1767	March	4	John, Son of Thos & Mary Leuton
1767	February	28*	W^{m}, Son of the Revd Mr Duncombe & Susanna his wife, was privately baptized
1767	April	3	Saml, Son of Mr Saml Porter, Organist of this Church, & Sarah his wife, was privately baptized April 3^{d}, & received into the Congregation ye 21st of D^{o}
1767	July	10	Isaac, Son of Isaac Sladden and Sarah his Wife
1767	July	16	Ann, Daughter of Colonel John Douglas & Mary his Wife
1767	July	30	Thos, Son of the Revd Mr Thos Freeman (Minor Canon of this Church), & Margaret his Wife, privately baptized July 30th, and rec^{d} into the Congregation the 7th of Sep^{t}
			Th^{o} Freeman, Sacrist
1768	February	18	Mary, daught^{r} of the Revd Mr John Tucker (Under Master of the Kings School) & Jane his Wife, was privately baptiz'd ye 18 of Feb., & receiv'd into the Congregation ye 15th of March
1768	October	5	Catharine Elizabeth Tatton, Daughter of the Revd Dr William Tatton, Prebendary of this Church, & Sarah his wife
1768	September	3*	Anna Maria, D^{r} of George & Sarah Philpot
1768	October	9	John, Son of the Revd Mr John Duncombe (one of the Six Preachers) and Susannah his wife
			W. Taswell, Sacrist
1769	July	9	Thomas, Son of John & Martha Preston
1769	July	23	Mary, Daughter of John & Mary Howell
1769	August	10	James-Kent, Son of Thomas & Mary Leutton
1769	September	23*	Jeremiah, Son of Jeremiah & Elizabeth Hatton
1769	August	17	Anne-Betty, Daught^{r} of ye Revd Mr Thos Freeman, (Min. Canon of this Church), & Margaret his wife, was privately baptized August 17th, & rec^{d} into ye Congregation ye 29th of Sept^{r}

* So in the original.

Year.	Month.	Day.	Names.
1769	September	3	Henry, ye Son of ye Revd Mr Francis Gregory (Min. Can. of this Church) & Elizabeth his wife, was privately baptized Sep. 3rd, & recd into ys Congregation ye 3rd of October following
			Richard Leightonhouse, Sacrist
1770	February	24	John, Son of Mr George Philpot, of the Archbishops Palace, and Sarah his wife, born Jan. 25
1770	February	9*	Catharine, Daughter of the Revd Mr John Tucker (Under Master of the Kings School) and Jane his wife, was privately baptized Feb. 9th, and receiv'd into the Congregation March 7
1770	June	17	Harriot, Daughter of the Rev. Mr John Benson, Prebendary of this Church, & Susanna his wife, was baptized privately on Sunday ye 17 of June, and receiv'd into ys Congregation the 4th of July following
			Fran. Gregory, Sacrist
1771	April	10	Ann, Daughter of Thomas and Elizabeth Allcorn
1771	May	24	Elizabeth, Daughter of Thomas & Mary Leutton
1771	July	19	Charles Ellis (A Negro, aged 35)
1771	September	4	Benjamin, Son of Edward & Elizabeth Smith (of the Archbishops Palace)
1771	October	12	William, Son of John & Mary Howell
			J. Airson, Sacrist
1771	November	25	Margaretta Maria, Daughter of the Revd Mr Thos Freeman, Minor Canon of this Church, and Margaret his wife, was born Nov. 18, privately baptized Nov. 25th, & received into ye Congregation ye 20th of Decr
1772	April	16	Ann Dow, aged 25, a Quaker Servant to Dr Benson, Prebendary of this Church
			Tho. Freeman, Sacrist
1772	June	28	Martha, base born Daughter of Martha Stevens
1772	August	17	John, Son of John Simmonds & Ruth his Wife, was privately baptized August ye 17th, & received into the Congregation ye 2d of September following
			Tho. Freeman, Sacrist
1773	March	27	Carolina, Daughter of the Revd Dr John Moore, Dean of this Church, and Catherine his wife
1773	May	6	Ann, Daughter of the Revd Mr Wm Taswell (Minor Canon of this Church) and Hannah his wife, was privately baptized May ye 6th, and received into the Congregation June ye 3rd
1773	September	12	Elizabeth, Daughter of Edward & Martha Smith
			Wm Taswell, Sacrist
1773	December	14	Mary, Daughter of Edward Hasted, Esq., & Ann his Wife, was privately baptized Dec. 14, received into the Church Jan. 8, 1774, by the names of Mary Barbara Bennett
1774	March	27	Thomas, Son of John Simmonds & Ruth his wife
1774	April	22	Mary, Daughter of the Revd Mr Joshua Dix (Minor Canon of this Church) and Martha his wife, born 25 March
1774	July	15	William, Son of the Revd Dr John Moore, Dean of this Church, and Catherine his Wife, was privately baptized July 15th, & received into the Congregation Aug. 6th
1774	August	13	Alice, Daughter of Thomas Allcorn & Elizabeth his wife

* So in the original.

Year.	Month.	Day.	Names.
1774	October	25	Harriot, Daughter of the Revd Mr Wm Taswell (Minor Canon of this Church) and Hannah his Wife
1774	October	27	Solomon, Son of John Royes & Sarah his Wife, of the Precinct of this Church
			J. Dix, Sacrist
1775	January	13	Rebecca Maria, Daughter of Thomas and Mary Leutton
1775	February	2	William James, son of Mr Samuel Potter (Organist of this Church) and Sarah his wife, was privately baptized
1775	March	3	John Wootton, Son of Edward Smith and Martha his Wife, of the Archbishop's Palace
1775	May	13	Maria, Daughter of Mr Robert Le Geyt (of the Archbishop's Palace) and Anna Maria his wife, was privately baptized
1775	August	27	Mary, Daughter of Jeremiah Hatton & Elizabeth his wife
1775	August	30	Mary, base born Daughter of Mary Woolcot
1775	October	25	Stephen, Son of John Simmonds & Ruth his wife
1775	November	9	Mary Broadley, an Adult
			Fran. Gregory, Sacrist
1776	January	2	Susanna Horn, an Adult, of the Archbishops Palace
1776	April	1	Phillip, Son of Mr Robert Le Geyt, of the Archbishops Palace, & Anna Maria his wife, was privately baptized April 1st, received into the Congregation May 7th
1776	February	15	Joshua, Son of the Revd Mr Joshua Dix (Minor Canon of this Church) & Martha his wife, born Jan. 21st
			John Airson, Sacrist
1777	January	24	Francis, Son of Edward Smith (of the Archbishop's Palace) and Martha his Wife
1777	February	17	Thomas, son of Thomas & Mary Leutton
1777	March	3	Elizabeth, Daughter of Thomas Allcorn & Elizabeth his Wife
1777	July	13	Joseph, Son of John Simmonds and Ruth his Wife
1777	August	31	William, Son of Mr Robt Legeyt, of the Archbishop's Palace, & Anna Maria his Wife, born Aug. ye 30th, privately baptized Aug. 31st, and rec^{d} into the Congregation Oct. 9th
			Tho. Freeman, Sacrist
1777	October	23	Caroline, Daughter of the Revd Mr William Taswell, Vicar of Aylsham, in ye county of Norfolk, and Hannah his wife, was privately baptiz'd October 23^{d}, & receiv'd into ye Congregation Dec. 4th
1778	March	15	William, Son of Bartholomew & Mary Elvy, was privately baptized Mar. 15, receiv'd into ye Congregation March 19th
1778	August	29	Joseph, son of Jeremiah Hatton & Elizabeth his Wife, was privately baptiz'd Augst 29th, received into ye Congregation Oct. 17
1778	October	27	Edward, Son of Joshua & Martha Dix, born Sep. 29
			J. Dix, Sacrist
1778	November	27	James, Son of Thomas & Mary Saffery
1778	December	14	Henry, Son of John & Hannah Jagger
1779	February	7	William, Son of the Revd William Chafy, Min^{r} Canon of this Church, and Mary his Wife, resident in the Arch-Bishop's Palace, was born and privately baptized Feby the 7th, & received into the Congregation March 10
1779	March	19	Wootton, Son of Edward Smith (of the Arch-Bishop's Palace) & Martha his wife
1779	June	17	Bartholomew, Son of Bartholomew & Mary Elvy

Year.	Month.	Day.	Names.
1779	September	8	Robert, Son of Joshua Dix, Minor Canon of this Cathedral, & Martha his wife, born Sepᵗʳ 8ᵗʰ, & received into the Congregation Sepᵗʳ 29ᵗʰ following
1779	November	6	George, Son of George Philpot (of the Arch-Bishop's Palace) & Penelope his wife
			J. Ford, Sacrist
1779	November	29	James, son of James Ford, Minor-Canon of this Church, & Dorothy his wife
1780	January	15	William, Son of Benjamin & Mary Batt
1780	January	16	John Monins, Son of Mʳ Robert Le Geyt, of the Archbishop's Palace, and Anna Maria his wife, was privately baptized Janʸ the 16ᵗʰ, and received into the Congregation Febʸ the 18ᵗʰ
1780	April	25	Ann, Daughter of John Jager & Hannah his Wife
1780	April	29	Horatio, Son of the Honorable & Revᵈ Dʳ James Cornwallis, Dean of this Church, and Catharine his Wife, born March 27
1780	June	16	George, Son of John Simmonds & Ruth his Wife
1780	July	9	Catherine, Daughter of John Springall & Mary his Wife
1780	July	16	John, Son of the Revᵈ William Chafy, Minor Canon of this Church, and Mary his wife, born & privately baptized July the 16ᵗʰ, and received into the Congregation Augˢᵗ 10ᵗʰ
1780	July	30	George Finch, Son of Jeremiah Hatton and Elizabeth his Wife
			William Chafy, Sacrist
1781	May	5	William, Son of the Rev. James Ford (Minor Canon of this Church) and Dorothy his Wife
1781	May	17	Robert, Son of John Jager & Hannah his Wife
1781	July	17	Martha, Daughter of Edward Smith (of the Archbishop's Palace) and Martha his Wife
1781	September	19	Mary, Daughter of John Springall & Mary his Wife
1781	October	21	Jacob Christopher, Son of Jacob Schnebbelie & Carolina his Wife, born Jan. 7, 1780
1781	October	21	Robert Blemell, Son of Jacob Schnebbelie & Carolina his Wife, born Sepʳ 16, 1781
			Fran. Gregory, Sacrist
1782	February	17	Mary, the Daughter of Thomas & Mary Saffery, privately baptized February 17ᵗʰ & received into the Church Feb. 24ᵗʰ
1782	March	30	Elizabeth Ann Blunden, Daughter of Benjamin and Mary Batt
1782	May	5	Henry, Son of John Simmons & Ruth his wife, privately baptized May 5ᵗʰ, & received into the Congregation July 29ᵗʰ
1782	June	8	Mary, Daughter of the Revᵈ James Ford (Minor Canon of this Church) and Dorothy his wife, privately baptized June 8ᵗʰ, & received into the Church July 10ᵗʰ
1782	June	20	Frances, Daughter of the Revᵈ William Chafy (Minor Canon of this Church) and Mary his wife, privately baptiz'd June 20ᵗʰ, & received into the Congregation July 16ᵗʰ
1782	August	27	James, Son of Bartholomew & Mary Elvy
			John Airson, Sacrist
1783	February	24	Sarah, Daughter of John Springall & Mary his Wife
1783	August	11	Elizabeth, Daughter of the Revᵈ John Tucker, Master of the Kings School, and Sarah his wife, born Aug. 10ᵗʰ

Year.	Month.	Day.	Names.
			privately baptized Augst 11th, & received into the congregation Sep. 19th
1783	May	13*	John, Son of John Jager & Hannah his Wife
1783	September	8	Elizabeth, Daughter of Edward Smith, of the Archbishop's Palace, & Martha his Wife
			Tho. Freeman, Sacrist
1784	January	31	James, Son of the Revd William Chafy, Minor Canon of this Church, & of Mary his Wife, privately baptized Jan. 31st, & receiv'd into the Congregation March 25th
1784	July	18	William, Son of Benjamin Batt & Mary his Wife
1784	July	29	Frances, Daughter of the Revd Joshua Dix (Minor Canon of this Church) & Martha his Wife, born ye 25th of June
1784	September	24	George, Son of John Jagger & Hannah his Wife
			J. Dix, Sacrist
1785	April	14	Ann, Daughter of Bartholomew and & Mary Elvy
1785	June	5	William, Son of the Revd James Ford (Minor Canon of this Church) & Dorothy his wife, was privately baptized June 5th, & received into the Congregation ye 13th following
1785	July	5	Charles, Son of John & Ruth Simmonds
1785	November	6	Elias, Son of Benjamin & Mary Batt
			J. Ford, Sacrist
1786	March	29	Philip Gurney, an adult Mulatto, of Philadelphia, in North America
1786	July	20	Thomas, son of John Jager & Hannah his Wife
1786	September	4	Edward John Winterbottom, Son of the Revd Edward William Whitaker (Second Master of the King's School) and Mary his Wife, was privately baptized Sept^{br} the 4th, & received into the Congregation Sep^{br} the 26th
			William Chafy, Sacrist
1786	November	27	James, Son of John Springall & Mary his Wife
1786	December	24	Sophia Ursula, Daughter of the Rev. William Chafy (Minor Canon of this Church) and Mary his Wife, born Decr 14th, privately baptized Decr 24, and receiv'd into the Congregation Jan^{ry} 22^{d}, 1787
1787	April	15	Thomas, Son of William & Sarah Green, privately baptiz'd at the Dean'ry
1787	May	10	Dorothy, Daughter of the Revd James Ford, Minor Canon of this Church, and Dorothy his Wife
1787	June	10	Mary, Daughter of Henry & Ann Gee
1786	November	18	John, Son of Sr Thomas Hyde Page, Knight, and Dame Mary Albinia his Wife, born at Montpellier, in the South of France, Novr 18, 1786, and privately baptiz'd the same day by the Revd Mr Adair, a Clergiman of the Established Church of England, was received into the Congregation in this Church July 17, 1787
1787	August	1	Helen, Daughter of the Revd Joshua Dix, Minor Canon of this Church, and Martha his Wife, born June 29
1787	August	15	Philip Henry, Son of Henry Kemp and Susanna his Wife
			Fran. Gregory, Sacrist
1788	February	1	Sarah, Daughter of John Jager & Hannah his Wife
1788	March	3	Richard the reputed Son of John Monins, of the Archbishops Palace, by Sarah Trice

* So in the original.

Year.	Month.	Day.	Names.
1788	February	25*	Mary Ann, Daughter of the Revd J. Francis, second Master of the King's School, & Mary his Wife, was born Decr 6th 1787, privately baptized Feb. 25th 1788, and received into the Congregation the 16th Oct^{r}
1788	June	25	Charles, Son of John Abbot & Susannah his Wife, was privately baptized June 25th & received into the Congregation the eighth day of August
1788	August	8	John, Son of the Revd Joshua Dix, Minor Canon of this Church, & Martha his Wife, born July the 2nd
1788	August	28	Mary Ann, Daughter of Henry & Susannah Kemp
1788	September	3	Henry, Son of John & Ruth Simmonds
1788	November	13	Edward, base-born son of Anna Marsh from the Archbishop's Palace
			Tho. Freeman, Sacrist
1788	December	7	Henry, Son of Henry & Ann Gee
1789	February	16	Elizabeth, Daughter of William & Sarah Green
1789	March	22	Edward, Son of Edward & Sarah Smith, of the Archbishop's Palace
1789	March	24	James, Son of the Rev. Wm Gregory, one the Six Preachers of this Church, and Catharine his Wife, was privately baptized March 24th—receiv'd into the Congregation April 27th
1789	July	26	John, Son of John Wrightson & Elizabeth his Wife
1789	July	14	Champion Edward, son of Champion Branfill, Esqr and Charlotte his Wife, was privately baptized on July 14th—receiv'd into the Church Aug. 10th
1789	September	3	Harriott, Daughter of William & Ann Welby, of the Arch-Bishops Palace
1789	September	16	Charles, Son of the Revd James Ford, Minor Canon of this Church, and Dorothy his Wife
1789	September	29	Richard, Son of the Revd Joshua Dix, Minor Canon of this Church, & Martha his Wife, born August 23rd
			Joshua Dix, Sacrist
1789	November	12	Mary, Daughter of John Monins, Esqr, and Sarah his Wife, privately baptized November the 12th. Received into the Church December 25th
1790	January	1	Henry, Son of Henry Humphry Sandys & Helen his wife
1790	February	20	Sarah, Daughter of William & Sarah Green
1790	April	2	Charlotte, Daughter of John and Ruth Simmonds
1790	April	17	Eliza, Daughter of the Rv^{d} John Francis (Second Master of the King's School) and Mary his Wife, born March 23rd, and privately baptized April 17th
1790	May	31	Mary Ann, Daughter of John & Hannah Jager
1790	August	8	William Roy, son of William & Catherine Groombridge. From the Archbishop's Palace
1790	August	22	George, Son of the Revd William Gregory (one of the Six Preachers of this Church) and Catharine his Wife, was privately baptized August 22nd, & received into the Church September 20th
1790	December	12	Martha, Daughter of the Rev. Wm Chafey, Minor Canon of this Church, and Mary his Wife, born Dec^{br} 7th, privately baptized Dec^{br} 12th, and received into the Congregation January the 25th, 1791
1790	December	27	Thomas, Baseborn Son of Mary Bye (Poor)

* So in the original.

Year.	Month.	Day.	Names.
1791	January	16	Sarah, Daughter of Edward and Sarah Smith, of the Arch-Bishop's Palace
1791	February	24	William James, son of James and Esther Blackley
1791	March	14	Charles, Son of William and Ann Welby
1791	April	1	William, baseborn Son of Sophy Tanner
1791	October	10	Charlotte, Daughter of William and Mary Vidgen
			William Chafy, Sacrist
1791	December	31	Catharine, Daughter of the Revd William Gregory, Rector of St Andrew's, in the City of Canterbury, and Catharine his Wife, was privately baptized Decr 31, 1791, and received into the Church, Feb. 7th, 1792
1792	January	10	Jemima Elizabeth, Daughter of Champion Branfill, Esq., and Charlotte his Wife, was privately baptized Jan. 10th, and receiv'd into the Congregation Feb^{ry} 20
1792	February	27	William, Son of John Monins, Esq., of the Archbishop's Palace, and Sarah his Wife, born Feb^{ry} 20th
1792	June	16	William, Son of John and Elizabeth Wrightson
1792	June	28	Elizabeth, Daughter of John & Hannah Jager
1792	July	9	Elizabeth Isabella, Daughter of the Revd Henry John Todd, Minor Canon of this Church, and Anne his Wife
1792	September	9	Jane Sophia, Daughter of Henry & Ann Gee
1792	September	23	Elizabeth Mary, Daughter of William and Anne Welby
			Fran. Gregory, Sacrist
1792	December	6	Thomas Francis, Son of Edward and Sarah Smith, of the Archbishop's Palace
1793	March	4	James Studwell, son of William and Mary Vidgen
1793	April	26	Robert, Son of James Ford, Minor Canon of this Church, and Dorothy his wife, was privately baptized April 26, and received into the Church May 23
1793	November	15	Charles, Son of the Revd Joshua Dix, Minor Canon of this Church, and Martha his Wife, born Octr 5th, baptized & received into the Church Novr 15th
			Tho. Freeman, Sacrist
1794	May	12	Mary Georgina, Daughter of the Revd Henry John Todd, Minor Canon of this Church, and Ann his wife, was privately baptized May 12th, and receiv'd into the Congregation June 18th
1794	May	20	William, Son of the Revd William Gregory, Rector of St Andrew's, in the City of Canterbury, and Catharine his Wife
1794	June	15	Sarah, Daughter of Edward & Sarah Smith, of the Arch-Bishops Palace
1794	June	27	Susannah, D^{r} of John Jager & Hannah his Wife
1794	July	29	Harriott, Daughter of Wm Stacey Coast, Esqr, & Hester his Wife, born 6th May preceding
1794	August	24	Herbert, Son of the Revd Dr Folliott Herbert Walker Cornewall, Dean of this Church, and Anne his Wife, born July 21st, privately baptized August 24th, & receiv'd into ye Congregation Sept^{br} 27th
1795	January	12	George Oliver Evans, Son of Evan Evans & Amy his Wife
1795	January	11*	Martha Jemima, Daughter of the Revd Wm Chafy (one of the Minor Canons of this Church) & Mary his Wife, born Dec^{br} 31st 1794, privately baptized Jan^{ry} 11th 1795, & receiv'd into the Congregation March the 10th

* So in the original.

Year.	Month.	Day.	Names.
1795	October	23	Elizabeth, Daughter of William & Mary Vidgen
1796	April	12	Martha Ann, Daughter of Edward and Sarah Smith, of the Arch-Bishops Palace
1796	August	5	John, Son of John & Hannah Jager
			William Chafy, Sacrist
1797	January	24	George, Son of Thos & Elizabeth Gilbert
1797	March	22	Eliza Mary, daughter of Evan and Amy Evans, was privately bapt^{d} March 22, & received into the Congregation the 30th of April
1797	April	17	Sarah, daughter of Valentine & Sarah Smith, of the Archbishop's Palace, was privately bapt^{d} April 17th, & rec^{d} into the Congregation May 29
1797	April	18	Charles, Son of William & Sarah Johnston, of the Archbishop's Palace, was privately bapt^{d} April 18th, & was received into ye Congregation May 1st
1797	April	29	Maria, daughter of William & Mary Vidgen
1797	May	1	Catherine, daughter of the Revd Henry John Todd & Anne his wife, was privately baptized May 1st, & rec^{d} into the Congregation June 8th
			Henry John Todd, Sacrist
1797	November	26	John Freeman, Son of John George and Margaretta Maria Wood, was born Novr 19th, privately baptized the 26th of the same month, & rec^{d} into the Church Decr 27th
1798	April	12	Elizabeth, Daughter of Edward Smith and Sarah his Wife, of the Archbishop's Palace
1798	June	10	Elizabeth, Daughter of John Tiddeman & Mary his Wife
1798	September	4	John, Son of William & Elizabeth Wiltshier, of the Archbishops Palace
1798	September	6	Robert John, Son of John Scott, Esq., & Elizabeth his Wife
1798	October	14	Elizabeth Mary, Daughter of James London, of the Archbishop's Palace, and Elizabeth his Wife, born Sepr 16
			Fran. Gregory, Sacrist
1799	January	21	Sarah, Daughter of John Monins, Esqr, and Sarah his Wife, of the Precincts of the Archbishops Palace, was born Jan 14th, privately baptized the 21st, & received into the Church March 2nd
1799	March	9	Sarah, Daught^{r} of William and Sarah Johnson, privately
1799	April	13	William Henry, Son of William and Mary Vidgen
1799	May	16	George, Son of John & Hannah Jager
1799	June	18	Hannah, Daughter of the Revd Henry John Todd & Anne his Wife, was privately baptized June 18th. Rec^{d} into the Church July ye 15th
1799	August	6	Joseph, Son of Samuel & Mary Botle, a Soldier
1799	August	6	James, Son of James & Mary Dedman, a Soldier
1799	October	2	William Harrison, the supposed Son of Thomas Harrison and Jane* Coulter, from St Paul's
1800	February	20	Mary Catherine, Daughter of Edward Smith and Sarah his Wife, of the Arch-Bishop's Palace
1800	March	4	Henry, Son of Benjamin & Ann Revill, of the Royal Artillery
1800	January	30†	Edward, Son of John Monins, Esqr, and Sarah his Wife, of the Arch-B—p^{s} Palace, born Jany 26th, privately baptized 30th D^{o}, & receiv'd into ye Congregation March 8th following

* The word Ann erased, and Jane written over.
† So in the original.

Year.	Month.	Day.	Names.
1800	July	13	William, Son of John & Mercy Baynes, one of the Bell-Ringers of this Church. Born in Burgate Parish
1800	September	14	Austin, Son of Valentine Austin Smith & Sarah his Wife, of y[e] Arch B—ps Palace
1800	September	14	James, Son of Andrew & Elizabeth Forrest, of 14th Regm[t] Light Dragoons
1800	October	2	Jane, Daughter of William & Elizabeth Wiltshier, of y[e] Arch-Bishops Palace
1800	October	10	Jane Packman, Daughter of Francis Smith and Elizabeth his Wife, of the Arch-B—ps Palace
			Joshua Dix, Sacrist
1800	December	6	Maria, Daughter of William & Mary Vidgen
1801	January	6	Thomas Edward Chafie, Son of the Rev[d] W[m] Chafy, Minor Canon of this Church, and Mary his Wife
1801	March	3	Frederic John, baseborn Son of Charlotte Thomsett, born in the Almonry (Extra-parochial), being not well, and no duty at the Time at S[t] Paul's, the nearest Church
1801	April	26	Henry Edwin, Son of William and Sarah Johnson
*	June	13	Jane, daughter of the Rev[d] Henry John Todd & Anne his wife, was privately baptized June 13th & received into the Congregation June 30th
1801	March†	25	Henry, Son of John Monins, Esq[r], of the Arch-Bishop's Palace, and Sarah his Wife, was born March the 21st, privately baptized March the 25th and received into the Congregation July the 9th following
1801	August†	16	Harriot, Daughter of Thomas and Catherine Parnell
1801	July†	9	Robert Horace, Son of John Scott, Esq[r], and Elizabeth his wife, was privately baptiz'd July the 9th & received into the Congregation Aug. 22nd following
1801	June†	22	John Allen, Son of Michael and Martha Allen, of the Seventh Regim[t] of Dragoons, privately
			William Chafy, Sacrist
1801	December	21	Robert, Son of William & Sarah Powell
1802	February	28	Louisa Charlotte Margaret, dau[r] of the Rev[d] Henry William Champneys of the Precincts & Lucy his wife, born Feb[y] 27th, priv[y] bapt[d] Feb[y] 28. Received into the Congregation June 28th
1802	March	7	Mary Ann, dau[r] of William & Ann Hacker, of the Arch-bishop's Palace, privately
1802	July	3	Henry, son of William & Jane Smith
1802	July	30	Thomas, son of Thomas & Catherine Parnell
1802	August	1	Charles Haire, son of John & Mary Ann Walter, Privately. From the Archbishop's Palace
1802	August	30	Mary Ann, dau[r] of Valentine & Sarah Smith, of the Archbishop's Palace, privately bapt[d] Aug 30th, Rec[d] into the Congregation Sep[tr] 5th
1802	September	13	William, son of Rigden & Isabella Swain, privately
1802	November	7	Thomas, son of William & Olly Roswell
1802	September†	6	Harvey, Son of John George Wood & Margaretta Maria his wife, born in the Parish of S[t] Mary-la-bonne, London, Aug[t]. 31st, privately baptized September 6th, & received into Church y[e] 18th of November following
1803	April	5	John, Son of William & Elizabeth Wiltshire, of the Arch-bishop's Palace

*** In the original no year is affixed to this entry. Query 1801.**
† So in the original.

Year.	Month.	Day.	Names.
1803	May	19	Charles Hare, Son of John & Mary Ann Walter, born the 7th of July 1802
1803	May	19	Elizabeth, Daughter of William & Elizabeth Webster, born 13th Sept. 1800
1803	November	4	Edmund, son of John and Mary Tiddeman
1803	September*	21	Sarah, Daug^{r} of William & Sarah Johnson
			Tho. Freeman, Sacrist
1803	December	4	Rosa Dietrichstein, Daughter of Mr John George Wood & Margaretta Maria his wife, born October 21st, & privately baptized Decr 4th. Received into the Congregation Jan^{ry} 31st
1803	December	13	Jane Anna, Daughter of the Revd Philip Legeyt & Jane his wife, was privately baptized
1803	December	3*	Alicia, Daughter of John Scot, Esqr, & Elizabeth his wife, born Octr 27, 1803, baptized 3 Dec^{r}
1804	September	2	John, Son of William and Mary Deane
1804	October	17	John, Son of John Tiddeman & Mary his wife
1804	November	14	Mary Elizabeth, Daughter of Thomas & Mary Bradshaw
			T. A. Mutlow, Sacrist
1805	April	10	Henrietta Mary, Daughter of the Revd Henry William Champneys & Lucy his Wife, of the Precinct of this Church, born April 9th, & privately baptized April 10th
1805	April	12	Elizabeth, Daughter of James Saffery & Mary-Ann his wife, privately baptized April 12. Received into the Congregation May 7th following J. Dix, Sacrist
1805	June	19	John, Son of John Need, Esqr, of Sherwood Hall, in ye County of Nottingham, and Mary his Wife; privately
1805	September	19	Eliza, Daughter of W^{m} & Elizabeth Wiltshire, of the Arch-Bishops Palace
1805	November	22	Harriet, Daughter of Thomas & Dells Starr
			J. Dix, Sacrist
1806	February	23	George, Son of William & Sarah Johnson
1806	June	29	Henry Charles, Son of Thomas & Mary Bradshaw
1806	July	11	Emily Catharine, Daughter of ye Revd Henry-William Champneys and Lucy his Wife, born July ye Eleventh, 1806, and privately baptized the same day
1806	September	11	James, Son of William and Elizabeth Bowers, was privately baptized
1806	November	16	John George, Son of John George Wood and Margaretta Maria his Wife, was born Nov. 9, and privately baptized the 16th, 1806
1806	November	16	James Sanders,† Son of William and Sarah Wheeler
			Tho: Freeman, Sacrist
1807	May	6	Mary Jane, Daughter of Henry & Harriot Hunter, born Ap^{l} 20th, 1806
1807	June	21	William, Son of Thomas & Mary Bradshaw, of the Arch-Bishop's Palace
1807	November	25	George, Son of Henry & Hanna Bremen, 2^{d} Regim^{t} Light Dragoons. King's German Legion
			J. Dix, Sacrist
1807	December	11	Thomas Wyllie, Son of Captain Matthias & Hannah Maria Sisk, Sojourners, born Aug. 20th, 1806, & received into the Congregation the 11th of Dec^{r}, 1807

* So in the original.

† In the original the name has been John Saunders, the word "John" has been obliterated and "James" substituted, and the letter "u" crossed out.

Year.	Month.	Day.	Names.
1807	December	14	Thomas, Son of William & Sarah Johnson, privately baptized 14th Decr, 1807, & received into the Congregation Jany 24th, 1808
1808	January	24	Ann, Daughter of William and Sarah Wheeler
1808	January	26	George-Culmer, Son of George & Sarah Simmonds, privately baptized 26th Jany, & received into the Congregation February 23rd, 1808
1808	February	20*	Harriet, daur of Thomas & Mary Wright, born Jany 7th, baptized Feby 20, 1808, Omitted by Mr Yeates (as stated by the Father.) W. Bennett
1808	January	18†	Powys, Son of Thomas & Dells Starr, privately baptized January 18th, & received into the Congregation April 26th, 1808
			Jno. Yeates, Sacrist
1808	September	3	Langton-Edward, Son of the Revd Walter Brown, Prebendary and Vice-Dean of this Cathedral, and Eliza his Wife, born August 3rd and baptized September 3rd, 1808
1808	September	3	Thomas Phipps Amian, Son of the Revrd Henry William Champneys, Vicar of St Mary Bredin in this City, and Lucy his Wife, born & privately baptized September 3rd, 1808
1808	September	26	Jane, Daughter of the Revd John Yeates, Minor Canon of this Church, and Jane his Wife, born September the 9th and baptized privately the 26th of September, 1808, and received into the Congregation November 14th, 1808
1808	October	3	Thomas-Monins, Son of Thomas Barnett, Esqr, Captain 96th Regt of Infantry, and Mary his Wife, born September the 6th, 1808
			J. Yeates, Sacrist
1808	December	11	Maria, Daughter of William & Mary Pursey
1808	December	24	Elizabeth, Daughr of Charles and Rebecca Anne Simmons.
			T. A. Mutlow, Sacrist
1809	January	17	Mary, Dr of Thomas & Mary Wright
1809	May	6	Henry Jay, Son of Arthur & Ann Stammers
1809	June	18	Louiza Elizabeth, Daughter of Thomas & Hannah Marden, of the Archbishop's Palace
1810	June	11	Ann Starr, Daughter of Thomas & Dells Starr, born March 11th
1810	July	29	Charles Norley, Son of Charles & Ann Norley
1810	August	16	Elizabeth Bates, Daughter of William & Mary Bates, of the Archbishop's Palace
1810	October	12	Sarah Simmonds, Daughtr of George & Sarah Simmonds, of the precincts
			J. Radcliffe, Sacrist
1810	December	20	Mary Sophia, daur of the Revd Henry William Champneys & Lucy his Wife, born Decr 20th, 1810, & baptized the same day
1811	January	27	William, Son of William & Mary Purssey
1811	August	25	Ann, daur of Charles & Ann Norley
1811	September	19	Sarah, daur of Thomas & Mary Wright
			W. Bennett, Sacrist

* This entry is interlined and in another handwriting. † So in the original.

Year.	Month.	Day.	Names. Residence and Profession of Father.
1812	June	7	Thomas & George, twin Sons of Thomas & Mary Macgill, brought from the parish of Northgate
1812	December	27	Sophia, Daughter of William and Mary Purssey

END OF THE CHRISTENINGS IN THE THIRD REGISTER.

1813	February	20	Edward Geoffrey John, Son of Henry William & Lucy Champneys, of the Precincts of the Arch Bishops Palace, Vicar of St Mary Bredin, in the City of Canterbury
1813	May	26	Martha, Daughter of Thomas & Mary Wright, of the Precincts, One of the Vesterers of the Cathedral
1813	June	3	Radcliffe John, Son of William & Hannah Abbot, of the Precincts, Proctor
1814	January	27	John Levett, Son of Thomas & Charlotte Julian Bennett, of the Precincts, Clerk, Rector of St Alphage & V. of St Mary, Northgate, born Decr 20th, 1813
1815	April	28	Hannah, daughter of Thomas and Mary Wright, of the Precincts, Vesterer
1815	May	28	William, Son of William & Mary Mockett, of the Precincts, Grocer
1815	September	17	Charlotte Julian, daughter of Thomas & Charlotte Julian Bennett, of the Precincts, Clerk, One of the Minor Canons of this Cathedral, Rector of St Alphage, V. of St Mary, Northgate
1815	October	9	William, Son of Thomas & Jane Pettman, of the Precincts, Carpenter
1816	April	8	Edward, Son of Aduet & Charlotte Norley, of the Precincts, Carpenter
1816	July	3	Frances, Daughter of Thomas & Mary Wright, of the Precincts, Vesterer
1816	November	3	Elizabeth Sarah, Daughter of William & Elizabeth Anne Monins, of the Precincts, Lieut. in the 18th Reg^t of Hussars
1817	May	22	Charlotte Julian, Daughter of Thomas & Charlotte Julian Bennett, of the Precincts, Minor Canon of this Church
1817	September	8	Emma Harriet, Daughter of John & Minerva Birt, of the Precincts, Head Master of the Kings School
1817	November	5	Charles James Hornby, Son of Henry William & Lucy Champneys, of the Precincts, Vicar of St Mary Bredin, Canterbury
1817	December	29	Hugh Josceline, Son of Hugh & Mary Percy, of the Precincts, Prebendary
1818	April	13	Charlotte, Daughter of Thomas & Mary Wright, of the Precincts, Vesterer
1818	September	30	John William, Son of John & Elizabeth Metcalfe, of the Precincts, Clerk*
1818	November	9	William Henry, Son of John & Minerva Birt, of the Precincts, Clerk
1819	August	9	Francis Levett, Son of Thomas & Charlotte Julian Bennett, of the Precincts, Minor Canon of this Church. Born May 21st

* One of the Minor Canons of the Cathedral.

Year.	Month.	Day.	Names. Residence and Profession of Father.
1820	January	28	Charles Cuyler, Son of Henry & Lætitia Anderson, of the Precincts, a Lieut. in the 69th Regt of Foot
1820	March	6	Catherine Louisa, daughter of John & Minerva Birt, of the Precincts, Clerk
1820	April	6	Henry, Son of Edward & Sarah Nicholson, of the Precincts, Shoemaker
1820	November	13	Eleanor Etheldreda, daughter of John and Elizabeth Metcalfe, of the Precincts, Clerk
1821	May	8	Kate, daur of George & Eliza Austin, of the Precincts, Painter & Gilder
1821	June	11	Eloisa Maria, daur of Thomas & Charlotte Julian Bennett, of the Precincts, Clerk, Minor Canon of this Cathedral
1821	July	26	Edward Phillips, son of John & Minerva Birt, of the Precincts, Clerk
1822	January	10	Charlotte Adams, daughter of William & Catherine Adley, of the Precincts, Plumber & Glazier
1822	March	3	John Nicholas, Son of John & Sarah Parks, of the Precincts of the Arch Bishops Palace, Grocer
1822	April	10	Charles, Son of William Pitman & Fanny Jones, of the Precincts, Clerk
1822	July	25	Maria Elizabeth (born May 9th), daughter of John & Elizabeth Metcalfe, of the Precincts, Clerk
1822	October	17	Isabella Jane, daughter of Robert & Elizabeth Ambler, of the Precincts, Schoolmaster
1823	May	5	William De Chair, Son of George & Mary Ann Baker, of the Deanery, Canterbury, Barrister at Law
1823	August	22	George (born Feb. 15th, 1821), Son of George & Eliza Austin, of the Churchyard, Precincts, Carver & Gilder
1823	August	22	Henry George (born March 19th, 1823), Son of George & Eliza Austin, of the Churchyard, Precincts, Carver & Gilder
1824	January	22	Joseph Powell, Son of John & Elizabeth Metcalfe, of the Precincts, Clerk
1824	June	21	Frances Hervey, daughter of John & Minerva Birt of the Precincts, Clerk
1824	July	6	Anne (born Feb. 14, 1824), daughter of the Honble John Evelyn and Catherine Elizabeth Boscawen of the Green Court, Clerk, Prebendary of this Cathedral
1824	October	7	Charlotte Augusta, daughter of the Honble George and Frances Pellew, of the Green Court, Clerk, Prebendary of this Cathedral
1824	October	12	Paris Lewis Grant, Son of Henry & Lætitia Anderson, of the Precincts, Staff Adjutant
1825	January	23	William Holtom, Son of the late Thomas & Charlotte Julian Bennett, of the Precincts, Clerk
1825	February	10	Jemima (born Xtmas-day, 1824), daughter of George Parry & Jane Bonham Marriott, of the Precincts, Clerk*
1825	June	18	Mary Eamonson, daughter of John & Elizabeth Metcalfe, of the Precincts, Clerk
1825	June	26	Amelia, daughter of William & Elizabeth Fell Chalk of Dover, a Clerk of the Customs
1825	August	14	Elizabeth (born Feb. 10th, 1825), daughter of George & Eliza Austin, of the Precincts, Carver & Gilder

* A Minor Canon of the Cathedral.

Year.	Month.	Day.	Names. Residence and Profession of Father.
1825	October	6	Lucy Pauli, dau^{r} of Thomas Thorpe & Elizabeth Delasaux, of the Precincts, Attorney
1825	October	28	Emma Anne, Daughter of William Pitman & Fanny Jones, of the Precincts, Clerk in Holy Orders
1826	January	2	Elizabeth Martha, Daughter of Edward & Sarah Nicholson, of the Precincts of the Arch Bishop's Palace, Shoemaker
1826	August	22	Henrietta Agneta, Daug^{r} of the Honble George & Frances Pellew, of the Precincts, Prebendary, born June 20th
1826	October	30	Robert, Son of John & Elizabeth Metcalfe, of the Precincts, Clerk
1827	January	27	Catherine, Daughter of George Parry & Jane Bonham Marriott, of the Precincts. Born Octr 9th, 1826. Clerk in Holy Orders
1827	July	17	Jane, Daughter of William & Harriett Roots, of St Mildred's Parish, Canterbury, Cornfactor
1827	December	25	Hugh (born Octob. 13th), Son of George & Eliza Austin, of the Precincts, Architect
1828	June	5	Alice Eamonson, Daughter of John & Elizabeth Metcalfe, of the Precincts, Clerk
1828	November	9	Ellen (born Sep. 11th), dau. of Frederick & Martha Pearce Rouch, of the Precincts, Clerk
1829	February	17	Henrietta (born Decr 4th, 1828), Daug^{r} of George Parry & Jane Bonham Marriott, of the Precincts, Clerk
1829	March	10	Henry Edwd, the Son of the Honble George and Frances Pellew, of the Precincts, late a Preb^{y}, now Dean of Norwich
1830	February	3	Thomas Frederick (born Sep^{tr} 29th, 1829), Son of George & Eliza Austin, of the Precincts, Architect & Surveyor
1830	May	14	Elizabeth Anne Eamonson, daughter of John and Elizabeth Metcalfe, of the Precincts, Clerk
1830	November	1	Emma Burchell (born Sep. 19th, 1830), Daughter of William Spencer Harris & Martha Braham, of the Precincts, Clerk*
1831	January	10	Georgiana Maria (born Novr 14, 1830), Daughter of George Parry & Jane Bonham Marriott, of the Precincts, Clerk
1831	May	25	Sarah Frances, D^{r} of John and Sarah Johnson, of the Barracks, P^{l} Q^{r} Master 7th Dragoon Guards
1831	June	25	Herbert Richard, Son of John & Augusta Peel, of the Precincts, Preb^{y} of this Cathedral
1831	October	31	Agnes Eamonson, dau^{r} of John & Elizabeth Metcalfe, of the Precincts, Minor Canon
1832	July	5	Eleanor, Daughter of James and Sarah Turmaine, of the Precinct of the Archbishop's Palace, Sadler (*sic*)
1832	December	3	Douglas Spencer (born Octr 6th), Son of William Spencer Harris & Martha Braham, of the Precincts, Clerk
1832	December	19	Augustus Frederic Peel, Son of George Parry & Jane Bonham Marriott, of the Precincts, Born October Tenth, 1832, Clerk
1833	January	7	Hugh, Son of John Evelyn & Catherine Elizabeth Boscawen, of the Precincts, Prebendary of the Cathedral
1833	December	12	Frederick, Son of James & Sarah Turmaine, of the Precincts, Sadler (*sic*)

* A Minor Canon of the Cathedral.

Year.	Month.	Day.	Names. Residence and Profession of Father.
1834	January	26	George (born Novr 15, 1833), Son of John & Jessey Cooke,* of the Precincts. Father a Servant
1834	May	5	Lucy Curteis (born March 23^{d}), Daughter of John & Elizabeth Metcalfe, of the Precincts, Clerk
1834	June	12	Harriett Fanny (Born Feby 7th, 1832), Daughter of George & Eliza Austin, of the Precincts of the Arch-Bishop's Palace, Architect & Surveyor
1834	June	12	Frederick (Born July 29th, 1833), son of George & Eliza Austin, of the Precincts of the Arch Bishop's Palace, Architect & Surveyor
1834	October	2	Cockburn Peel (born August Eleventh), Son of George Parry & Jane Bonham Marriott, of the Precincts, Clerk
1835	February	1	George, Son of John & Anna Filmer, of the Precincts, Gardener
1835	March	28	Edward Martin (born Feby 6th), Son of William Spencer Harris & Martha Braham, of the Precincts, Clerk
1836	June	28	Leonard Broune (Born May 19th), Son of Anby & Ann Dorothea Elizabeth Beatson, of the Precincts, Second Master of Kings School
1837	June	1	Anne, Daughter of Arthur Bastard Eastabrooke & Ann Mervyn Holdsworth, of Widdicombe, Devon, Esquire
1837	July	6	Harriet Dunning, an adult in the 19th Year of her age, of the Precincts, a servant
1837	July	24	Lucy Chapman, Daughter of William Spencer Harris and Martha Braham, of the Precincts, Clerk
1837	November	9	Geoffrey Lewis (Born Sep^{t} 11th), son of George & Eliza Austin, of the Precincts of the Archbishop's Palace, Architect & Surveyor
1838	February	4	John, Son of John Cooke & Jessey Silcock, of the Precincts, Apparitor of the Archdeacon's Court
1838	August	2	Frances Julia (Born June 25, 1838), Daughter of George Parry & Jane Bonham Marriott, of the Precincts, Clerk
1838	November	7	Ellen Castle (Born Oct. 3rd, 1838), Daughter of Herbert Castle and Ellen Southey, of the Precincts, Harbour Master at Demerara
1839	May	30	Horatio George, Son of Horatio and Louisa Maunsell, of the Precincts, Clerk, Prebendary
1839	July	4	Walter Francis, Son of Francis & Alice Dawson, of the Precincts, Clerk, Prebendary
1840	March	28	Charlotte Gertrude, Daughter of William Spencer Harris & Martha Braham, of the Precincts, Clerk
1840	June	5	Katharine Russell (Born April 28), Daughter of George and Emily Frances Wallace, of the Precincts, Head Master of the Kings School
1840	October	5	Arundel (Born May 31st, 1840.), Son of Alfred Boydell & Mary Eliza Lambe, of New Bond Street, in the Parish of St George's, Hanover Square, London, Wine Merchant

* Attached to this page and referring to this entry is a statutory declaration, made on the fourteenth day of September, 1836, by the Father, whose name is entered as John Cooke, when it ought to be John Cooke *Silcock*. The declaration states that the father, John Cooke Silcock, was the son of William and Ann Silcock, and was baptized at Thompson in the county of Norfolk on the 27th of March, 1798. He subsequently assumed the name of Cooke, and inadvertently described himself on his marriage by the name of John Cooke only, instead of John-Cooke Silcock.

Year.	Month.	Day.	Names. Residence and Profession of Father.
1840	November	3	Thomas Crawford, Son of John & Ann Brampton, of Hoath, Miller
1841	March	2	Henry Thomas, son of Mark & Catherine Teal, of the Precincts, Porter at the Gate
1841	July	15	Emily Frances, Daughter of George and Emily Frances Wallace, of the Precincts, Head Master of the King's School
1841	November	16	Emily, Daughter of Patrick & Kezia Elizabeth McGuire of Northgate, in The Barracks, Serjeant Major in the 21st Regiment of Foot
1842	August	16	Henry, twin son of William and Emily Octavia Deedes, of the Precincts (usual abode Sandling in Saltwood), Gentleman
1842	August	16	Edward, twin son of William and Emily Octavia Deedes, of the Precincts, (usual abode Sandling in Saltwood), Gentleman
1842	December	13	Lucy Ann, Daughter of William & Mary Finn, of the Precincts, Servant
1843	March	27	George Archdale, Son of George & Emily Frances Wallace, of the Precincts, Head Master of the King's School
1843	August	30	Frances Waldegrave, Daughter of William Spencer Harris & Martha Braham, of the Precincts, Minor Canon of the Cathedral
1844	April	11	Elizabeth Catherine Wastell, Daughter of Frederick & Elizabeth Finn, of the Precincts of the Archbishop's Palace, Tailor
1844	June	28*	William, (Born May 12th, 1844), son of George and Emily Frances Wallace, of the Precincts, Head Master of the King's School
1844	June	28	Archdale Todd, (born May 12th, 1844), Son of George and Emily Frances Wallace, of the Precincts, Head Master of the King's School
1845	January	6	Anne Myrrah, Daughter of Ambrose & Myra Neate, of the Precincts, Gardener
1845	March	6	Helen Christiana Catharine, Daughter of Mark & Catharine Teal, of the Precincts, Porter
1845	April	18	Frederick George, Son of Frederick & Elizabeth Finn, of the Precincts of the Archbishop's Palace, Tailor
1845	June	3	Georgina (an Adult) Daughter of John & Hannah Goodwin, of the Precincts, Ship Agent
1845	September	25	John Newport, Son of John & Harriott Eastes, of the Precincts, Lay Clerk & Music Seller
1846	January	29	Emily Charlotte, (Born Dec. 21, 1845) Daughter of George & Emily Frances Wallace, of the Precincts, Head Master of the King's School
1846	April	21	Amelia Angela, Daughter of Francis & Amelia Eliza Burdett, of the Barracks, Major 17th Lancers
1846	September	30	George Hatton, son of Mark & Catherine Teal, of the Green Court, Gate Porter
1847	July	19	Harriet Jane (Four years old), Daughter of William & Harriet Strike, of Rye, Officer of Customs
1847	August	15	Harry Wright, Son of Henry & Hannah Russell, of the Precincts, Carver & Gilder
1847	September	22	Emily Sarah, daughter of Thomas & Sarah Stock, of Bilgaum (?), Bombay, Assistant Adjutant General, H. E. I. C. Service

* This date has been altered from the 27th to the 28th.

Year.	Month.	Day.	Names. Residence and Profession of Father.
1847	September	27	Jessie Caroline Fraser, Daughter of George and Emily Frances Wallace, of the Precincts, Head Master of the King's School
1848	December	1	Mary, Daughter of George and Mary Wells, of the Precincts, Labourer
1849	May	20	(Private), Richard Charles, Son of Charles William & Maria Keng, of the Precincts, Artist
1849	June	24	Alfred, Son of Stephen & Charlotte Maple, of the Precincts, Servant
1849	August	13	Cicely, daughter of William and Ann Smith, of the Precinct of the Archbishop's Palace, Watchmaker
1849	August	24	Gordon Taylor Bentinck, Son of Alfred Sidney & Leonora Wigan, of Brompton, Gentleman
1849	September	17	Augusta Dottin, Daughter of William Nelson & Mary Hutchinson, of the Precincts, L[t] Col[l] of The Grenadier Guards
1849	October	27	Mary Ellen Edith, dau. of Henry George & Mary Ellen Austin, of the Precincts, Surveyor
1850	April	7	Thomas James, Son of Henry & Hannah Russell, of the Precincts, Carver & Gilder. (Born Feb[y] 12th, 1850)
1850	November	17	William, Son of William & Emily Walker, of the Precincts, Coachman to The Dean
1850	December	25	William, (Born Oct. 18, 1850), Son of George & Emily Frances Wallace, of the Precincts, Clerk, Head Master of the King's School
1851	April	8	Isabella, daughter of William and Ann Smith, of the Precinct of the Archbishop's Palace, Watchmaker
1851	August	3	Edwin Richard, son of Mark & Catherine Teal, of the Green Court, Bell Ringer
1852	March	30	Charlott Catherine, daughter of Robert Manners & Cecilia Isabella Croft, of the Green Court, Gentleman
1852	July	5	Amy, daughter of William & Ann Smith, of the Precinct of the Archbishop's Palace, Watchmaker
1852	November	30	Herbert, son of George and Emily Frances Wallace, of the Precincts, Head Master of the King's School
1853	March	29	Herbert Lascelles, Son of Henry Lascelles and Mary Isabel Jenner, of the Precincts, Minor Canon of the Church
1853	May	29	William, Son of William & Mary Norman, of the Precincts, Bell Ringer
1853	June	22	Edward Norton, Son of Edward Norton & Sarah Anne Ford, of Palace Street . . . .
1853	October	5	John S[t] George Nelson, Son of John & Matilda Byrne, of the Artillery Barracks, Officer in the 4th Light Drags.
1854	January	8	Maria, Daughter of Charles & Maria Hauston (or Hanston) of the Barracks, Canterbury, Gun Maker
1854	March	21	Owen, Son of Thomas Evance & Maria Jones, of the Precincts, Organist
1854	March	21	Amy Elizabeth Ann, Daughter of Mark & Catherine Teal, of the Precincts, Verger
1855	November	6	Edwin Denys, Son of Robert & Octavia Frances Hake, of the Precincts, Minor Canon of this Cathedral
1855	December	26	Elizabeth Jane, D[r] of George & Sarah Kennett, of the Ville of Christ Church, Gardener
1856	June	17	Mary Mildred, D[r] of Benjamin & Mary Waters, of the Cathedral Precincts, Servant

Year.	Month.	Day.	Names. Residence and Profession of Father.
1856	August	11	Walter Eustace Gerald, Son of Francis Angel & Louisa Smith, of the Cathedral Precincts, Minor Canon of this Cathedral
1856	September	4	Marian Emma, Daughter of Thomas & Emily James, of the Precincts, Vesturer of the Cathedral
1856	September	12	Constance, Daughter of Charles Laurence & Emily D'Aguilar, of Barton House, Major of The Royal Horse-Artillery
1856	November	22	Mary, Daughter of John James & Mary Brenchley, (or Branchling), of Canterbury, Major in the Royal Artillery
1857	January	22	Sarah Ann, Daughter of George and Sarah Kennett, of the Precincts, Gardener
1857	June	3	Lewis Francis, Son of Robert & Octavia Frances Hake, of the Precincts, Minor Canon of this Cathedral
1857	September	16	George William, Son of George & Mary Ann Kay, of the Precincts, Soldier (deceased)
1857	September	27	Henry Charles Chivers, Son of Charles Frederick & Mary Ann Jordan, of the Precincts of the Archbishop's Palace, Engineer in the Royal Navy
1857	November	4	Donald, Son of Thomas Evance and Maria Jones, of the Precincts, Organist of this Cathedral
1858	January	19	Ellen, daughter of Benjamin & Mary Waters, of the Precincts, Servant
1858	February	5	Edith Spencer, daughter of John Bachelor & Ellen Sophia Kearney, of the Precincts, Clerk, one of the Masters of the King's School
1858	February	12	Thomas William, Son of Thomas & Emily James, of the Precincts, Vesturer
1858	April	4	Mary Jane, dau[r] of George & Elizabeth Kenward, of the Precincts, Ostler
1858	April	14	Ambrose, (Adult,) Parents not known, being a man of Colour, native of South Carolina. Baptized by Henry Alford, Dean
1859	January	27	Norman Leslie Angel, Son of Francis Angel & Louisa Smith, of the Cathedral Precincts, Clerk
1859	May	26	George John, Son of George & Sarah Kennett, of the Precincts, Gate Porter
1859	May	31	William Henry De Courcy, Son of William John & Louise De Courcy Chads, of Canterbury Barracks, Major in the 64th Reg[t] Foot
1859	October	1	Oswald, Son of Samuel & Rosalie Harradon, of S[t] Mary's Parish, Islington, East India Merchant
1859	October	9	Grace Ursula Cotgrave, Daughter of William Roberts & Alicia Mary Farmar, Barton House, Cant[by], Brevet-Major of 82nd Reg[t]
1859	December	23	Harriet Mary, Daughter of Thomas & Emily James, of the Precincts, Vesturer of the Cathedral
1860	March	6	William, Son of Stephen & Amelia Waters, of Horsmonden, Kent, Draper
1860	April	10	Ormond Butler, Son of Robert & Octavia Frances Hake, of the Precincts of Christ Church, Minor Canon of this Cathedral
1860	April	23	Frederick Ernest William Cheesman, Son of William Henry & Ann Hart, of S[t] Andrew's, Canterbury, Pensioner
1860	May	8	Frances Sarah, Daughter of Chamberlain Henry & Matilda Hinchcliff, of S[t] George's, Canterbury, Captain in the 64th Reg[t] of Foot

Year.	Month.	Day.	Names. Residence and Profession of Father.
1860	July	17	George Balfour, Son of Alfred Picton & Lucy Georgina Bowlby, of St George's, Canterbury, Major in the 64th Regt of Foot.
1860	August	17	Edwy Athelwald, Son of John Bachelor & Ellen Sophia Kearney, of the Precincts, Clerk; one of the Masters of the King's School
1860	September	1	Violet Gertrude Angel, Dr of Francis Angel & Louisa Smith, of the Cathedral Precincts, Minor Canon of this Cathedral
1860	November	13	Henry Thomas, Son of George & Sarah Kennett, of the Precincts, Porter
1861	March	14	Charles Ephraim, Son of Thomas & Emily James, of the Cathedral Precincts, Vesturer of the Cathedral
1861	July	21	Catherine Mariah, Dr of Adolphus & Catherine Frances Bigg, of the Infantry Barracks, Keeper of the Canteen
1861	August	10	Guy Edward Wentworth, Son of Peter & Catherine Mary Withington, of the Dane John, Captain of the 7th Dragoon Guards
1861	August	19	Caroline Annie, Dr of Thomas Fagge & Caroline Jane Hawke, of Clarence Road, Herne Bay, Gentleman
1861	November	25	George Evan, Son of Thomas Evance & Maria Jones, of the Mint Yard, Precincts, Organist of this Cathedral
1861	December	6	Alfred Elliott, Son of Alfred Picton & Lucy Georgina Bowlby, of the Infantry Barracks, Major of the 64th Regt of Foot
1862	January	16	Robert Francis, son of Robert Francis & Sarah Ann Obey, of the Green Court, Porter at the Gate
1863	March	11	Emily Mary, dau. of George & Sarah Kennett, of the Precincts, Gate-Porter
1863	March	18	William Joseph, Son of William Spencer Hawksworth & Mary Cooper, of the Precincts, Captain in the 70th Regt
1863	May	25	Godfrey, Son of John Streatfield & Frances Lipscombe, of the Mint Yard, Precincts, Under Master of the King's School
	*August	18	Leila Beatrice Angel, Daughter of Francis Angel & Louisa Smith, of the Precincts, Clerk, Minor Canon of the Cathedral
	*October	10	Arthur Holmes, Son of Joseph Williams & Margaret Wilson Blakesley of the Precincts, Canon of this Cathedral Church
	*December	31	Jessie Martha, Daughter of Thomas & Emily James, of the Precincts, Vesturer
(1864)	*March	16	Mary Frances, Daughter of John & Henrietta Cockerell, of the Dane John, Army
	*April	11	Harriette Grace Newman Bewsher, Daughter of George Hendy & Catherine Edith Herbert Du Pré Pooley, of the Cathedral Yard, Army
	*July	4	Edith Mary, Daughter of Augustus Henry & Augusta Mary King, of Barton House, R.H. Artillery
(1865)	*January	16	Charles George, Son of William Everard & Fanny Elizabeth Lucy, of Wincheap, Father, Station Master L.C.D.†

* The years are omitted in the original. † London, Chatham, and Dover Railway.

Year.	Month.	Day.	Names. Residence and Profession of Father.
1865	February	14	John William, Son of Robert Francis & Sarah Ann Obey, of the Precincts, Porter
1865	March	16	Emma Shortridge, Dr of John Streatfield & Frances Lipscombe, of the Mint Yard, Precincts, Under-Master of the King's School
1865	August	9	Ralph George Elliott, Son of Ralph William Elliott & Frances Joanna Forster, of the Cathedral Precincts, Barrister-at-Law
1865	October	17	William Henry, Son of William Samuel & Louisa Sarah Grigg, of the Ville of Archbishop's Palace, Fruiterer
1865	October	26	Mabel Catherina Mary Angel, Daughter of Francis Angel & Louisa Smith, of the Cathedral Precincts, Minor Canon of this Cathedral
1866	July	9	Frederick Percy, Son of Thomas & Emily James, of the Cathedral Precincts, Verger
1866	December	6	Maurice John, Son of John Streatfeild & Frances Lipscomb, of the Cathedral Precincts, Under Master of the King's School
1867	March	30	Francis Wyndham, Son of George Crespigny & Jennetta Caroline La Motte, of Barton Fields, Rector of Denton
1867	March	27*	Charles Thomas, Son of William Samuel & Louisa Sarah Grigg, of Palace St., Greengrocer. P.B.†
1867	May	7	Frances Mary, Daughter of Edward & Julia Mary Golds, of Palace Street, Draper
1867	July	28	Edwin James Diddams, Son of James & Emma Harris, of Palace Street, Saddler
1868	March	12	Walter John, Son of William Samuel & Louisa Sarah Grigg, of Palace Street, Greengrocer
1868	April	12	Cresacre George, Son of Allen Page & Eliza Harriet Moor, of the Precincts, Canterbury, Clerk
1868	June	23	Ellen, Daughter of Edward & Julia Mary Golds, of Palace Street, Draper
1868	June	25	Lilian Victoria Angel, Daughter of Francis Angel & Louisa Smith, of the Cathedral Precincts, Clerk in Holy Orders
1869	January	17	Anthony Francis, Son of Ralph William Elliott and Frances Joanna Forster, of the Precincts of the Cathedral. Barrister-at-Law, (Died Aug. 19, 1871)‡
1869	April	27	Susanna, Daughter of Thomas & Mary Fairway Peen, of the Precincts of Canterbury Cathedral, Farmer, an adult, aged 16 yrs
1869	May	17	Susanna, Daughter of George & Sarah Hempstead, of the Precincts of Canterbury Cathedral, Soldier, Adult, aged 15 yrs
1869	December	4	Amy, Daughter of George & Eleanor Longman, of Canterbury Barracks, Veterinary Surgeon
1870	May	22	Horace Frank, Son of John Browning & Emma Jane Lott, of the Ville of The Archbishop's Palace, Musician
1870	June	24	Edward Stanley Lord, Son of John Forward & Emily Tafe, of South Hackney, London, Journalist
1870	July	14	Bertha Matilda, Daughter of Edward & Matilda Parry, of the Cathedral Precincts, Bishop Suffragan of Dover

* So in the original. † Private Baptism. ‡ Added in pencil.

Year.	Month.	Day.	Names. Residence and Profession of Father.
1870	September	5	Ada Howell, Daughter of George Henry & Ellen Weatherman, of Westbere, Accountant
1871	May	9	Arthur George, Son of John & Ann Hartley of Palace Street, Fishmonger
1871	August	6	Hatherley George, Son of Allen Page & Eliza Harriet Moor, of the Precincts, Canterbury, Clerk
1871	December	26	Ellen Maude Lillie Studdy, Daughter of Alfred Freeman Studdy & Ellen Studdy, of Palace Street, Schoolmaster
1872	March	2	Ethel, Daughter of George & Eleanor Longman, of The Barracks, Vet^{ry} Surgeon
1872	June	7	Edith May, Daughter of Robert Jenkin & Mary Hannah Hatcher (or Hatchett) Terry, of Lydd, Gentleman
1872	August	10	Bertha Mary, Daughter of Ralph William Elliott & Frances Joanna Forster, of the Cathedral Precincts, Barrister-at-Law
1873	April	21	Rhoda Maude, daughter of John & Ann Elizabeth Hartley, of Palace St., Fishmonger
1873	July	27	Henry George, Son of George Westover & Harriet Cross, of Havelock Street, Grocer
1873	October	20	Montague, Son of Harry Daniel & Harriett Mary Good, of St Dunstan's Terrace, Civil Engineer
1873	November	26	Charles, Son of Edward & Matilda Parry, of the Precincts, Bishop of Dover
1874	January	17	Isabel Marguerite Melville, Daughter of Henry Sykes & Mary Louisa Thornton, of Hacklinge, Kent, Gentleman
1874	May	16	Mabel Carew, Daughter of Arthur Carew & Frances Katrine Hunt, of St Sepulchre's, Lieutenant 5th Lancers
1874	July	2	Frank, Son of George & Eleanor Longman, of the Barracks, Veterinary Surgeon
1874	August	2	Hugh Buller, Son of Ralph William Elliot and Frances Joanna Forster, of the Cathedral Precincts, Barrister-at-Law
1874	November	29	Henry Samuel Frank, Son of Walter & Elizabeth Williams, of Northgate, St Mary's, Lay Clerk of the Cathedral
1874	November	29	Ethel Matilda, Daughter of Joseph Hodgson & Ellen Higgins, of St Dunstan's, Lay Clerk of the Cathedral
1875	January	10	Cecilia Catherine, Daughter of Allen Page and Eliza Harriet Moor, of St Clement's, Truro, Clerk
1875*	April	25	Henry Watson Sykes, Son of Henry Sykes & Mary Louisa Thornton, of Hacklinge, Kent, Gentleman
1875	August	29	Harriet Mary Eleanor, Daughter of Theodore Fitzgerald & Harriet Leah Bull, of St George's Parish, Tutor
1875	September	12	Maude Marion, Daughter of James Albert & Sophia Birch, of 13 Cossington Road, Lay Clerk of the Cathedral
1876	January	16	Adaline Wetherelt, Daughter of Joseph Hodgson & Ellen Higgins, of St Dunstan's, Lay Clerk of the Cathedral
1876	January	17	Willie Barnard, Son of John & Ann Elisabeth Hartley, of the Ville of Archbishop's Palace, Poulterer & Fishmonger.
1876	May	6	Inglis Sykes, Son of Henry Sykes & Mary Louisa Thornton, of Hacklinge, Kent, Gentleman
1876	August	15	Kate, Daughter of George & Eleanor Longman, of the Barracks, Veterinary Surgeon

* In the original this entry follows that of January 17, 1876, but as there is a note of the omission, it is here placed in chronological order.

Year.	Month.	Day.	Names. Residence and Profession of Father.
1876	November	24	Maud Ethel Margaret, Daughter of Lionel Thomas & Eliza Margaret Alsager Spens, of 3 Watling Street, Lieut. 3rd Buffs
1877	April	19	Mildred Gurney, Daughter of James & Georgiana Mangan, of St Mildred's Rectory, Canterbury, Clerk in Holy Orders
1877	August	31	Meriel Mary, Daughter of Henry Sykes & Mary Louisa Thornton, of Hacklinge, Kent, Gentleman

MARRIAGES.

Year.	Month.	Day.	Names.
1583	December	8	William Arnolde & Repentance Pownoll
1587	January	17	Roper Blundell and Elizabeth Elam
1588	June	4	Thomas Boys and Sara Roger
1592	September	12	Thomas Consant and Judith Cocks
		*	Martin Fotherbie and Margaret Winter
		*	John Manne and Marie Simpson
1599	December	17	George Marson and Magdalen Primount
1602	May	2	Edward Ward and Cuce (Luce?) Wysman
1603	May	14	Thomas Evens, Minister and Elizabeth Hares
1606	May	1	John Sheparde and Elizabeth Pickell
1606	May	4	Mathew Tomlen and Anne Smythe
1607	December	8	Samuell Nicoles and Margaret Vowell
1608	January	31	Daniell Gooking and Marye Birrde
1609	July	4	Richard Martin and Elizabeth Birrde
1613	May	30	John Thimble and Ann Master
1613	February	22	George Knatchbull and Jone Gilbarde
1614	June	1	Robart Hill, Doc' in deuinitie & Mrs Margaret de Sarauia
			I, John Shepherd was chosen Sexten the xxvth day of November 1614
1615	May	1	William Saint and Catheren Hallett
1616	July	22	Christopher Mann and Mary Rogers widdowe
1616	August	11	Symon Whitt and Anne Jacksone
1616	February	10	Robart Moyle and Prissilla Fotherbye
1616	February	20	William Tonstall and Marye Jacsonne
1618	April	20	Walter Pergiter & Mary Masters
1618	March	15	Harton Drayton and Marie French
1619	April	29	John Spencer and Marie Swinford
1619	October	7	John Barnard marryed Marie Martin
1619	December	7	John Player married Elisabeth Masters
1620	February	12	Thomas Curle and Margett Bunce
1620	February	12	Thomas Jacksone and Anne Colfe
1621	October	18	Peeter Symonds & Cisly Marson
1622	September	16	William Nethersoull & Marget Euerard
1622	September	1†	Steeuen File, of Deall, & Ann Joh'son, of West beere
1624	July	29	Josua Ellis, of Wesmester, & Margaret Nayler, of Christ Church
1625	January	28	William Best, of this Church, & Annis Doo, of Chartham
1625	February	21	Mr William Watts & Mrs Dorothy Vaughan
1625	February	27	William Den, of the parish of Bridge, & Bennett Clarke, of this Church
1627	December	26	Beniamin Jackson & Marget Marson
1628	February	17	Thomas Rammell, of Nunnington, and Elizabeth Griffin, of this church
1629	June	1	John Ludlow and Eedeth Wilks, their banes hauing bin askt in this church
1630	February	17	Charles White, Viccar of Beaskboorne, and Francis May, of this Churche

* The dates omitted in the original. † So in the original.

Year.	Month.	Day.	Names.
1632	June	24	Thomas Seimore and Anne May
1632	August	19	Thomas Hovenden and Rachel Simpson
1632	October	9	Jacob Church and Jane Baker, of Westwell
1632	October	30	John Wafforde and Godly Spicer
1632	October	15*	William Dale and Mary Denly
1632	November	19	James Grewer and Priscilla Rosell
1632	January	29	Mr Ham'on Leucknor and Mrs Damaris Kingsly
1633	May	2	Adam Cleater and Mary Dale
1633	September	5	Mr Henry Deeringe and Mrs Mary Sanders
1633	September	10	Mr Thomas Cater and Elizabeth Dunkin
1634	June	12	William Somner and Elizabeth Thurgar
1634	January	27	Mr Paule Pettit maried Ms Anne Meriwether by license
1634	February	1	Mr Richard Gibbons maryed Margaret Browne by license
1635	April	13	Mr Robert Bargraue maried Mrs Elisabeth Paten, by license
1635	May	19	Isaack Raner married Susanna Greene, by license
1635	July	20	Robert Fuller maryed Apherie Pitt
1635	September	13	Samuell Clercke, Doctor in diuinity, married Ms Katherine Simpson, by license
1635	February	18	Mr William Haward and Mrs Mary Hamon', by license
1636	July	21	Mr Nicholas Knight and Mrs Jone Lawes, by license
1636	December	27	Mr Thomas Coppin and Mrs Anne Bargraue
1636	January	19	Thomas Bunce and Sarah Elseter
1636	January	24	Sr Thomas Culpepper and ye Lady Streinghfoord
1638	June	24	George Hardeman, of the parish of Boughton, and Mary Brett, widow, of this Church
1638	January	31	Thomas Kiborne and Susanne Hoforde
1639	April	18	Mr Thomas Munnings and Mrs Anne Shrubsoll
1639	July	18	Thomas Beere and Mary Smithet
1639	October	10	John Bellinger and Margaret Berry
1639	January	30	Edward Mills, Gent: and Mtris Elizabeth St Nicholas
1639	March	19	Richard Forstall and Mary Jeffery
1640	July	5	Leonerd Morris and Ann Mace
1640	July	9	Jeames Wreake (alias) Reake and Joane Clinton
1640	October	8	William Standing, of ye Parish of Beakes-Borne, and Katherin Planner, of Christ Church, Cant:
1640	January	18	Humphry Gardiner, Esquier, in Cambridgeshire, and Helen Wyld, of the Arch Bishops palace in Cant: by License
1641†	September	5	Thomas Wraith, of St Georges, Cant: and Mary Sedwick
1640*	March	22	Mr Edward Boys and Mrs Mary Herne, by Licence
1641†	October	7	Ralfe Jukinson and An' Lane
‡		9	Thomas Faulkner and Eliz: Laurence, by Licence
‡		14	Thomas Filden and Katharine Niccoll, by licence
‡		26	Edward Packer and Sara Morris, by Licence
§	December	17	Mr John Tuck and Elizab: Marsh, Wid: by Licence
§†	March	13	Peter Spratling and An' Hobkins, by Licence
1642†	April	11	Stephen Leeds and Mary White, by Licence
§†	May	2	Isaak Allbery and Elizabeth Spicer
§	July	10	James Luccas and Joan Bradford, of the Arch: B: pallace
§	October	6	John Pim'e, of Ashford, and Jane French, Wid: by licence
1643†	April	10	Edward Jeffery and Jone Pinke
§†	April	13	Edmund Saare and Anne Hukin
1643	September	29	Thomas Happar and Margaret Allen

* So in the original. † Overwritten in the original.
‡ In the original the year and month is omitted, query October.
§ In the original the year is omitted.

Year.	Month.	Day.	Names.
1644	June	24	Thomas Masters married Margaret Balden, by license
1644	October	8	Mr Robert Sprakeling married Mrs Rebecca Lamming
1645	May	26	Moyses Flood married Anne Tonge
*	May	26	Thomas Haward married Hester Kingston
*	June	19	Thomas Best married Mary Seluy
1645	July	7	John Holyday married Alice Case
1645	March	2	Mr Nicholaus Bix married Mrs Elisabeth Benson
1646	October	12	Thomas Pepper married Susanna Wilks, by license
1646	October	13	Dan'iell Bennet married Elisabeth Saunders
1647	July	8	John Talor married Elisabeth Roe
1647	October	4	Adam Ramsha married Mary Bennitt
1647	October	14	Richard Norwood married Margaret Hesleby
1647	November	1	William Beane married Alfery Giles
1647	November	18	Robert Bate married Susanna Allen
1647	November	20	William Preble married Elisabeth Rutland
1647	November	25	James Pilcher married Margaret Browning
1648	May	30	Mr Nicholas Simpson married Mrs Mary Rous
1648	July	2	Mr Richard Gibbon married Mary Lambe
1649	April	10	Thomas Dunck married Thomizin Saint
1649	April	14	Simon Parker married Elisabeth Wollet
1649	May	15	Walter Grant married Mary Stather
1649	June	26	Ambrose Starke married Mary Golfinch
*	July	16	John Cocke married Jane Findall
1649	June†	28	John Yeomans married Sarah Powre
1649	July	22	Thomas Weeks married Joane . . . . .
*	October	28	Thomas Wise married Katherine Chilto'
1649	March	5	Mr Daniell Cucko married Elisabeth Ludd
1650	June	5	John Culmer, of Deale, married Joane Masey, of London
1650	August	5	John Lucket married Martha Johnson
1650	October	15	John Keeler married Mary Broekman
1650	November	24	Marke Fowtrell married Susan Coife‡
1651	May	29	Francis Sanders, marchant, married Elisabeth Williams, in Christchurch, Canterb:
1651	May	1†	George Pilcher married Helen . . . . .
1651	June	23	Edward Stanner married Dorathy Swinford
1651	June	26	Edward Smith married Clemens Roberts
1651	June	30	Henery Frin' married Martha Slany
*	October	27	Richard Ambrose married Isabell Maxted
1651	October	30	Mr Thomas Papillon married Jane Brodnax
1651	October	31	Edward Ambrose married Grace Young
1651	July†	17	Ezekiell Parker married Katherine Bollard
1651	October†	12	William Sander married Mary Stadman
*	November	22	Thomas Foulks married Katherine Brittan
*	December	6	Mr Frederick Primerose married Mary Monyns
*	December	22	Lawrence Legatt married Jane Parker
*	January	1	William Parker married Martha Parker
*	January	3	Gregorie Smisson married Jane Greene
*	January	12	Richard Carter married Sarah Adcock
1651	February	24	Mr Robert Morrice married Anne Saint
1651	March	6	William Bing married Ellenor Page —
1652	May	5	Edward Masters married An'e Simons
1652	February†	10	Mathew Hopkin married Margaret Martin
1652	April†	8	Bartholomew Hornden married Joane Paye
1652	June	7	John Pointer married Katherine Pittock
1652	June	24	Alexander Steddy married Mary Lowe

* The year omitted in the original. † So in the original. ‡ Probably Colfe.

Year.	Month.	Day.	Names.
1652	July	8	Thomas Payne married Jane Wilson
*	August	31	Anthony Knowler married Mary Bishop
*	September	24	Simon Wate married Mary Wise
1652	October	5	Thomas Allen married Mary Spencer
1652	November	23	Thomas Chaper married Alice Smith
1652	October†	11	John Filpott married Mary Spaine
1653	April	14	John Millar married Elisabeth Joanes
1653	May	19	George Scott married Susanna Jarman
1653	June	7	William Ratleffe married Dorathy Mascall
1653	July	7	John Eltindon married Mary Reader
1653	July	7	Richard Seward married Sarah Dann
1653	August	26	Mr James Heath married Mrs Alice Finch, in Christchurch, Canterburie
1653	September	15	Richard Silkwood married Anne Hope
*	September	22	Michaell Page married Elisabeth Horsfeele
*	September	26	John Ladd married Katherine . . . .
*	September	28	Thomas Bridgeway married Elisabeth Lee
*	September	29	Richard Moone married Benedicta Rolfe
1654	March	26	William Enins married Anne Wood
1654	March	28	William Hen'eker married Anne Tong
1654	April	6	Isaac Sayres married Elisabeth Mott
1654	July	3	William Austin married Anne Reeue
1654	July	26	Thomas Watson married Elisabeth Castle
1654	October	31	Thomas Hesill married Elisabeth Goulding
1654	December	30	John Smith married Dorathy Reue
1655	April	23	John Dade married Ellen Auenell
1655	October	8	Anthony Stather married Ben'itt Baker
1655	October	11	Aaron Morris married Mary Knowler
1655	October	12	Richard Bucke married Anne Yewell
1655	February	14	Philip Bussher married Dorathy Denn
1656	August	3	Robert Hartwell marryed Ann Meed
*	September	9	William Manger marryed Constant Weston
*	September	11	John Hayward marryed Patience Taylor
*	October	6	William Younge Marryed ffrancis Royall
*	October	12	John Hubbert Marryed Mary Terry
*	October	8†	Mr William Broadnax Marryed Mrs Mary Diggs
*	October	14	James Knell Marryed Elizabeth Berry
*	November	1	Richard Mount Marryed Ann Burvell
*	November	3	Thomas Rigden Marryed Katherine ffrench
*	November	13	ffrederick Primrose Dr of Phisicke marryed Mrs Ann Gibbon
*	January	31	Jeffery Barbet marryed Margaret Coife‡
*	March	3	Mr John Marsh marryed Mrs Mary Groane
*	March	3	Thomas Bayly marryed Mary Knight
1656	March	5	Philip Busher marryed Ann Hopkins
1657	March	30	Mathew Coope marryed Rachaell Tall
*	March	30	John Mount marryed Elizabeth Haskin
*	May	18	John Cock, of Chislet, marryed Francis Hock
*	July	21	Henry Johncock marryed Priscilla Kennett
*	September	21	John Jarman marryed Alice Marsh
1657	October	1	Thomas ffox marryed Elizabeth ffox
*	October	22	Mr William Butler marryed Joane Justice
*	October	24	John Hills Marryed Jane Swinford
*	October	25	James Boulderson marryed Judith Ashman

* The year omitted in the original. † So in the original.
‡ Probably this should be Colfe.

Year.	Month.	Day.	Names.
*	January	5	Symon Carter marryed Sarah Harnington
1658	April	29	William Smith Marryed Jane Beare
1658	May	1	Jonas Deeringe Marryed Mary Seed
1658	May	18	John Waddell marryed Mary Saint
1658	June	1	John Combs Marryed Katherine Vance
1658	June	9	William Sutton marryed Sarah Bosle
1658	June	17	Mr John Crane marryed Francis Elliot
1658	July	8	Mathias Gray marryed Anne Tilman
1658	July	8	William Rayston Marryed Joane Becham
1658	July.	22	Richard Smalewood marryed Katherine Wise
1658	October	4	James Russell Marryed Jane Chilman
1658	October	14	Stephen Balducke marryed Susanna Hoddeman
1658	October	25	Thomas Smith marryed Susanna Chandler
1658	October	30	Thomas Gill marryed Margaret Spencer
1658	November	10	Richard Bayman marryed Hannah Curlinge
1658	November	27	Thomas Boulden marryed Ann Andin (or Audin)
1658	January	29	Edward Hurst marryed Elizabeth Pollin
1658	February	13	Paule Harris marryed Ann Barnes
1658	February	15	Thomas Godfrey marryed Anne Knowlden
1658	February	26	John Kennitt marryed Mary Baker
1658	February	26	Peter Keturum marryed Elizabeth ffrancis
1658	March	2	Stephen Gisard Marryed Mary Honus
1658	March	5	George Chilman marryed Mary Row
1659	April	11	William Philpot marryed Susan Sprat
1659	May	4	Joseph Page marryed Anne Hills
1659	June	11	William Beekes marryed Anne Chilman
1659	June	13	George Beane marryed Afery Welsmith
1659	June	27	Edward Epps marryed Katherine Hall
1659	July	14	John Pearson marryed Anne Gilvin
1659	July	14	Stephen Sargant marryed Anne Younge
1659	July	23	Robert Jell marryed Anne Harvie
1659	August	18	John Clerke marryed Anne Patrick
1659	September	22	John Hopper marryed Elizabeth . . . .
1659	September	29	John Coller marryed Elizabeth Howell
1659	October	15	Lawrance Ellis marryed Elizabeth Starke
1659	October	8†	Silvester Gray marryed Mildred Adams
1659	October	20	Thomas Parker marryed Elizabeth Gray
1659	October	22	Robert Dad marryed Alice Gamon
1659	October	24	Richard Coosens marryed Mary Cheeseman
1659	October	29	John Rayment marryed Elizabeth Greeneleafe
1659	October	24†	John Muns marryed Sarah Saphra
1659	November	10	Thomas Talor marryed Sarah Atherlo
1659	November	10	James Moate marryed Alice Barton
1659	November	22	Thomas Wilson marryed Mary Ale
1659	November	28	Edward Gray marryed Joane Barnes
1659	December	1	Mr William Sumner marryed Barbara Browne
1659	December	26	Stephen Ellin marryed Mary Hills
1659	December	28	Thomas Muggoll marryed Margaret Browne
1659	February	23	Richard Constance marryed Alice Goare
1659	March	20	Israell Moone marryed Alice Noble
1660	April	10	Thomas Brockwell marryed Margaret Gibson
1660	April	22	William ffuller marryed Mary Knight
1660	May	8	William Baker marryed Mildred Vincent
1660	June	7	Thomas Hetherington marryed Anne Crow

* The year omitted in the original.
† So in the original.

Year.	Month.	Day.	Names.
1660	July	9	John Parker marryed Elizabeth Coulegate
1660	July	9	John Pomerow marryed Margaret Hodgman
1660	July	10	Abell Tirry marryed Mary Johnson
1660	July	23	Nicholas Lee marryed Mary Bottle
1660	July	31	John Parker marryed Alice Hall
1660	August	20	Isaac Pilcher marryed Joane Winford
1660	October	9	Thomas Hodgman marryed Mary Hayward
1660	November	15	John Hooker marryed Mildred Spaine
1660	December	26	Thomas Emptage marryed Christian Hogbin
1660	January	11	William Not marryed Joane Blackman
1660	February	14	Robert Jessard marryed Anne Chambers
1661	June	18	Henry Cob marryed Anne Cockerton
1661	July	28	Thomas Davis marryed Mary Hills
1661	December	12	Abraham Hooke and Mary George
1662	April	7	William Pising the Younger, a member of this Church, and Alice Leese
1662	April	13	Vallentine May and Susanna Foach
1662	May	6	Mr Blase Whyte, one of the Minor Cannons of this Church, and Mrs Susanna Wright, Widow
1662	September	16	Mr John Somner and Mris Ann Tressar widdow were married together by the Deane, and by Licence
1662	October	27	Thomas Young and Mary Russell
			{ Here occurs a carefully erased entry, but upon examination it proves to be a Baptism written by mistake among the Marriages }
1662	January	15	Mr John Crane and Mris Elisabeth Carter widdow were maried together by Mr Alday
1662	February	24	Edward Sympson and Jane Norwood
1662	February	26	Michaell Impett (or Finpott) and Ann Sisely
1663	April	9	George Nerne and Elisabeth Nicholls
1663	July	2	Richard Burges and Mary Beagle
1663	July	13	Richard Spayne, Widdower, and Susanna Lamb, Widdow
1663	August	2	Mr Joseph Roberts and Mris Elisabeth Lee
1663	August	3	Robert Howell and Ann Nicholls
1663	August	27	Stephen Whyte and Mary Acton
1664	May	10	John Wonstall and Vrsula Cockerton, were married together in ye Quire
1664	December	8	Joseph Highstreete, and Elisabeth Warren, Widdow, by Lycence
1664	December	29	Edward Sym'ons and Elisabeth Lake, by Lycence
1664	January	5	John Jiggins and Ellen Wotton, by Lycence
1665	March	26	Dr John Bargraue, Prebend of this Church, and Mris Frances Osborne, Widdow, by Lycense, being Easter day
1665	May	11	John Smyth and Mary Knolden, by Lycense
1665	May	17	Richard Smith and Mary Skinner
1665	July	30	*Vallentine Ashenden and Jane Wilkins
1665	September	5	John Knowler and Susanna Sole
1665	September	13	Thomas Smyth and Elisabeth Coppin, Widdow
1665	September	28	Vallentine Wraith and Afra Foart
1665	October	2	Richard Barrington and Ann Safery
1665	October	14	Henry Bycraft and Mary Flackton
1665	November	2	Robert Sampson and Mary Jenkins
1665	November	9	Henry Pannell and Ann Woodland
1665	December	26	Mr Sidney Dawson of Westenhanger, and Catherine Harlenstone, of Fordich, were married in ye Quire by a licence

* This entry has been overwritten.

Year.	Month.	Day.	Names.
$166\frac{5}{6}$	January	26	Nicholas Maskoll and Sarah Philpot
1666	July	30	John Cocks, of Beaksborne, and Sicely Giles, of Westgate Parish
1666	October	14	Thomas Spicer, of Dover, and Elizabeth Troward, servant to Mr Aldey, Prebend of this church
1666	December	13	Thomas Whyte and Elizabeth Chapman, both of Deale
1666	February	5	Mr John Buck and M^{ris} Joane Aucher
1667	May	11	John Arnold and Catherine Kempe
1667	June	16	Mr William Kingsly and M^{ris} Priscilla Fotherby were married together by Mr Alday, then Vice-deane
1667	October	9	John Bridges and Susanna Lowd
1669	July	1	Mr Thomas Knowler and Mrs Jane Parker were married in ye Choire
1669	January	20	Henery Reade and Elisabeth Ellis
1669	January	20	Thomas Beuerton and Margaret Fisher
1669	February	3	Thomas Saffery and Jane Nokes
1670	April	4	Thomas Browning and Ann Best
1670	June	6	Robert Terry and Elisabeth Leese
1671	May	11	John Whitlocke & Anne Jacob, by Lycence
1671	July	17	Mr John Valavine & Mary Wakeman married in y^{e} choire by lycence from y^{e} facultie office
$167\frac{1}{2}$	February	19	Mr Thomas Fidge and Mrs Hester Twyman, by a Lycence
1673	April	6	John Leawsly and Mary Woodward, by a Licence
1673	July	29	Symon Conyers and Mary Seare, by way of Lycense
1673	October	7	Thomas Sturges and Elisabeth Streeting
1673	March	10	George Sumner and Elizabeth Barton married in ye Choire by D^{r} Du Moulin, by Licence from ye faculty office
1674	September	10	Peter Scrivinor and Sarah Marden, of this Precincts, in the Choire, by Lycence
1675	July	22	Henery Osbiston and Ann Austen, in the Choire, by Lycence from the Faculty Office in London
1675	September	30	Mr John Ockman and M^{ris} Ann Lamb
1676	April	6	Mr Hale, of London, and Mrs Mary Kingsley, in ye Quire
1676	July	17	John Pack, of East Malling, & Rebecka Greenhill, of Stockbury
1676	September	3	William Browning, of the Parish of St George the Martyr, in the City of Canterbury, and Mary King, of the Parish of St Stephen, Virgin, by a Licence
1676	January	25	Robert Sampson, Lay Clerk, Widd^{r}, and Ann Chaffer, Mayden, of the Precincts of ye Bishop's Pallace
1677	May	17	John Hills, of Reculver, and Elizabeth Hatcher, of Staple
1677	June	7	Mr James Broome, Vicar of Newington, neer Hyth, and Priscilla Johnson, of Y^{e} Precincts of Chr. Church, in ye Quire
1677	July	26	Mr John Cullen, Vsher of ye Free Schoole, and Anne Harrison
1677	July	31	Thomas Tindall, of Sutton Vallance, & Mary Becket, of ye same Parish
1678	May	26	John Mace & Elizabeth Aldridge
1678	November	3	Solomon Rendoll & Susan Fuller
1678	November	12	William Reignolds & Elizabeth Austin
1679	August	7	Thomas Reade & Elizabeth Harnett, both of the Precincts of this Church
1679	September	23	Richard Davies, of the p'cincts of this Church, and Martha ffriend, of ye Monastery of Whitefriers
1680	May	11	Michael Bigg, of Davington, & Joanna Culling, of ye precincts of this Church

Year.	Month.	Day.	Names.
1680	October	4	Paul Skelton of St Mild. Cant., & Mary Jeffery, of the Bishop's Pallace
1680	November	25	James King, of Westbeere, & Elizabeth Lovell, of Hearne
1680	February	5	Mr Francis Turner, Citizen of London, & Mrs Hester Bargrave, of ye p'cints of this Church
1680	March	24	Phillip Penn, of Thannington, & Mehittabela Hilder, of St Mildreds, Canterbury
1681	April	25	Mr Charles Kilbourne, Minor Canon of this Church, and Mrs Mary Waddington, of the P'cincts of the Bishop's Pallace
1681	May	29	Morris Horner and Susanna Best, both of the precincts of this Church
1681	September	12	Mr John Elvye, of the p'ish of St Andrew, and Elizabeth Pysing, of the precincts of this Church
1681	July*	5	Stephen Ligny and Sarah Creed, both of Harty
1681	October	20	Edward Browne and Susan Reely, both of the parish of Ash
1681	December	26	Stephen Ledger & Elizabeth Stredwick
1682	April	9	John Wingate, of St Pauls Parish, & Mary Stroud, of ye Preci'cts of this Church
1682	June	14	Henry Cullen & Elizabeth Cademan, both within ye Liberties of this Church
1682	July	16	Mathew Munday & Jane Mills
1682	December	12	John Paine And Mary Ladd
1683	May	3	Edward Martin, of the Parish of Northgate, and Sarah Godden, of the precincts of this Church
1683	May	30	John Apps and Mary Jolly, both of the parish of Hawkhurst
1683	June	25	Richard Derrier and Jane Hills, both of the parish of St Lawrence, in the Isle of Thannett
1683	September	30	Dudley Soane and Mary Russell, both of the precincts of this Church
1683	October	7	Christopher Goatly and Elizabeth Kirke, Widdow
1683	October	30	Mr Paul Loftie and Mrs Hellen Turner
1683	November	4	Thomas Gilbert and Elizabeth Skeene
1684	April	27	Egid. Barham & Eliz. Woodroffe, of ye Parish of St Margarett
1684	April	30	Richard Drinker & Elianor Bryhtll (or Mychell), of ye Precincts of this Ch.
1684	December	9	William Burgesse, of Bethersden, and Allice Tucker, of the same
1684	November*	26	William Clarke, of Chartham, and Mary ffrend, of the precincts of this Church
1684	December	14	John Winter and Sarah Justice, both of the City of Canterbury
1684	January	22	Gabriell Turner, of Chilham, and Mary Snoath of Molash
1684	February	3	Michaell Symmons, of All Saints, and Ann Hart, of ye p'cints of this Church
1685	August	2	Henry Proud, of Wickham, and Catherine Knight, of the Precincts of this Church
1685	September	9	Christopher Goffe & Diana Richardson, both of Dover
1685	November	12	Joseph Hawker and Ann Stokes, both of Woodnesborough
1685	December	29	Herbert Randolph, Esq., of ye Citty of Canterbury, & Mary ye daughter of John Castillion, D.D. & prebend of ye Cathedrall
1685	January	17	James Eafry, of St Peters Parish, & Sarah Badcock, of ye precincts of this Church

* So in the original.

Year.	Month.	Day.	Names.
1686	March	28	John Burges, of St Mary Northgate, & Elizabeth Hubbert, of ye precincts of y^{s} Church
1686	September	23	William Barber & Margaret Muns, both of ye precincts of y^{s} Church
1686	September	30	Gilbert Knowler & Eliz. Juxon, both of this Citty
1686	October	28	Robt Sayer of Nonnighton & Mary Harriss (or Harrisson), of Northbourne
1686	December	9	Robert Sturgeon, of Queenborough, and Ann Curtis, of Milton, near Sittingborne, by Licence
1687	June	20	John Ellis, of St Dunstans, & Ruth Marable, of the Precincts of the Bish. Pallace, by Banns
1687	September	29	Thomas Powell, of St Andrewes Parish, and * Elizabeth Carry, of the Precincts of Chris. Church, Cant.
			Charles Kilbourne, Sacrist

END OF THE MARRIAGES IN THE FIRST REGISTER.

1687	December	26	Mr John Cripps and Mrs Margarett Fotherby
1688	April	22	Richard Hills, of Sturrey, and Martha Lees, of Eastling
1688	July	3	William Bouldes, of Deal, and Mary Smith, of the precincts of this Church
1688	September	17	John Bradford and Elizabeth Harteley, both of Upchurch
1688	September	18	William Waterer, of Milton, and Sarah Barron (or Barrow), of Maidstone
1688	October	4	Joseph Powell and Ann Potts, both of St Margaretts, in Canterbury
1688	October	7	John Elphick, of Holy Cross, Westgate, and Elizabeth Tiddiman, of Thannington
1688	November	15	John Penny, of Chatham, and Ann Snoades, of Rainham
			Tho. Johnson, Sacrist
1688	November	29	Thomas Paine & Elizabeth Tucker, of Hougham
1688	December	29	Edward Bullocke & Mary May, both of Canterbury
1689	June	11	Richard Argar & Mary Down, both of Postling
1689	July	23	William Brumbrick & Susanna Batcheller, both of Sandwich
1689		†	Valentine Austin . . . . †
1689	October	22	Thomas Philpott & Anne Fox, both of St Stephens
1689	October	24	John Johnson & Margaret Jenkin, within ye Precincts of this Church
1689	October	29	Daniel White, Esqr & Anne Kingsley, of ye Precincts of this Church
1689	November	28	John Marlier, of St Mildreds, & Eliz. Herst, of ye precincts of this Church
1690	May	28	Andrew Bland, of St Paul's, Shadwell, and Elizabeth Roberts, of Deal, by licence
1690	October	9	John West & Anne Adams, both of Nackington
			S. D'Evereux, Sacrist
1690	November	27	George Joade and Susan Baker, both of St Laurance in Than^{t}
1690	January	13	Andrew Gray and Sarah Mote, booth of Holy Crosse, West Gate, in the City of Cant.
1690	January	15	William Barfitt, of Harbledown, and Ann Cullen, of the liberty of Christ Church
1690	February	19	Alexander Forbis, a Souldier, and Susannah Dabelly, of Christ Church

* Preceding Elizabeth is the name Mary erased. † Blank in the original.

Year.	Month.	Day.	Names.
1690	February	27	John Swaine, of Rye, and Margaret Sole, of St Dunstons, near Cant.
1691	April	18	John Dudley, of Halton, in Oxfordshire, and Mary Sherman, of Christ Church, Cant.
1691	May	21	William Curling and Margery Abbott, booth of Romans gate in the Iland of Thannett
1691	November	10	Robert Rabbett, of Boughton Munchelsea, and Frances Brown, of Langley
			Charles Kilburne, Sacrist
1691	December	22	William Munn and Mary Taylor, both of Milton next Sittingbourn
1691	January	7	Stephen Ketherell and Mary Williams, both of Sandwich
1691	January	12	Edward Austen and Ann Nash, both of St Margaret's at ye Cliffe, neer Doner
1692	April	7	Thomas Barrett and Mary Selden, both of the City of Cant:
1692	April	28	Stephen Chapman, of Sittingbourne, and Ann Sanders, of the Precincts of this Church
1692	June	9	Thomas Gosby and Elizabeth Barrow, of Brookland
1692	August	23	Joseph Hasell, of Kennington, and Dorothy Gill, of Mersham
1692	September	27	John Dawson, of St Martin's, & Mercy Baker, of the precincts of the Arch-Bish: Pallace
1692	October	4	Norton Goatley, of Molash, and Mary Wanstall, of Challock
1692	October	11	Abraham Bean, of Great Mungeham, and Mary Brown, of ye same
1692	October	20	Richard Taddy and Mary Maxted, both of St Laurence, in Thannett
			Tho. Johnson, Sacrist
1692	December	27	Thomas Solley, of Sittingborn, and Alicia Coodd
1692	January	31	Thomas Smith and Mary Baker, of St John Bapt: in the Iland of Thannett
1693	March	27	Mr Charles Hardress, of Cambrige, and Mrs Elizb: Reeues, of Holy Crosse, in Canterbury
1693	May	25	John Gilbert, of St Marg^{ts}, in Can^{t}, and Mary Knowler, in the Precincts of Ch^{t} Church, Can^{t}
1693	July	6	Roger Taddy and Elizb: Mussared
1693	August	7	Charles Brown, of Wapping, and Phœbe Jewell, of Deal
1693	October	17	Thomas Gurney, of Shoulden, and Jane Pordage, of Woodnesborow
1693	November	8	Dauid Gill, of Sheldwhich, and Ann Spencer, of Selling
			Charles Kilburne, Sacrist
1694	April	10	Thomas Lypeatt* and Mary Heneq,* by licence
1694	July	8	Thomas Gibbon & Ann Johnson, both of Canterbury, by licence
			S. D'Evereux, Sacrist
1694	January	10	Thomas Proud, of ffeuersham, and Martha Eastland, of the Precincts of this Church
1694	January	21	Mr Thomas Hunt and the Lady Elizabeth Aucher, by licence
1694	February	3	Thomas Gray and Martha Smith, by licence
1695	October	10	Thomas Crispe and Hannah May, by Banns
			Tho. Johnson, Sacrist
1695	January	14	John Williams & Elizabeth Milles, by licence
1695	January	26	John Remish and Anne Tritton, by Banns

* The name overwritten in the original.

Year.	Month.	Day.	Names.
1696	June	25	*Henry Mount, of this Ch., & Joanna Perry, of this Church by Banns
1696	August	16	*Mr Michael Wilson, of London, & Mrs Hester Fidge, of Elham, by licence
			R. Cumberland, Sacrist
1696	November	16	*James Wishart, of Canterbury, and Elizabeth Bruce, of the same, by Licence
1697	May	6	*Thomas Jeffery, of Milton next Sittingborne, and Ann Dorne, of Gillingham, by License
1697	July	7	*David Dean, of Boxley, and Mary Spice, of Alington, by Lycence
1697	September	26	*Benjamin Longly, of Canterber: and Ruth Tadhunter, of Cht Church, Cant., by Lycense
			Charles Kilburne, Sacrist
1698	September	4	*John Stanton, of London, and Dorothy Harnaby, of the precincts of this Church
1698	September	20	*John Gregory and Ann Hussey, both of Stelling, by licence
1698	October	3	*John Trepsack, Clerke, and ffrances Row (alias Kenchley), Widdow
			Tho. Johnson, Sacrist
1698	January	5	Henry Godfrey, Esq., & Mrs Catharine Pitty (or Pitts), of ye precincts of this Church, by licence
1698	January	29	John Thornley, of St Andrew's, Cant: & Catherine Wyburne, of ye Precincts of this Church
1699	March	26	Thomas Redwood, of St Lawrence, in ye Isle of Thanet, & Thomasin Fletcher, of St Peter's in ye said Island, by licence
1699	June	1	John Barton & Anne Mons, both of Sandwich, by licence
1699	June	4	John Bedwell, of ye Precincts of ys Church, & Elizabeth Holdstocke, of Harbledown, by Banns
1699	July	11	William Edridge, of London, & Anne Hunt, of Canterbury, by Licence
1699	July	13	Adam Fowle & Anne Howland, both of Canterbury, by Licence
1699	October	1	John Cooke, of Nackington, & Mary Benefield, of ye Precincts of this Church, by Banns
1699	October	3	*Simon Adams, of Preston by Faversham, & Ann West, of ye Precincts of this Church, by Banns
1699	November	21	Benjamin Wootton & Joan Rigden, both of Fordwich, by Licence
			Rob. Cumberland, Sacrist
1699	December	14	John Atwood, of Harbledown, & Elizabeth Deward, of ye precincts of this Church, by licence
1699	January	8	William Milward, of Thanet, & Elizabeth Monday, of Littlebourn, by licence
1700	April	7	Edward Burgess & Martha King, both of ye precincts of this Church
1700	April	24	George Emptage & Mary Sprackling, both of St Peter's Parish in Thanet, by licence
1700	May	4	John Brown & Ann Sturges, both of Sturry, by licence
1700	May	7	Thomas Bridges, of Birchington, & Elizabeth Pattison, of Chisllet, by licence
1700	May	20	James De La Croix & Martha Lamb, both of Dover, by licence

* Overwritten in the original.

Year.	Month.	Day.	Names.
1700	May	30	William Ewell, of Hearn, & Elizabeth Underdown, of Fordwich, by licence
1700	July	7	Abraham Newenham, of Nonnington, and Ann Pain, of ye precincts of this Church, by licence
1700	October	1	William Curling & Dorothy Wise, both of ye Parish of Throughley, by licence
1700	October	13	Henry Deward & Elizabeth Olive, both of ye precincts of this Church, by licence
1700	October	15	William Whiting, of Chisllet, & Elizabeth Austin, of Fordwich, by licence
			S. D'Evereux, Sacrist
1700	November	28	John Kennett, of St John's in Thanet, & Ann Sampson, of Sturrey, by licence
1700	February	18	Thomas Hearn, of St Mary Bredin in Cant., & Elizabeth Knight, of ye Precincts of this Church, by Licence
1701	May	15	Robert Gyles & Elizabeth Churchman, both of Chislet, by licence
1701	July	6	John Baker, of Thanington, & Susanna White, of ye Precincts of this Church, by Banns
1701	July	15	John Smith & Elizabeth Dally, both of East-Church in Shepey, by Licence
1701	July	17	Thomas Millison, of St Paul's, Cant: & Sarah Bills, of ye Precincts of this Church, by licence
1701	August	13	John Trigg, of Deal, & Mary Bigg, of St Mary Bredman, Cant: by licence
1701	September	7	Thomas Griggs, of Birchington in Thanet, & Elizabeth Blanderry, of Sturrey, by licence
1701	October	7	John Paramour & Mary Wallbanks, both of ye Precincts of this Church, by Banns
1701	October	14	George Curling & Alice Tickner, both of St Lawrence in Thanet, by licence
1701	November	23	Henry Hunt, of St Martin's, Cant: and Elizabeth Bean, of Fordwich, by licence
			Robert Cumberland, Sacrist
1701	December	11	Thomas Court, of St Steuen's, husbandman, and Elizabeth Young, Widow, of St Dunston's, by licence
1702	April	16	Mr Thomas Maunder, Rector of Tylmanstone, and Mary Randolph, of St George's in Canterbury, by License
1702	October	7	Obadiah Grew, of St Grigories, weauer, and Sarah Webb, of the Lord Archbishop's Palace, by Banns
1702	October	8	William Kendall, yeoman, & Mary Pickard, booth of Sturry
1702	November	12	William Cooke, of Sturry, Miller, and Elizabeth Fowle, of Queenborowe Charles Kilburne, Sacrist
1703	May	13	Robert May, of Holy Crosse, Westgate, & Mary Pennall, of the precincts of this Church, by licence
1703	June	23	Richard Walker & Catherine Read, both of Woodnesborow, by licence
1703	July	1	James Mantle, of Wickham, and Mary Maxted, of the Precincts of the Arch Bps Pallace, by Banns
1703	July	11	Thomas Smithson, of St Mildred's, and Ann Philpott, of St Margaretts, by licence
1703	October	28	Gilbert Knowler, of Hearne, Gent: & Mrs Honywood Denn, of Kingston, by licence
1703	November	23	Daniel Shoveler, of Bishopsbourn, & Mary fferris, of the Precincts of this Church, by Banns
			Tho. Johnson, Sacrist

Year.	Month.	Day.	Names.
1703	January	13	Thomas Taylor, of St Paul's in Cant: & Sarah Taylor, of Fordwich, by licence
1704	April	15	Christopher Curd, of Bleane, & Mary Denne, of Chislett, by licence
1704	April	20	John Page, of Milton near Sittingbourn, & Catherine Moore, of St Margaretts, by Licence
1704	April	22	John Godden, of City of Cant: Gent., & Ann Kay, of St Margaret, by Licence
1704	June	7	Daniel Frank,* of St Andrew's, Cant., & Ann Bedingfeild, of the precincts of ys Church, by Banns
1704	October	2	†William Ares, of Tilmanstone, & Rebecca Cullen, of the precincts of the Bishop's Palace, by banns
1704	October	16	Tho. Lyneal, of St Peter's, Joyner, & Ann Wootton of St Margaret's, by Licence
1704	October	22	Robert Jull, of Chillham, & Jane Stone, out of the Precincts of the Bps Palace, by Banns
			James Henstridge, Sact
1704	November	28	John Baxter & Mary Dolly, both of St Paul's, Cant: by Licence
1705	July	3	John Upton, of St Mary Magdalen's, Cant: and Elizabeth Rogers, of ye precincts of this Church, by Banns
1705	September	16	William Johnson, of ye Arch Bishops Palace, & Gertrude Rothwell, of ye Precincts of this Church, by Licence
1705	September	30	Thomas Shrubsole, of Bishopsbourne, & Mary West, of ye precincts of this Church, by Banns
1705	October	11	William Nash & Hannah Carter, both of Adisham, by Licence
1705	October	11	William Woodwar, of Staple, & Elizabeth Paramore, of Shepardswell, by Licence
1705	October	14	Henry Court, of Thanington, & Ann Adams, of ye Precincts of this Church, by Banns
			Robert Cumberland, Sacrist
1705	January	18	John Turner, of Aldington, & Mary Catchpole, of the Precincts of this Church, by Banns
1705	January	31	Richard Scott, of Boughton under Bleane, & Elizabeth Lent of St Margaret's in Canterbury, by Licence
1706	March	30	George Kidder, of St George, Cant., & Dorcas Fowle, of St Margaretts, Cant., by Lycence
1706	June	13	John Alban (?) and Elizabeth Beane, (?) both of Debtford, by Lycence
1706	July	29	Luke Breese (or Bruse,) & Martha Langram, both of Queenborough, by Licence
1706	September	7	Thomas Middleton & Elizabeth Martin, both of Deal, by licence
1706	September	29	Richard Beane & Mary Reakes, both of Sturry, by licence
1706	October	1	John Peirce, of Northgate, Cant., & Elizabeth Ladd, of the Precincts of this Church, by banns
1706	October	3	Andrew Beane & Eliz. Jefford, both of Chislett, by Licence
1706	November	1	Stephen Taylor, of Fordwich, & Mary Gibbs, of Wickhambreux, by lycence
1706	November	5	Alexander Watson, of All Saint's, Cant: & Sarah Stevens, of ye Precincts of ye Bishop's Palace, by Banns
			James Henstridge, Sacrist
1706	December	25	Edward Highstead, of Westwell, and Sarah Ansell, of the Precincts

* Date and name overwritten in the original.

† This entry is entirely overwritten in the original.

Year.	Month.	Day.	Names.
1706	January	21	William Elucy, of Stassfeild, and Sarah Tumms, of Eastling
1706	February	13	Peter Tombling, of S[t] Alphage, and Frances Godden, of S[t] Peter's, by lycence
1706	February	23	Daniel Chandler, of All Saintes, and Elizab: Franckling, of the Precincts, by licence
1706	February	23	Geruice Louell, of Herne, and Mary Frampton, of y[e] Bish: Pallace, by Lycence
1707	May	6	John Bowles and Mary Emerson, of S[t] Laurence, in the Iland of Thanett, by Lycence
1707	June	2	James Tapley and Elianor Lauce, of Stroode, by lycence
1707	July	3	John Goodwin and Mary Headach, booth of Folkstone, by lycence
1707	September	18	Richard May, of Ash, and Sarah Roome, of Adisham
1707	September	23	James Jekin and Elizabeth Neale, both of Queenborow, by lycence
			Ch: Kilburne, Sacrist
1707	November	27	John Pilcher and Mary Taylor, both seruants within the precincts of this Church, by Banns
1707	December	13	John Chapman and Rebecca Oates* or (Gates,) both of ffolkstone, by licence
1707	January	5	Matthew Godfrey and Jane Allen, both of Holy Crosse, by licence
1707	February	5	Isaac Mockett and Elizabeth Kirby, both of S[t] Peter's, in Thanett, by licence
1707	February	16	Richard Solley and Elizabeth Baxted, both of Eastry, by licence
1708	April	4	Richard Philpott, of Hackington, and Elizabeth Busher, of the Precincts of this Church, by licence
1708	April	15	Thomas Cullen and Elizabeth Mackley, both of Ashford, by licence
1708	June	10	Richard Spratbrow, of Sturry, and Ann Tritton, of Stodmarsh, by licence
1708	June	19	James Streeting and Jane Jarvis, both of Whitstable, by licence
1708	June	20	John Kingsland and Jane Minge, both of Luddenham, by licence
1708	September	7	Matthew Bunce, of Hoathfield, & Elizabeth Copland, of the same, by licence
1708	September	25	Thomas ffowl, of S[t] Margaretts, & Margery Everden, of the precincts of this Church
1708	October	21	Edward Adams and Deborah Taylor, both of Westwell
1708	October	26	Simon Hunt, of Great Chart, and Martha Butcher, of Bethersden, by licence
1708	November	5	William Brissenden and Lucy Brissenden, both of Cranbrooke, by licence
			Tho: Johnson, Sacrist
1708	December	23	William Fox, of Seasalter, & Elizabeth Coultrope, of y[e] same parish, by Lycence
1708	January	20†	Thomas Beale & Margaret Phosier,† both of Whitstable, by Lycence
1708	January	25	George Wilson & Ann Cockman, both of Whitstaple
1708	March	1	Richard Taddy & Catherine Tuckness, both of S[t] Laurence, in y[e] Isle of Thanett, by Licence

* Written over an erasure in the original.
† The date and the name "Phosier," overwritten in the original.

Year.	Month.	Day.	Names.
1709	March	28	Matthew Browne, of St Peter's, Cant: & Jane Davis, of Wingham, by licence
1709	April	28	Thomas Miles and Elizabeth Fox, both of Seasalter, by licence
1709	June	18	John Goatley & Dorothy Lukin, both of St Mary Magdalene, in ye City of Cant: by licence
1709	June	26	John Ward & Sarah Romell, both of Northborne, by licence
1709	June	27	Stephen Hall and Anne Browne, both of Whitstaple
1709	July	28	William Richardson & Mary Draper, both of Whitstaple, by licence
1709	August	3	*Samuel Prescott, of Gustone, & Mary Pitt (or Pott,) of Fordwich, by licence
1709	July†	11	John Lewis, Vicar of Minster, in ye Isle of Thanett, & Mary Knowler, of St George's, Cant: by licence
1709	October	2	*John Coates & Ann Court, both of the precincts of this Church, by licence
1709	October	4	*John Harrison, of Rothervill in Sussex, & Mary Barham, of Ashford, by licence
1709	October	6	*John ffriend and Hester Hedgcock, both of Saltwood, by licence
1709	October	9	*James Read, of Hern Hill, & Elizabeth Saundes, of the Precincts of this Church, by Banns
1709	October	15	*John Austen & Catherine Rickesin, both of St Mary's in Sandwich, by licence
1709	October	10†	John Hermon, of Milton, & Mary Preston, of Seasalter, by licence
1709	October	28	*Jacob Widdick & Mary Cory, both of Whitstaple, by licence
1709	November	3	*John Cumberland, Vicar of Leisdowne, & Mary Tickner, of Feversham, by Licence
			Ja: Henstridge, Sacrist
1709	December	19	Searles Middlemas & Elizabeth Court, Both of Chartham, by Licence
1709	December	28	Henry Tiddiman & Mary Furse, both of Canterbury, by Licence
1709	January	5	John Watkins & Mary Fleming, both of Cant: by Licence
1709	January	17	Richard Bunce, of Newington, & Mary Sedger, of Harrietsham, by Licence
1709	January	17	Philip Margot, of St Gyles in ye fields, London, & Anne Dauborne, of Cant., by Licence
1709	January	19	Stephen Buckhurst & Elizabeth Haffenden, both of St George's, Cant., by Licence
1709	January	21	William Fox & Thomasin Hopkins, Both of Nackington, by Licence
1709	January	22	Richard Marsh, of Sturrey, & Jane Kilham, of ye Precincts of this Church, by Banns
1709	January	28	Thomas Fowle, of St Margaret's, Cant: & Frances Bennett, of Sturrey, by Licence
1709	February	13	Daniel Godfrey Swan & Sarah Tickner, Both of St Lawrence in Thanet, by Licence
1709	February	18	Ambrose Starke & Elizabeth Deane, Both of Chislet, by Licence
1710	April	17	Benjamin Wootton, of Fordwich, & Ann Evans, of ye Precincts of ye Arch Bishop's Palace, by Banns

* These entries are overwritten in the original.
† So in the original, the entry has been overwritten.

Year.	Month.	Day.	Names.
1710	June	15	Edward Hoare, of St Mary Bredman, Cant., & Mary Watson, of ye precincts of ye Arch Bishop's Palace, by Licence
1710	July	4	Thomas Jennings, of Fordwich, & Susanna Farriers, of ye Precincts of ye Arch Bp's Palace, by Licence
1710	July	29	William Juge & Mary Spickett, both of St John's in Thanet, by Licence
1710	August	16	Thomas Foster, of St Lawrence, & Sarah Smith, of Birchington in Thanet, by Licence
1710	August	22	Roger Pilcher, of ye Citty of Rochester, & Sarah Law, of Faversham, by Licence
1710	September	30	John Randalph, of Kennington, & Mary Ellis, of Fordwich, by Licence
			Rob. Cumberland, Sacrist
1710	December	3	George Laming and Ann Constant, both of St John's in Thanet, by Lycence
1710	February	16	Robert Hammon and Elizabeth Estes, both of St Mildred's, by Licence
1711	April	3	James Leggat, of St Andrew's, and Ann Hikes, of Holy Crosse, by Licence
1711	April	23	Mathew Browne and Mary Wattson, of St Peter's in Cant.
1711	May	31	John Webb and Mary Hills, of Ash
1711	August	14	Edward Constant and Mary Sauidge, both of St John Bap^{t} in the Island of Thant., by Lycence
1711	October	25	Robt May, of St Peter's, Cant: and Catherine Benefeild, of Nackington, by Lycence
1711	October	28	John Lewes and Sarah Gray, both of Holy Crosse, Westgate, by Lycence
1711	October	3*	George Grimes, of Cripple Gate, London, and Ann Beuerton, of Holy Crosse, by Lycence
			Ch. Kilburne, Sacrist
1711	November	26	Thomas Claringbold and Ann Peirce, both of Hougham, by licence
1711	November	28	William Wanstall, of Chilham, and Martha Bing, of Doddington, by licence
1711	January	22	John Hurst, of St Peter's in Thanett, and Mary Ricard, of the precincts of this Church, by Banns
1711	January	22	William Overy and Martha Scott, both of Tenham, by licence
1711	February	23	Sammuell Mayden, Soldier in the Regiment of Marines, and Elizabeth Burgar, of St Mary, Northgate
1711	February	28	John Coxon and Mary Emerson, both of St Lawrence in Thanett, by licence
1711	March	3	Thomas Kingsland, of Luddington, & Elizabeth Worham (or Norham), of ffaversham, by licence
1712	March	25	John Clerke, of St Margarett's parish, and Mary Holnesse, of the precincts of this Church, by licence
1712	April	15	John Saywell, of Bredhurst, and Elizabeth Bensted, of Bredgar, by licence
1712	April	21	Archibald Hamilton and Catherine Humble, both of St Mary's in Sandwich, by licence
1712	April	26	Joseph Upton and Hannah Carter, both of Minster in Thanett, by licence
1712	May	1	Robert Austen, of Little Mongham, & Elizabeth Kitchen, of Waldershiere, by licence

* So in the original.

Year.	Month.	Day.	Names.
1712	June	12	James Sharpe and Mary Maylam, both of Bethersden, by licence
1712	June	14	John Bradly, of Wingham, & Jane Goodburne, of Goodnestone, by licence
1712	June	23	*John Bushell and Jane Tapsell, both of Monkton in Thanett, by licence
1712	June	24	Richard Maundy, of Sandwich, and Susanna Harrison, of St Alphage in Canterbury, were married by Dr Sydall, by licence
1712	June	28	Simon Evernden and Elizabeth Kilham, by Banns
1712	July	5	Richard Philcott and Mary Carpenter, both of Thanington, by licence
1712	July	19	Thomas White, of Brookland, and Bridgett Butcher, of Brensett, by licence
1712	September	15	Gerhard Selby, of Wapping in Middlesex, & Hester Turner, of All Sn'ts in Canterbury, by lic.
1712	October	2	*John Adams and Ann Stains, both of Chislett, by licence
1712	October	14	John Rabson and Mary Redford, both of Sandhurst, by licence
1712	October	18	Gilbert Aldridge, Soldier in the Marine Regiment, and Sarah Kember, of the Parish of St Margarett, by licence
1712	October	28	John Smith and Elizabeth Goodwin, both of Faversham, by licence
1712	November	24	Abraham Ducro, of St Stephen's, and Mary Olive, of the Precincts of this Church, by Banns
			Tho. Johnson, Sacrist
1712	February	9	William Austen & Elizabeth Daniel, both of this precinct, by licence
1712	March	21	John Walk & Margarett Minnis, both of Romney, by licence
1713	April	9	Benjamin Macare, of ye City of Cant., & Martha Middleton, of ye Precincts of this Ch: by licence
1713	July	11	Thomas Hatton, of Hyth, & Elizabeth Drayton, of Chart, by licence
1713	September	29	John Pimm, of St Dunstan's, Cant., & Rejoice Epps, of ye Precincts of this Church
			Ja: Henstridge, Sacrist
1713	December	26	William Court, of Elham, & Mary Seldon, of Nunnington
1713	January	9	Daniel Upton & Elizabeth Carter, both of Sheldwich
1713	January	13	Thomas Gill, of St Mildred's, & Susanna Shrubsole, of the Precincts of this Church
1713	January	26	Richard Rippon, of ye City of Cant., & Mary Hook, of ye Precincts of this Church
1714	March	27	James White, of St Mildred's, & Thomasin Head, of ye Arch Bp^s^ Palace
1714	March	30	Thomas Rolfe & Elizabeth Woodham, both of Monkton, in Thanet
1714	May	20	Henry Watson & Susanna Jordan, both of Folkstone
1714	June	8	John Bowtell, of Woolwich, & Susanna Gyles, of Milton
1714	June	12	Robert Danes & Amy Brown, both of Maidstone
1714	June	15	Henry Wood & Elizabeth Rolfe, both of Elham
1714	June	19	William Cockernutt & Mary Burbridge, both of the Precincts of this Church
1714	June	20	Michael Billingherst, of Beaksbourn, & Sarah Thomson, of ye Precincts of this Church

* Overwritten in the original.

Year.	Month.	Day.	Names.
1714	July	8	Thomas Bushel & Mary Down, both of Stourmouth
1714	July	21	Stephen Ward & Susanna Blackbourn, both of Thanington
1714	July	26	Joseph Nicholls, of Acrise, & Mary Court, of Swinfield
1714	September	12	John Fagge, of Littlebourne, & Elizabeth Ummer, of ye Precincts of this Church
1714	September	29	Thomas Pierce, of ye Precincts of this Church, & Mary Church, of St Alphege
1714	October	10	Richard Cousins, of Folkestone, & Ann Wraith, of ye Precincts of this Church
1714	October	16	George Pilcher & Ann Tadhunter, both of Nackington
			Robt Cumberland, Sacrist
1714	December	30	Peter Blackborne, of Deal, and Mary Butteris, of the same
1714	February	5	Henry Brockman, Gent., of Cheriton, and Mrs Elizabeth Randolph, of the Precincts of the Bishopps Pallace
1715	March	27	John Brattle, of St Georis Parish, and Mary Jagger, of the Precincts
1715	April	17	William Clarke, of St George's, and Mary Davis, of the Precincts
1715	May	9	Henry Greenstreet, of Baughton under the Bleane, and Elizab: Willcock, of Feucsh.
1715	May	28	William Ward, of St Mary, Northgate, and Mary Rayner, of St Paules
1715	June	18	William Ayerst, of Hawkhirst, and Mary Bowyer, of Horsmenden
1715	October	8	Thomas Wilkins and Mary Gold, both of the Arch Bish. Pallace
1715	October	27	William March and Sarah Heeler, both of Barham
			Ch. Kilburne, Sacrist
1715	December	10	James Cheesman and Susanna Pilcher, both of Nackington, by Mr Devereux
1715	January	26	William Wait and Ann Caner [or Cauer].
1715	February	4	William ffilmer and Margarett Stubblefeild, both of Otterden
1715	February	14	John Terry and Susanna Stundley, both of Eastling, by licence
1715	March	17	Samuel ffly, of St Andrews, & Margarett ffriend, of this Church
1716	March	25	Stephen Philpott, of Hackington, and Elizabeth Jaggar, of the precincts of this Church
1716	April	3	Isaac Foucate, of St Dunstan's, and Jane Grooe, of St Mary Northgate
1716	May	12	William Hall and Jane Halfing, both of St Mary's in Sandwich
1716	May	25	Thomas Day and Mercy Parsons, both of Staplehurst
1716	June	9	George Curling, of St Laurence, Than: & Mary Castle, of St Pet: Sandw: by licence
1716	June	23	James Sherlock and Sarah Benny, both of Petham, by licence
1716	July	24	John Hammond and Susanna Stokes, both of Swinfeild, by licence
1716	September	20	Thomas Perry, D.D., Canon of Christchurch in Oxford, and Elizabeth Lukin, of the Parish of St Margaretts, Canterbury
1716	September	25	Robert Minnis and Ann Tookey, both of New Romney, by licence
1716	September	27	Thomas Walker and Elizabeth Barton, both of St Peter's, Cant: by licence

Year.	Month.	Day.	Names.
1716	October	2	Thomas Denn, of Petham, & Hester Sandum, of the Precincts of this Church, by Banns
1716	October	6	John Bird and Sarah Tucker, both of Staple, were married by Mr Arch Deacon
1716	October	29	John Stace, of Smeeth, And Benedicta Austen, of Adisham, were married by Mr Arch Deacon
1716	November	3	Henry Bennett, of St Andrew's, and Margarett Watson, of St Margaretts Parish, by licence
1716	November	10	John Hewson and Elizabeth Gittens, both of ffolkstone, by licence
			Tho: Johnson, Sacrist
1716	December	8	Anthony Baker & Margaret Hall, both of ffolkstone
1716	December	31	George Lettice, of St Peter's in Thannet, & Thomasine Laws, of ffolkstone
1716	January	22	John Southee & Elizabeth Pettman, both of Ickham, by Licence
1716	February	8	William Rice & Elizabeth Martin, both of St Mary Bredman
1716	February	14	Richard Stroud, of Wickham, & Hester Silke, of Ickham, by licence
1716	February	14	William Munns, of Preston by Wingham, & Ann Moyse, of Chislett, by Licence
1716	February	21	Thomas Denne & Sarah Holnes, both of St Margts, Cant:
1716	March	23	Edward Baker, of Wingham, & Mary Bing, of Wickham breux
1717	March	25	Jacob Sharpe & Elizabeth Nethersole, of St Margts, Cant by licence
1717	April	20	Robert Newhouse, of ye City of Cant: & Joan Norrington ?, of St Margaret's in ye said City, by licence
1717	May	7	John Word, of Stourmouth, & Elizabeth Carre, of the same, by licence
1717	October	10	John Penny, of Minster in ye Isle of Thanet, & Eliz: Jarvis, of Birchington, by licence
1717	October	3*	Mr William Gosling & Hester Thomas, both of ye precincts
1717	November	11	Robert Knock & Sarah Keete, both of Minster in ye Isle of Thanett
			Jam: Henstridge, Sacrist
1717	December	5	Augustine Taylor & Catherine Smith, both of Lydd
1717	December	28	Thomas Curling, of East Langdon, & Ann Monday, of ye same
1717	January	2	Edward Jones, of London, & Esther Harris, of Deale
1717	January	19	John Rayner, of Brabourne, & Mary Cullen, of ye Precincts of this Church
1718	April	14	Edward Randall & Margaret Boykett, both of St Mildred's, Cant:
1718	May	3	John Clarke & Elizabeth Pope, both of ye Precincts of this Church
1718	June	4	John Cooke, of Eastry, & Sarah Cock, of Staple
1718	October	8	Richard Baker, of Brookland, & Elizabeth Ford, of Aldington
1718	October	9	John Lott & Mary Adams, both of Sturrey
1718	November	11	Robert Dakein, of ye City of Cant., & Frances Fowle, of St Margaret's, Cant:
1718	November	23	Simon Hall, of ye City of Cant: & Mary Newport, of St. Andrew's, Cant:
			Robt Cumberland, Sacrist

* So in the original.

Year.	Month.	Day.	Names.
1718	December	18	George Friend, of the Precincts of Christ, and Elizabeth Clifford, of St Andrew's
1719	April	4	Peter Dalman, of St Mary Northgate, and Elizabeth Turner, in the Precincts of Christ Church
1719	April	27	Alexander Hauker of St George's, and Mary Dixon, of Ch^t Church, Cant.
1719	September	8	Richard Chapman, of Cheriton, and Mary Tournay
1719	October	21	William Cotter, and Mary Westfield, both of St Maries, in Douer
			Ch: Kilburne, Sacrist
1720	August	6	Richard Johnson, of Norton, and Elizabeth Tong, of Ospringe, by licence
1720	August	6	William Adams and Philadelphia Saffery, both of St Margarett's parish, by licence
1720	August	13	Thomas Petman and Susanna Simmonds, both of Herne, by licence
1720	September	7	George Broadbridge, of Boughton under Blean, and Mary Shore (or Short), of the par^{sh} of St Marg^{ts}, by Lic.
1720	September	8	Robert Martin, of Ash, and Martha Reader, of Staple, by licence
1720	September	24	William Sawyer and Elizabeth Amis, both of Boughton Blean, by licence
1720	September	30	William Derby, of Chislett, and Baldock,* of Sturry, by licence
1720	October	18	Henry Tiddeman, of Lower Hardresse, and Ann Maxted, of St Marg: Cant: by licence
1720	October	31	John Rows and Mary Hunt, both of Leeds, by licence
1720	November	5	Andrew Monrow, of St Mildred's, and Dorothy Rose, within the Precincts of this Church, by licence
1720	November	10	William Wildbore, of Bredgar, and Margaret Higham, of Newington near Sittingbourn, by licence
1720	November	14	Gabriell Merriott and Mary Overy, both of Milton neer Sittingbourn, by licence
1720	December	12	William Pembrooke, of St Paul's, Cant: & Mary Hardres, of ye precincts of this Church
1720	December	30	William Beer, of Hoth, & Elizabeth Bushell, of Birchington
1720	June†	14	Thomas Rouse, of ye City of Canterb: & Elizabeth Elvey, of ye precincts of this Church
1720	January	21	‡John Burchett & Jane Tadhunter, both of Nackington
1720	February	7	‡John Elrinton, of Kingston, & Mary Hayward, of St Mildred's Cant:
1720	February	7	‡John Shipthorp, of Dunkirk, & Ann Rothbourne, of Faversham
1720	February	28 (?)	‡William Allen & Margarett Austen, both of Wye
1720	February	21	‡Edward Broadbridge, of Boughton under Bleane, & Mary White, of Feversham
1720	February	21	‡Thomas Cramp & Mary Whitehead, both of St John's, in ye Isle of Than^t
1721	April	10	‡James Claris, of St Alphage, Cant: & Mary Villiers, of ye precinct
1721	May	30	‡Robert Ellis, of Doddington, & Abigail Six, of Holy Cross, Westgate, Cant:

* So in the original.
† This entry has been overwritten, June is probably an error, it should be January.
‡ These entries are overwritten in the original.

Year.	Month.	Day.	Names.
1721	August	6	*Richard Coates, of Staplegate, & Mary White, of ye Bishop's palace
1721	August	20	*Thomas Corbest (or Corbett) & Mary Gibson, both of ffolkestone
1721	September	21	*William Peene, of Dover, & Mary Harvey, of Eythorne
1721	October	3	*Robert Jagger, of St Mildred, Cant: and Elizabeth Simmonds, within ye precincts of this Church
1721	October	5	*William Dunnings, of Bridge, & Jane Morris, of ye precincts of this Church
1721	October	16	*Thomas Tillett & Elizabeth Cotter, both of St Mary's, in Douer
1721	October	23	William Pierce & Margery Simkin, both of Postling
1721	November	4	John Davison, of All Saints, Cant: & Mary Pack, of ye precincts of this Church
1721	November	6	William Bourne & Jane Amis, both of Littleborne
			Jas: Henstridge, Sacrist
1721	January	11	Ralph-Sherwood Plott, of Newington, Gent., & Frances Tassell, of Faversham
1721	January	29	Thomas Cullen & Elizabeth White, both of Blean
1722	April	4	James Philips, of Sturrey, and Elizabeth Walker, of Westbeer
1722	July	6	Thomas Bayly & Mary Pickle, both of Deale
1722	July	23	Thomas Lelandle & Susanna Polhill, both of St James's, Dover
1722	August	21	Valentine Cantis, of St George's, & Mary Cantis, of St Andrew's, Cant.
1722	August	21	John Dunkin, of Stonar in Thanet, & Bennett Barker, of St Peter's, Sandwich
1722	September	26	Thomas Marshal, of Linxted, & Elizabeth Reader, of Otterinden
1722	October	1	Augustine Reynolds & Catherine Taylor, both of Littlebourn
1722	October	1	Thomas Pepper, of Bearsted, & Sarah Mosely, of Egerton
1722	October	3	Thomas Burr, of Brenset, & Ann Maylam, of Kenardington
1722	October	12	William Waters & Mary Henly, both of Bethersden
1722	October	25	Simon Gilbert, of Aldington, & Ann Desmoulin, of St Andrew's, Cant:
			Rob: Cumberland, Sacrist
1722	January	29	William Palmer, of Culham, in Oxfordshire, and Sara Walters, of the Præcinct of this Church, by M^{r} Le Hunt
1722	February	4	John Mellsted, of Patrixborn, and Mary Godfrey, of the Præcinct of this Church, by Banns
1723	(April	25)	George Knowler, of St Paul, Canterbury, & Mis Anne Elstob, of ye Archbishop's Palace, on St Mark's day
1723	May	28	Joshua Sayer & Ann De Hane, both of Deal
1723	June	4	Anthony Smith, of Canterbury, & Mary Southouse of St Mary, Dover
1723	June	4	Thomas Beer, of Preston by Feversham, and Elizabeth Harnet, of Feversham
1723	June	5	Walter Tilby and Elizabeth Amos, both of the Parish of Raynham
1723	June	21	John Adams, of Sturrey, & Mary Ladd, of Hern
1723	July	29	Thomas Smith & Madlock Dad, both of Folkstone
1723	August	29	Philip Price & Elizabeth Hawkins, both of Wye

* These entries are overwritten in the original.

Year.	Month.	Day.	Names.
1723	September	30	Dudly Soan & Hannah Walkup, both of the Precinct of this Church
1723	October	2	William Michelborn, of ye City of Canterbury, & Catherine Adams, of the Precinct of this Church
1723	October	7	William Foreman, of ye Parish of Addisham, & Elizabeth Silk, of the Bishop's Palace
			John Gostling, Sacrist
—1723	February	13	Thomas Gray & Ann Page, both of St Andrew's Parish, in Canterby
1723	February	14	John Hammond & Elizabeth Rigsby, both of East Church
1723	February	18	Richard Holness & Ann Gors, of the Parish of Harbledown
1724	April	5	William Nutt, of St Margaret's Parish, and Rebecca Ladd, of the precincts of this Church
1724	April	5	John Rowe, of Northgate, & Elizabeth Agar, of the Precincts of this Church
1724	April	13	Thomas Sandwell, of Sandwich, and Margaret Sherwood, of the Precincts of this Church
1724	May	25	Isaac Burton, of St Alphege, & Elizabeth Foord, of St Margarets, in Canterby
1724	July	2	Joseph Monds, of Sturry, & Margaret Tadhunter, of the Precincts of this Church
1724	August	27	Henry Wallis & Ann Diggs, both of St John Baptist's, in the Isl of Thanett
1724	September	26	Thomas Ellett & Sarah Savell, both of Bredhirst
1724	October	4	William Impit, of St Paul's Parish, and Martha Coleman, of the Precincts of this Church
1724	November	24	John Holman & Margaret Stoddard, of Littleborne
			Simn D'Evereux, Sacrist
1724	January	5	Thomas Lees and Ann Curtis, both of the Precincts of this Church
1724	January	9	Sampson Dambs and Susannah Mitchell, of St James in Douer
1725	April	6	Thomas Palmer, of St Mary Magdalene, and Rebecca Drury, of St Margaret's
1725	June	9	John Shipwash, of Boughton Aluph, and Ann Juss, of Crundall
1725	June	26	Robert Holliday and Susan Franck
1725	July	7	Benjamine Watson, of Wansworth, in Surrie, and Priscilla Simpson, of St Maries in Douer
1725	July	21	Robert Turner, of All Sts, and Mary Saffery, of St Paul's
1725	September	30	Richard Dowker and Ann Harrison, of St Marie Bredman
1725	December	15	Peter Corne and Elizabeth Long, both of St Clement's, Sandwich
1725	December	18	William Whiting, of Chislett, & Pleasant Burt, of Reculver
1725	February	18	Thomas Pope, of Thanington, and Eliz: Earle, of Nackington, by Mr D'Evereux
1725	March	8	John Read and Jane Holness, both of St Margaret's parish, by Licence
1726	April	23	Richard Hedgecock and Mary Merlin, both of Faversham, by licence
1726	July	2	Thomas March, of Elmsted, and Ann Boykett, of St Mildred's, Cant., by licence
1726	July	5	John Harvy, of Eythorn, Gnt, and Margarett Maud, of Boughton Alluph, by Dr Graudorge, by licence
1726	July	11	William Sisly, of Linton, and Barbara May, of Hunton, by Licence

Year.	Month.	Day.	Names.
1726	July	16	Thomas Godden and Tabitha Crouch, both of Newnham, by Licence
1726	July	30	Christopher Pack, M.D., of St Margarett's Parish, and Mary Randolph, of the Precincts of this Church, by the Rd Dean, by licence
1726	August	7	Richard Perkins and Mary Pysing, both of St Mary Magdalen Burgate, by Dr Terry, by virtue of a licence
1726	October	1	Sammuell Nash and Elizabeth fford, both of Adisham, by licence
1726	November	3	Herbert Taylor Clerke, and Mrs Mary Wake, by Mr Le Hunt (by virtue of a Licence directed to this Church) Tho: Johnson, Sacrist
1726	January	3	Aaron Fryer & Elianor Carlin, both of Great Chart, by licence
1726	January	28	Clement Hogben, of St John, Isle of Thannett, & Mary Brown, of St Peter's, Cant.
1726	February	7	Richard Constant & Hannah Stoddard, both of Chislett, by licence
1727	April	2	William Bullock, of ye parish of St Paul, & Elizabeth Tiddeman, of the pr'cincts of this Church
1727	May	22	Thomas Pain & Ann Bean, both of Ospringe
1727	July	6	Henry Paschal & Ann Green, both of St Mary's, in Dover
1727	August	4	Armand Squire, of St Mary Magdalene, Cant: & Hester Burine, of St Mildred's, Cant:
1727	July*	27	Richard Botting, in the City of Cant., & Ann Holcomb, of ye precincts of this Church
1727	September	10 (or 19)	Isaac Sandy, of Chartham, & Mary Sandy, of Harbledown, by Mr D'Evereux
1727	October	8	John Stone & Jane Plummer, both of All Saints, Cant.
1727	October	10	Thomas Godwin, of Chilham, & Mary Walker, of ye precincts of this Church, by licence
1727	January	23	John Pysing, of St Andrew's, Cant., & Elizabeth Jennings, of ye Precincts of this Church
1727	January	29	John Corne & Sarah Bubbars, both of Sandwich
1727	March	3	Joseph Chandler, of St Andrew's, & Ann Neam, of Littlebourne
1728	April	16	Abraham Bubbars & Rebekah Long, both of Sandwich
1728	June	26	William Kennett, of Folkstone, & Priscilla Lacey, of Deale
1728	August	24	James Whiddett & Jane Whiddett, both of Harbledown
1728	September	12	Nicholas Hatton of Dover, & Elizabeth Cunning, of Deale
1728	October	16	George Banfield, of St Andrew, & Mary Hunt, of ye Archb Palace
1728	October	28	Daniel Kebell & Mary Horne, both of Ash
1728	December	2	John Horn, of St Margaret's, & Susan Tritton, of St Georgs Parish
1728	December	21	Nicholas Knight, of Charing, & Ann Greenstreet, of Norton
1728	December	26	George Browish & Mary Carlin
1728	January	2	Vincent Underdown, of Dover, & Jane Hussey, of All Saint's parish, in Canterbury
1728	February	17	William Pilcher & Mary Bates, of Littlebourn
1729	April	7	John Fayerman, of Nackington, & Sarah Jordan, of Bridge
1729	April	9	Alexander Steddy & Ann Mompus, of the Precincts of this Church

* So in the original.

Year.	Month.	Day.	Names.
1729	June	15	John Woodwar, of Eastry, & Mary Honess, of St Mary's in Sandwich
1729	July	13	James Jorden, of Newington, & Elizabeth Cawldor, of the Precincts of this Church
1729	October	21	John Swiffington, of Ospringe, and Elizabeth Bushel, of Harbledown
1729	November	20	Richard Dowker, of St Mary Bredman, & Susan Nepecher, of St Alphege in Canterbury
1729	November	27	Stephen Six & Ann Colf, both of the Parish of St Margaret in Canterbury
1729	December	18	William Lake, of the Parish of St George in Canterbury, and Margaret Baker, of the Precinct of this Church
1729	December	26	Ambrose Rose and Sarah Church, both of Monkton in Thanet
1729	January	1	William Allen, of the Precinct of this Church, and Margaret Pittinton, of the Parish of St Mary Magdalene in Canterbury
1729	February	2	John Hubbard, of Sturry [written so in the Licence by mistake for Stelling], & Ann Lambe, of Stelling
1729	February	12	Bryan Bentham, of Sheerness, and Eliz: Belke, of the Precincts of this Church
1730	April	21	Henry Horne & Sarah May, both of Ash
1730	July	14	John Springfield & Ann Somersale, both of Borden
1730	September	4	James Jeudvine, of the City of Canterbury, and Hester Hibone, of the precinct of St Gregory's, near Canterbury
1730	October	4	Giles Bret & Susan Miles, both of Elham
1730	December	9	John Blancha of St Alphage, Cant., & Elizabeth Tivesane (?), of the precinct of this Church
1730	January	2	James Newenden, of Egerton, & Margaret Pope of Charing
1730	January	16	Thomas Beard & Catherine Martin, both of Swinfeild
1730	January	26	John Pilcher, of Whitstaple, & Ann Wile, of ye A.Bp^s palace
1730	February	25	Mr William Bedford, Rector of Beaksborne, & Mrs Susan Knowler, of ye precinct of this Church.
1730	February	25	Charles Delmar, of All Saints, Cant: & Ann Holness, of ye precinct of this Church
1731	April	6	Thomas Upton & Magdalene Lebeup, both of ye City of Canterbury
1731	May	20	Thomas Barker, of ffaversham, & Martha fforeman, of Hernhill
1731	May	29	James Neighbour, of Harbledown, & Eliz: Skelton, of ye precincts of this Church
1731	June	17	Henry Roberts, of Bobbing, & Elizabeth Perkins, of Milton near Sittingbourne
1731	July	10	Francis Marsh, of Shoulden, & Elizabeth White, of Deal
1731	July	13	Bateman Carrick, of Halstow, & Esther Taylor, of St Peter's in ye Isle of Thannett
1731	July	29	Edward Elphick, of St Margaret's, Cant., & Elizabeth ffox, of All Saints, Cant.
1731	August	2	George Guy, of Rainham, & Mary Thompson, of Rochester
1731	September	7	John Scholes (?) & Elizabeth Hamond, both of Eastchurch in ye Isle of Sheppay
1731	September	13	John Barrow & Joanna Higgs, both of Sittingbourne
1731	September	14	Robert Brook & Elizabeth Keys. both of Minster in Thannett

Year.	Month.	Day.	Names.
1731	September	26	John Keys, of Minster in ye Isle of Thannett, & Susanna Hall, of Ash
1731	October	16	George Savage, of Stone, near ffaversham, & Mary Berry, of Offspringe
1731	November	2	James Streeting, of Hernhill, & Ann Huene, of All Saints, Cant.
1731	November	10	Richard ffrend & Mary Johnson, both of Postling
1731	November	24	Edward Gurney, of Swinfeild, & Ann Pain, of Adisham
1731	February	18	James White & Ann Bridger, both of Deale
1731	March	1	Henry Thomson, of Ospringe, and Sarah Goodborne, of Faversham
1732	April	13	William Saxby, of Hedcorne, & Elizabeth Staply, of Leeds
1732	May	3	John Carter & Mary Harty, both of Birchington in Thanet
1732	May	6	John Shrubsole, of Chartham, & Sarah Sainty, of Harbledown
1732	June	24	Henry Burton, of Chilham, & Mary Johncock, of this Church
1732	June	29	Robert Petman, of Westgate, & Mary Andrews, of Hinxhil
1732	July	15	John Smith & Mary Gilbert, both of Smarden
1732	July	27	Nicholas Knight, of Charing, & Mary Bunce, of Faversham
1732	August	13	John Upton, of Hastings, & Susanna Bowes, of ye Precincts of this Church
1732	September	23	John Kedman & Elizabeth Culmer, both of Chislet
1732	October	7	John Benifield & Sarah Holt, both of Hernhill
1732	October	7	Francis Neame, of Birchington, & Elizabeth Jenken, of Minster
1732	October	24	Henry Wraith, of St Nicholas, & Elizabeth Collard, of Chislet
1732	October	28	Matthew Sankey, of Harbledown, & Mary Chambers, of Ash
1732	November	11	Ward Slater, of Alkham, & Elizabeth Chandler, of Maidstone
1732	November	12	William Johnson & Elizabeth Chambers, both of ye Precincts of y^s^ Church
1732	November	20	Thomas Staines & Elizabeth Stace, both of Hern
1732	December	23	Henry Squire, of Hernhill, & Margaret Bunce, of Faversham
1733	March	31	Joshua Drayson & Elizabeth Lippeat, both of Swacliffe
1733	April	5	Richard Allen & Mary Penn, both of ye Precincts of this Church
1733	October	8	Richard Edwards & Margaret Fowle, both of ye Precincts of this Church
1733	October	11	Samuel Halward, of Bridge, & Mary Pilcher, of ye Precincts of this Church
1733	October	20	Thomas Knowler & Catherine Bear, both of Chistlet
1733	November	10	Thomas Wiessum & Mary Chamberlain, both of Hearn

THE END OF MARRIAGES IN THE SECOND REGISTER.

1733	January	3	Gervase Waddington & Berthula Walton, both of St Mary's Parish in Dover, by licence
1733	February	2	Thomas Wanstal and Ann Gardner, both of Beaksborn, by licence
1733	February	26	John Oakinful, of Herbaldown, and Ann Saddleton, of St Alphege Parish in Canterbury, by licence

Year.	Month.	Day.	Names.
1734	April	15	Anthony Hills, of Ashford, and Catharine Pool, of Maidstone, by licence
1734	May	14	Thomas Brunger and Susan Hope, both of Biddenden, by licence
1734	June	24	John Hall, of Ospringe, and Ann Underdown, of Town Sutton, by licence
1734	July	2	William Rigden, of S[t] Mildred's, & Mary Rayner, of S[t] Margaret's Parish in Canterbury, by licence
1734	July	10	Thomas Atkison, of S[t] Mary Magdalene's Parish in Southwark, Mariner, and Sarah Smithers, of Deal, by licence
1734	July	13	William Slodden and Jane Moore, both of new Romney, by licence
1734	September	28	Edward May, of Ickham, and Elisabeth Young, of the Precinct of the Arch Bishop's Palace, by licence William Gostling, Sacrist
1734	November	9	Jacob Walter and Mary Newman, both of new Romney, by licence
1734	November	25	William Ayers and Abigail Dilnot, both of Tilmanstone, by licence William Gostling, Sacrist
1734	December	5	*John Newman, of New Romney, & Ann Kennett, of S[t] Mary in Dover, by Licence
†	February	10	*William Carter, of Elmsted, & Ann Epps, of Godmersham, by licence
†	December	12	*George Lacy, of Sturry, & Mary Taylor, of Littleborne, by licence
1734	January	4	*John Adams & Priscilla Marsh, both of Faversham, by licence
1734	February	12	*William Gemmett & Mary Stone, both of S[t] John Baptist in Thanett, by licence
1734	February	13	William Hart, of ffaversham, & Phebe Banett, of Davington, by licence
1735	May	3	Edward Tritton & Jane Austen, both of Wickham, by licence
1735	June	27	William Steadman, of S[t] Nicholas, & Elizabeth Jordan, of Birchington in y[e] Isle of Thannett, by licence
1735	July	10	John Bishop & Ann Bishop, both of Great Chart, by licence
1735	July	21	*Thomas Thunder & Martha Covell, both of Birchington in Thanett, by licence
1735	September	9	George Newman, of Rotherhith in Surry, & Elizabeth Clarabutt, of Deal, by licence
1735	September	23	John Carrington, of Queenborough, & Elizabeth Gransden, of Minster in Sheppy, by licence
1735	September	30	Stephen Homan, of Wickambreux, & Elizabeth Mussard, of Ickham, by licence
1735	October	1	Abraham Scoones & Elizabeth Hills, both of Leeds, by licence
1735	October	3	Robert Fright, of Tenham, & Mary Ellett, of Newnham, by licence
1735	October	15	James Otsirell & Mary Bennett, both of Westwell, by Licence
1735	October	21	Benjamin Chandler, of S[t] Andrew's, & Ann Dawking, of S[t] Alphage, by licence
1735	November	1	John Phillips, of Westwell, & Elizabeth Hubbell, of Hadlow

* Overwritten in the original. † No year in the original

Year.	Month.	Day.	Names.
1735	November	22	Thomas Castle, of St John Baptst in Than^{t}, & Mary Barber, of St Clement in Sandwich, by Licence
			James Henstridge, Sacrist
1735	December	11	William Wood, of Hyth, & Susannah Freind, of Sellindge, by Licence
1735	January	19	Daniel Godfrey & Mildred Bates, both of Faversham, by Licence
1735	January	26	John Keeppen & Elizabeth Drayson, Spinster, both of Sittingbourne, by Licence
1735	March	1	John Brattell, Batchelor, of St George's, & Elizabeth Claringbull, Spinster, of St Paul's, Canterbury, by Licence
1735	March	3	The Revd Mr James Evans, Under-Master of the King's School, & Hannah Kilburne, by Licence
1735	March	3 (or 8)	James Everden, of Chartham, Widower, & Elizabeth Carter, of Kenington, Spinster, by Licence, by Mr Henstridge
1736	May	1	Valentine Cock, of Hoth, Batchelour, & Elizabeth Ridgden, of Adisham, Widow, by Licence
1736	May	8	Thomas Nowers, of Halden, Batchelour, & Ann Rogers, of Wye, Spinster, by Licence
1736	May	13	John Foreman, of Hernhill, Batchelour, & Sarah Elliot, of Newnham, Spinster, by Licence
1736	May	25	Simon Brice, Batchelour, & Elizabeth Foreman, Spinster, both of Feversham, by Licence
1736	June	13	John Ellis, of St Dunstan's, & Elizabeth Percival, of the Precincts of Christ Church, by Banns, by Mr Evans
1736	July	26	John Nettleford, Batchelour, & Mary Slater, Spinster, both of Ashford, by Licence
1736	September	21	William Ireland, of Ashford, Batchelour, & Elizabeth Ertzberger, of Smeeth, Spinster, by Licence
1736	September	30	William Whiffen, Batchelour, & Elizabeth Sandy, Spinster, both of Bredhurst, by Licence
1736	September	30	William Beck, Batchelour, & Hannah Collins, Widow, both of Upchurch, by Licence
1736	October	2	William Lee, Batchelour, & Sarah Shaw, Spinster, both of Ruckinge, by Licence
1736	October	5	William Taylor, of New Romney, & Mary Moon, of the Precincts of Christ Church, by Banns
1736	October	11	John Curd, of Petham, & Ann Rogers, of the Precincts of Christ Church, by Banns, by Dr Donne
1736	October	21	William Turner, of Aldington, & Martha Quillanyton, (?) of the Arch-Bishop's Palace, by Banns
1736	October	27	William Bubb, of Tenham, Batchelour, & Hannah Saffery, of Harty in ye Isle of Shepy, Spinster, by Licence
1736	October	30	William Norris, Batchelour, & Mary Knot, both of Minster in Thanet, by Licence
			Tho. Buttonshaw, Sacrist
1736	December	6	John Tucker, Batchelour, & Eliz. Diplox, Spinster, both of Great Chart, by Licence
1736	February	3	Philip Loue, of Thanington, Batchelour, and Sarah Cowton, of Harbledown, Widow, by Licence
*	February	8	John Morne, Batchelour, & Ann Underdowne, Spinster, both of Deal, by Licence
*	February	19	John Coleman, of Godmersham, Batchelour, and Ann Bowles, of Walmer, Spinster, by Licence

* No year in the original.

Year.	Month.	Day.	Names.
*	March	3	Daniel Doingefield, Batchelour, & Mary Kennet, Spinster, both of Folkstone, by Licence
*	March	19	Tho: Wilson, Batchelour, & Mary Dunk, Spinster, both of St Lawrence in ye Isle of Thanet, by Licence
1737	March	26	Rich. Hart, of St Peter's in ye City of Cant., Batchelour, & Ann Constable, of ye Parish of Holy Cross in ye City of Cant., by Licence
1737	July	4	Simon Wing, of Eastwell, Batchelour, & Mildred Coast, of ye same place, Spinster, by Licence
1737	July	24	John Greenland, of Folkstone, Widower, and Sarah White, of Lyminge, Spinster, by Licence
1737	August	23	John Bendford, of Thanington, Batchelor, & Mary Malpass, of St Mary Breadman, Canterbury, Widow, by Licence
1737	August	29	John Holier, Batchelor, & Eliz: Gregory, Spinster, both of Faversham, by Licence
1737	September	12	Samuel Obree, Batchelor, & Margaret Horn, Spinster, both of St Mary Northgate, Canterbury
1737	September	12	John Hodges of Gravesend, Batchelor, and Ann Marsh, of Denton, Spinster
1737	September	24	Ambrose Stock, of Hearne, Batchelor, and Eliz. Ambrose, of Sturry, Spinster
1737	November	12	Adam Alexander, Batchelor, and Gidden Cornish, Spinster, both of Dover
			Robt: Jenkin, Sacrist
1737	December	†	James Powell & Ann Toker, by Licence, by Dr Holcombe
173⅞	February	14	Peter Richards, of Sturry, & Mary Hubbard, of Xt Ch. Cant., by Banns
173⅞	February	14	John Summersol & Alice Potten, both of Linxted, by licence
*	March	4	Joseph Lawrence, of Hucking, & Mary Weston, of Wormshill, by Licence
*	February‡	26	Robert Holness & Elizabeth Denne, both of Littlebourn, by Licence
173⅞	March	23	Nicholas Rayner, of . . . . ‡ & Mary Allott, of Xt Ch. Cant., by Licence, by Mr Griffith
1738	April	3	John White & Ann Boys, both of Littlebourn, by Licence
1738	April	6	Thomas Withers & Mary Cox, both of Nonnington, by Licence
1738	April	27	William Bennett, of Davington, and Martha Bunce, of Throwleigh, by Licence
1738	May	13	Abraham Raysell, of Sittingbourn, & Sarah Knowlden, of Milton, by Licence
1738	June	17	Daniel Jarvis, of Elmston, and Ann Rigden, of All Saints, Cant., Lic:
1738	July	11	Austen Neame, of Littlebourn, & Mary Hills, of Chilham, by Licence
1738	July	11	Abraham Landen, of Egerton, and Mary Pay, of Sarr, by Licence
1738	August	17	Richard Lilly, of Ashford, and Mary Franklyn, of Molash, by Licence
1738	May‡	31	Robert Jenkin, Minor Canon of this Church, and Catharine Blomer, by Dr Dawnay
1738	October	19	Richard Edwards and Mary Barns, Banns

* Year omitted in the original. † Date omitted in the original.
‡ So in the original.

Year.	Month.	Day.	Names.
1738	October	3*	John Roberts, of St Margaret's, & Jane Francis, of the Precincts of this Church, by Licence
1738	October	21	Samuel Simpson, of the Borough of Staplegate, & Mary Hasel, of Sturry, by Licence
1738	November	9	William Curling and Ann Shepardson, of St Lawrence in Thanet, by Licence
1738	November	5*	Edward Lawe, of Egerton, & Susan Elwy, of Hothfield
1738	November	22	James Fagg, of St Peter in Canterbury, & Mary Nichols, of the Precincts of this Church, by Licence, (by the Dean)
			Peter Vallavine, Sacrist
1738	December	24	The Revd Mr William Broderip, Minor Canon of this Church, & Elizabeth Terrey, of St Mary Bredman in ye City of Cant., Spinster, by Licence (by ye Dean)
1738	January	3	William Broadley, Batchelour, & Sarah Fox, Widow, both of St James, Dover, by Licence
1738	January	11	Henry Austen, Batchelour, & Elizabeth Stroud, Maiden, both of St Mary in Dover, by Licence
1738	January	24	Joseph Holness, Batchelour, of Canterbury, & Mary Chiddick, of Herne, Maiden, by Licence
1738	February	26	John Fowler, of Whitstable, Batchelour, and Dorothy Cook, of Thannington, Spinster, by Licence
1738	February	27	†Robt Main, Batchelor, & Barbara Clarke, both of Faversham, by Licence
1739	May	9	John Fisher, Batchelour, & Mary Fisher, Maiden, both of Faversham, by Licence
1739	May	25	Willm Parker & Jane Anderson, both of St Mildred in Canterbury, by License
1739	May	29	†Thos Binham, of Rolvenden, & Mary Clake, (?) of Guilldforde, in ye County of Sussex,* by Licence
1739	June	4	John Clover & Jane Griggs, both of Littlebourne, by Licence
1739	June	20	Thos Ashton, of St George's, Canterby, Batchelour, & Anne Gilbert, of St Mary Breadman, Maiden, by Licence
1739	September	16	Henry Jagger, of St Mildred's, & Elizabeth Hall, of ye Precincts, by Licence
1739	September	24	Thos Farney (or Farrley), Batchelour, & Mary Gore Maiden, both of Stalisfield, by Licence
1739	October	1	Robt Barker & Mary Kennet, both of Petham, by Licence
1739	October	2	†William Cheall, of All Saints, Cant., Batchelor, & Rebecca Penn, of Thannington, Widow, by Licence
1739	October	4	†Henry Knot, of Minster in Thanet, Widower, & Elizabeth May, of Wingham, Maiden
1739	October	8	†Isaac Crothall, of Ashford, Batchelour, & Mary Rasell, of Kennington, Maiden, by Licence
1739	October	11	†Thos. Glover, Batcher, & Sarah Farrow, both of Deal, by Licence
1739	November	8	†John Hills, of Denton, & Mary Denne, of Chilham
1739	November	10	†William Sharp, & Mary Barling, both of Westwell, by Licence
1739	November	20	†John Iverson & Anne Conchman, by Banns
			William Broderip, Sacrist
1739	December	17	James Bushell, of Woodnesborough, Batchelor, & Alice Horn, of Ash, Maiden, by Licence

* So in the original. † Overwritten in the original.

Year.	Month.	Day.	Names.
1739	January	1	James Mantle, of Sturrey, and Margaret Cooper, of Littleborn, by Licence
1739	January	25	Peter Bullock & Elisabeth Grant, both of Milton by Sittingborn, by Licence
1739	January	31	Joseph Rogers, of Sheldwich, & Elisabeth Knowles, of Wye, by Licence
1740	May	29	James Harman & Anne Weaver, both of Tenterden, by Licence
1740	June	12	William Turner, of Ham, & Deborah Macey, of Northbourn, by Licence
1740	June	22	William Stoddard & Elisabeth Goodbun, both of Littleborn, by Licence
1740	June	28	William Drayner & Elisabeth Jarman, both of Wye, by Licence
1740	June	29	John Carter, of Westbere, & Susanna Pratley, of the Precinct of this Church, by Licence
1740	September	30	Thomas Smith and Elisabeth Peen, both of Bapchild, by Licence
1740	October	1	Thomas Brown, of Newnham, & Mary Goatley, of Lenham, by Licence
1740	October	2	John Briscoe, of Friday Street, London, and Hannah Wightwick, of Marden, by Licence
			William Gostling, Sacrist
1740	November	29	Thomas Lamber, Batchelor, & Anne Horne, Maiden, both of Little Mongham, by Licence
1740	December	11	Benjamin Broomistone, of St Lawrence in Thanet, Widower, & Mary Taylor, of the Precincts of this Church, Maiden, by Licence, by the Revd Mr Deeds
1740	January	7	Henry Despain, of St Margaret's, Canterbury, Batchelor, & Mary Pysing, of the Precincts of this Church, Spinster, by Licence
1740	February	25	John Welling, of Dover, Widower, & Mary Chilmer, of the Precincts of this Church, Spinster, by Licence, by Mr Henstridge
1740	March	3	William Furner, Widower, & Anne Davy, Maiden, both of Stone in Oxney, by Licence
1741	March	26	Andrew Vere, Widower, & Susan Homee, Maiden, both of Holy Cross, Westgate, by Licence
1741	May	7	George Wrighte, of St George's, Westminster, London, Batchelor, & Joan Bushell, of Deal, Spinster, by Licence
1741	June	7	Stephen Gilham & Mary Holness, both of Harbledown, by Licence
1741	July	20	Thomas Woodnesse, of Little Mongeham, and Jane Fell, of Eastry, by Licence
1741	October	21	William Carr, of Ash, & Elizabeth Solly, of Staple, by Licence
1741	November	19	Charles Tassell (or Tatsell), of Norton, & Jane Lott, of Buckland, by Licence
1741	November	30	Henry Spain & Susan Nye, both of Nonington
			James Henstridge, Sacrist from Mid Sum'er
1741	December	12	John Barham, of Elham, & Mary Moore, of Folkstone, by Licence
1741	December	24	Steph. Sayers, of Littlebourn, & Marg: Minter, of ye Precincts of y^s^ Church
1741	December	29	Hen: Tickner & Mary Osbourn, both of Ramsgate, by Licence

Year.	Month.	Day.	Names.
174½	January	1	John Wethirelf, of Selling, & Mary Waters, of Godmersham by Licence
174½	January	28	Tho. Buckley, of St Alphage, Cant: & Sarah Manns (or Munns), of ye Palace of ye A. Bp.
174½	February	20	James Edwards, of Ash, & Mary Horne, of Eastry, by Licence
174½	February	25	Wm Ugen & Susan Page, both of Chartham, by Licence
1742	May	15	Tho. Grigson & Ann Holman, both of Ramsgate, by Licence
1742	May	19	John Wilson & Ann Cork, both of Lenham, by License
1742	June	29	William Sancroft & Sarah Medget, both of Wingham, by Licence
1742	August	30	Edward Barret & Mary Haywood, both of Canterbury, by Licence
1742	October	12	John Taylor & Ann Reynolds, both of Littlebourn, by Licence
1742	October	16	*Henry Southouse, of Owre, & Jane Munden, of Westwell, by Licence
1742	October	28	*George Gillow, of Walmer, & Mary Shepple, of Eythorne, by Licence
			Robt Jenkin, Sacrist.
1742	December	20	Henry Griffin, of St Bartholomew's, London, and Abigal Pappe, of Deal, by Licence
1742	December	28	John Langley and Elizabeth Brimsteed, both of Maidstone, Pr Lic.
1742	February	11	James Avery & Margaret Jacob, both of Newnham, Pr Licn
1742	February	28	John Pott & Ann Moverly, of Eastry, Pr licence
1742	March	18	William Eley, of Borden, & Susanna Underdown, of Toug, Pr Licn
1743	April	3	Thomas Mantle, of Bridge, and Mary Beesom, of the Precinct of Xt Ch., by Banns
1743	April	4	Samuel Balden, of Lenham, and Mary Dunk, of Kennington, Pr Licence
1743	April	7	Thomas Mitchell, of St James, in Dover, & Ellen Norwood, of St Mary, Dover
1743	May	17	James Mercer & Sarah Ady, both of Stockbury
1743	June	21	Henry Twisden & Mary Morphet, both of Tenterden
1743	June	24	John Charlton, of Linton, & Mary Eason, of ye City of Rochester
			Peter Vallavine, Sacrist
1743	August	9	Robert Joad & Hannah Allen, both of Ramsgate, by licence
1743	October	2	Mathew Hogman, of Sturry, & Susanna Pay, of Boughton Blean, by licence
1743	October	19	John Covirlid, of Westwell, & Ann Down, of Goodnestone, by licence
1743	October	20	John Bush & Rachael Rayner, both of Raynam, by licence
1743	October	31	Thomas Huggins & Elizabeth Anderson, both of Borden, by licence
1743	November	19	Edward Dunn, of Padlesworth, & Alice Mackett, of Newington, near Hythe, by Licence
1743	November	23	Richard Mackett, of Newington, & Jane Thomas, of Lyd, by licence
			James Henstridge, Sacst, from Mid Sumr

* Overwritten in the original.

Year.	Month.	Day.	Names.
1743	December	30	William Colley, of the Parish of Tong, & Elizabeth Turner, of the same, by Licence from Drs. Commons.
1743	January	7	Thos. Holness, Batchelor, & Hannah Jervis, Maiden, both of Birchington, by License
1743	February	1	Thomas Sillibourne, Widower, & Eliz: Haradee (?), Maiden, both of Great Chart, by Licence
1743	February	7	*Daniel Curling & Lucy Reed, both of Ramsgate, by licence
1743	February	24	*John Lawson (or Lavson), of Shellness, & Thomazin Moore, of Chatham, by Licence
1744	March	25	*Edward Snatt & Anne Read, of Linsted, by Licence
1744	April	3	Anthony Dive, of Tong, & Eliz: Swifington,* of Linsted, by Licence
1744	April	7	Edward Robinson & Susanna Bourn, both of Margate, by Licence
1744	May	2	William Pond, Batchelor, & Mary Robason, Widow, both of Margate, by Licence
1744	May	19	John Bissaker, of Portsmouth, & Mary Langley, of Deal, by Licence
1744	June	21	John Dunbrain, of St Mildred, & Susan Birch, Servant to Mrs Blomer, by Banns
1744	June	27	Edward Warner, of Borden, & Anne Knowlden, of Newington next Sittinbourn, by Licence
1744	July	22	John Honton & Christian Gascoyne, both of Eastchurch, in Sheppy, by Licence
1744	July	25	James Ellen, of Goodnestone, & Eliz: May, of Graveney, by Licence
1744	July	25	Joseph Clift & Mary Worthington, both of Dover, by Licence
1744	August	10	Samuel Corney & Mary Anne Kempster, both of Dover, by Licence
1744	August	20	Adam Palmer & Eliz: Terry, both of Canterbury, by Licence
1744	August	25	Henry Bridges & Frances Lancefield, both of the Præcincts, by License
1744	August	29	Henry Horne & Mary Court, both of Chislett, Pr Licence
1744	September	15	Edward Rumney, of Sturry, & Thomazine White, of Hearn, by License
1744	September	2†	Wm Belsey & Dorcas Friend, both of Eastrey, by licence
1744	September	15	Daniel Smith & Susanah Somes, Pr banns
1744	September	18	The Revd Mr Richd Marsh, Minor Canon of this Church, & Elizabeth Frend, of the Præcincts, Pr Licence, by Dr Ayerst
1744	November	5	Willm Pointing & Susan Down, both of Faversham, by Licence
1744	November	9	Stephen Springet & Jane Hart, both of Kennardington, by Licence
1744	November	13	John Ede & Frances Elven, both of the Præcts, by Banns.
1744	November	24	Daniel Parker, of Newnham, & Catharine Gibbons, of Bapchild, by Licence
			Wm Broderip, Sacrist.
1744	December	21	James Banks, of Canty, Widower, & Ann Ovenden, of St Mildred's, Spinster, by Licence
1744	December	26	James Osborn & Elizabeth Edwards, both of Deal, by Licence

* Overwritten in the original.
† So in the original.

Year.	Month.	Day.	Names.
1744	December	29	William Gibbs, of Elmstone, & Mababella Jennings, of Fordwich, by Licence
174$\frac{4}{5}$	January	15	Thomas Bromly & Catherine Philpot, both of Caple le Fern, by Licence
174$\frac{4}{5}$	January	24	Thomas Tapley & Mary Keet, both of Newington near Sittingbourn, by Licence
174$\frac{4}{5}$	January	29	John Bennet, of Canterbury, & Eleanor Barnes, of St Mildred's, Cant: by Licence
174$\frac{4}{5}$	January	29	William Spicer, of Canterbury, & Patience Boxer, of St Alphege, Cant., by Licence
174$\frac{4}{5}$	January	31	William Jubb, of Canterbury, & Hannah Gibbs, of All S^{ts}, Cant: by Licence
174$\frac{4}{5}$	February	3	Ozwell Stephens, of Canterbury, & Sarah Lowdell, of St Peter's, Cant: by Licence
174$\frac{4}{5}$	February	9	William Savin & Susannah Allen, both of Deal, by Licence
174$\frac{4}{5}$	February	11	John Stone & Elisabeth Blaxland, both of Bapchild, by Licence
174$\frac{4}{5}$	February	13	Timothy Gisup & Elisabeth Fry, both of Milsted, by Licence
174$\frac{4}{5}$	February	20	William Ansen & Sarah Hills, both of St Peter's in Thanet, by Licence
174$\frac{4}{5}$	February	25	William Wallar, of Ickham, & Susannah Benford, of Thanington, by Licence (by the Dean)
174$\frac{4}{5}$	March	18	Thomas Hulks & Sarah Poole, both of Bapchild, by Licence
1745	April	4	Richard Redwood, of Westgate, & Mary Marten, of St Andrew's, Cant., by Licence
1745	April	16	John Seath, of Wingham, & Ann Beake, of Wickham Breaux, by Licence
1745	April	18	James Roy and Susannah Norman, both of Sittingbourn, by Licence
1745	May	1	John Wyborn & Sarah Corner, both of Deal, with Licence
1745	May	9	John Mackerness & Susanna Friend, both of St Lawrence in Thanet, with Licence
1745	May	13	John Chambers, of Holy Cross, Westgate, & Jane Templeman, of St Peter's, Cant: by Licence
1745	May	15	John Denn, of Reculver, & Ann Taylor, of Littlebourn, by Licence, by Mr Gostling
1745	May	23	Thomas Myres, of Cant: & Ann Harris, of Boughton Blean, by Licence
1745	June	10	Francis Day and Ann Bayly, both of Sheerness, by Licence
1745	June	22	Daniel Keble & Elizabeth Horne, both of Ash, by Licence
1745	July	20	Thomas Knowler, of $Cant^{by}$, & Frances Knowler, of the Precincts of this Church, by Licence, by Mr Monins
1745	July	30	John Cook, of Bromfield, & Eliz. Atwood, of Hucking, by Licence
1745	August	3	John Evernden, of Ickham, & Mary Bing, of Wickham, by Lic.
1745	August	19	Thomas Langford & Elizabeth Chapman, both of Faversham, wth Licence
1745	August	29	John French & Martha Ralf, both of St Mary Mag^{d} Parish, Cant: by Lic.
1745	September	4	$Rich^{d}$ Whitnall & Margaret Bates, both of Tonge, by Lic.
1745	September	18	Valentine Homewood & Ann Newport, both of Elmsted, by Lic.
1745	September	28	Thomas Hawkes, of Woolwich, & Elizabeth Ladd, of Folkston, by Lic.
1745	October	23	Walter Tennant, of $Cant^{by}$, Gent:, & Jane ffoord, of St Mary Mag^{d}:, Cant:, by Licence

Year.	Month.	Day.	Names.
1745	October	26	James Clark & Mary Holtum, both of Chistlet, with Licence
1745	November	7	William Sutton & Mary Pilcher, both of St Mary's in Dover, by Licence Tho. Lamprey, Sacrist
1745	November	26	John Wilkinson, of Ospringe, & Anne Gifford, of Minster in Thanet, by Licence
1745	December	5	Peter Postlethwaite, of Portsmouth, & Anne Iggalden, of Deal, by Licence
1745	December	11	William Carter & Mary Hutton, both of Raynham, by Licence
1745	December	27	John Collingwood & Mary Rapley, both of Sheerness, by Licence
1745	December	30	John Sayer & Mary Herst, both of Hern, by License
1745	February	6	Vincent Rutter* & Anne Spice, both of St Dunstan's, Canterb^{y}, by Licence
1745	February	16	Edward Ladbury, of Rochester, & Frances Dale, of Holy Cross, Westgate, by Licence
1745	March	13	William King & Mary Smith, both of Dover, by Licence
1746	April	1	James Knight, of Harrietsham, & Cealer Knight, of Frinsted, by Licence
1746	April	9	James Eagar & Sarah Okeford, both of ye Precincts of this Church, by Banns
1746	April	19	John Hinds, of St Alphege, & Mary Lucas, of ye Precincts of this Church, by Bans
1746	April	23	John Towell, Serjeant in Gen^{ll} Harrison's Regiment, & Amy Russell, of St James's in Dover, Spinster, by Licence
1746	May	14	John Collins, of Milton, & Sarah Dane, of Linstead, by Licence
1746	June	8	Edward Smith & Alice Hilliard, both of Deal, by Licence
1746	June	14	Geofrey Abraham Hopeman, & Mary Smith, both of St Mary's, Dover, by Licence
1746	August	4	Benjamin Forrest, of Sandwich, & Anne Lettis, of St Peter's in Thanet, by Licence
1746	September	4	Peter Smith & Elizabeth Moverly, both of Ramsgate in ye Isle of Thanet, by License
1746	September	7	William Lott & Elisabeth Kingsford, both of Sturry, by Licence
1746	September	28	Jeremiah Cooper, of St Margaret's, & Elisabeth Kitchen, of ye A. B^{ps} Palace, by Licence
1746	September	28	Thomas Brazier, of St Peter's, & Elisabeth Booker, of St Lawrence in ye Isle of Thanet, by Licence
1746	October	5	Thomas Sneed, of Wingham, & Mary Booker, of St Mildred's, Cant., by Licence
1746	October	5	Richard Mount, of Cant'bury, & Jane Rolfe, of ye Precinct of this Church, by Licence
1746	October	12	Josias Cocke & Elisabeth Raven, both of Deal, by Licence
1746	October	20	Thomas Hutson & Elizabeth Pettit, both of Deal, by Licence
1746	November	21	Stephen Rose & Anne Bunce. both of Faversham, by Licence
1746	December	1	John Abbot, of Woodnesborough, & Mary Durban, of Eastry, by Licence
1746	December	12	George Davenport & Anne Kenny, both of Deal, by Licence

* Overwritten in the original.

Year.	Month.	Day.	Names.
1746	December	19	John Key & Elisabeth Fleet, both of ye City of Cant'bury, by Licence
			Richd Leightonhouse, Sacrist
1746	January	1	John Sayer, of Herne, & Elisabeth Abbott, of Ramsgate, by Licence
1746	January	4	Joseph Cook, a Marine, in Brigadier Pawlet's Regiment, and Eliz: Marsh, of St Dunstan, Canterbury, by Licence
1746	January	19	Isaac Anderson and Judith Tayler, both of Sittingbourn, by Licence
1746	January	30	David Bourne and Anne Taylor, both of St Lawrence in the Isle of Thanet, by Licence
1746	March	4	Henry Walker, of Pluckley, and Jane Dorman, of Charing, by Licence
1747	March	26	William Hunt, Batchelor, & Mary Waterman, Spinster, both of Lenham, by Licence
1747	April	2	Valentine Jewel, of Margate, Batchelor, & Mary Warman, of St Peter's in Sandwich, by Licence
1747	April	23	John Bissaker and Elisabeth Dendy, both of ye Precincts of this Church, by Banns
1747	May	11	Henry Hedgcock, Widower, and Mary Kelly, both of Lenham, by Licence
1747	May	19	John Warner, of Minster in the Isle of Sheppy, Widower, and Anne Crowther, of St Mary's, Whitechapel, London, Spinster, by Licence
1747	May	19	Nathaniel Belsey, of Nonnington, Widower, and Ellen Lushington, of Lydden, Spinster, by Licence
1747	June	25	James Martin, of Holy Cross, Westgate, and Margaret Sharp, of the Precincts of this Church, by Banns
1747	June	27	Henry Simmonds, Widower, & Martha Youmans, Widow, both of Margate, by Licence
1747	June	28	John Fletcher, of St Saviour's, Southwark, in the park, in the County of Surry, Widower, and Susanna Gill, of the parish of All Saints, Canterbury, by Licence
1747	August	31	John Vaughn, of Dovor, Batchelor, & Mary Grant, of St Mary's in Dovor, Spinster, by Licence
1747	September	8	Abraham Brown, of Canterbury, Batchelor, & Mary Cheesman, of St Mary Magdalen in Canterbury, Spinster, by Licence
1747	October	8	Matthew Hogman, of the Parish of Goodnestone, near Faversham, and Jane Headaway, of the Precincts of this Church, by Banns
1747	October	11	John Tritton & Eliz: Stone, both of Chislett, by Licence
1747	November	16	John Southee, of Ickham, & Mary Reynolds, of Littlebourn, by Licence
			Fran: Gregory, Sacrist
1747	December	29	Daniel Ford & Mary Mockett, both of St Peter's in the Isle of Thanet, by Licence
1747	January	9	Matthew Chandler & Margaret Stevens, both of Westgate, by Licence
1747	January	16	Richard Griggs, of Goodneston, & Mary Ballad, of Selling, by Licence
1747	February	4	Beaton Cowell & Elizabeth Baker, both of St John's in the Isle of Thanet, by Licence
1747	February	6	Thomas Mackney, of Shoulden, & Elizabeth Preston, of Gunstone by Dovor, by Licence

Year.	Month.	Day.	Names.
1747	March	14	George Rainier & Mary Casby, both of S[t] Lawrence in the Isle of Thanet, by Licence
1748	May	23	John Carter, of Dover, & Susanna Stone, of S[t] Peter in Sandwhich, by Licence
1748	September	15	Roger Strivens & Judith Elvyn, both of S[t] Lawrence in the Isle of Thanet, by Licence
1748	October	1	James Carter, of Dover, & Mary Burges, Ditt[o], by Licence
1748	October	3	Thomas Prior, of Ash, & Jane Bartlett, of Chillenden, by Licence
1748	October	6	Michael Wood & Elizabeth Strood, both of Tilmanstone, by Licence
1748	October	27	Michael Baker & Susanna Smith, both of S[t] Mary's in Dover, by License
			Rob[t] Ayerst, Sacrist
1748	November	26	John Laming, Batchelor, & Mary Noldred, Spinster, both of S[t] Lawrence in Thanet, by Licence
1748	December	28	Thomas Harnett, Batchelor, & Mary Knott, Spinster, both of Minster in Thanet, by Licence
1748	January	23	John Gransden, Batchelor, & Elizabeth Simpson, Spinster, both of Minster in the Isle of Sheppy, by Licence
1748	March	4	John Fright and Elizabeth Costen, both of Rodmersham, by Licence
1748	March	7	Stephen Read, Batchelor, & Sarah Tomson, Spinster, both of S[t] Lawrence in Thanet, by Licence
1749	April	22	Samuel Simmons, Batchelor, and Catherine Foart, Spinster, both of Sandwich, by Licence
1749	April	29	William Kelsey, Batchelor, & Sarah Long, Spinster, both of Swinfield, by Licence
1749	May	9	Thomas Thompson, Batchelor, & Mary Lee, Spinster, both of Womanswould, by Licence
1749	May	23	John Fryers, of the City of Canterbury, Widower, and Hope Barton, of All Saints, Canterbury, Spinster, by Licence
1749	June	24	Joseph Dell, of the Precincts of this Church, Batchelor, and Mary Browning, of Ratlesden, in the County of Suffolk, Spinster, by Licence
1749	July	20	William Turner, of Stalesfield, Batchelor, & Elizabeth Rook, of Otterden, Spinster, by Licence
1749	August	15	John Wildish, Batchelor, & Anne Ellis, Spinst[r], both of S[t] Dunstan, by Licence
1749	August	26	John Norrington, of Sturry, Batchelor, & Susanna Rogers, of Holy Cross, Westgate, by Licence
1749	September	12	John Baker, of Dover, Batchelor, & Ann Luck, of S[t] Andrew's, Canterbury, Spinster, by Licence
1749	September	12	Thomas Grant, of Milton near Sittingbourne, Batchelor, & Mary Prall, of Murston, Spinster, by Licence
1749	October	22	John Wootton, of Sturry, Batchelor, & Eleanor Kemp, of the Precincts of this Church, by Licence
1749	November	2	William Watson, of Widby, in Yorkshire, Batchelor, and Catherine Smith, of Dover, spinster, by Licence
			Fran: Gregory, Sacrist
1749	December	12	John Fowle, of the parish of S[t] Alphege, & Amy Waters, of the Precinct of this Church, by Banns
1749	December	14	William Cock, of S[t] Paul's in Canterbury, and Anne Wymock, of S[t] Peter's in Canterbury, by Licence
1749	December	18	Henry Warren, of S[t] John's in Thanet, & Elisabeth Hammond, of Minster in the said Isle, by Licence

Year.	Month.	Day.	Names.
1749	December	29	Nicholas Long, of St Laurence in Thanet, and Anne Pysing, of the City of Canterbury, by Licence
1749	January	14	Richard Drew and Elisabeth Drayton, both of St George's Parish in Canterbury, by Licence
1749	March	8	George Monger, of Feversham, Batchellor, and Elisabeth Costen, of Canterbury, Spinster, by Licence
1750	May	1	Peter Plomer, of the City of Canterbury, and Sarah Wellard, of the Precinct of this Church, by Licence
1750	June	5	John Revel, of Adisham, Batchelor, and Elisabeth Allen, of Littleborn, Spinster, by Licence
1750	June	15	Richard Gear, of Sandwich, Single man, and Mary May, of St Peter's in Sandwich, Single Woman, by Licence
1750	July	5	Edward Hooper, Widower, and Elisabeth Long, Spinster, both of Deal, by Licence
1750	August	27	Edward Jeakins, of Thornham, Batchelor, and Mary Redman, of Stockbury, Spinster, by Licence
1750	August	30	James Pheue, of the City of Canterbury, Batchelor, and Anne Johnson, of St Andrew, Canterbury, Spinster, by Licence
1750	September	16	William Seath, of the City of Canterbury, Batchelor, and Jane Finch, of the Precincts of the Cathedral Church of Christ, Canterbury, Spinster, by Licence
1750	October	2	John Francis, of Sutton by Dover, Batchelor, and Mary Dillnott, of Great Chart, Spinster, by Licence
1750	October	15	Richard Ruck, of Leeds, Widower, and Ann Skinner, of Broomfield, Spinster, by Licence
1750	October	30	Edward Freshwater, of Sheerness, Batchelor, and Judith Greengrass, of Eastchurch, Spinster, by Licence William Gostling, Sacrist
1750	December	1	Thomas Lake, of Bapchild, and Anne Swan, of St Peter's, Canterbury, by Licence
1750	January	9	Edward Muns* & Elizabeth Brown, both of Littlebourn, by Licence
1750	January	15	Russel Hodge and Jane Ayers, of Faversham, by Licence
1750	January	17	Richard Moon, of Swinfield, & Susanna Jolly, of Bishopsbourn, by Licence
1750	January	20	Robert Blaxland, of Thannington, & Anne Brewer, of Faversham, by Licence
1750	January	29	Bernard Egleson, of Chatham, & Anne Streeting, of All Saints in Canterbury, by Licence
1750	February	15	Thomas Roe & Elizabeth Bush, both of Thanington, by Banns
1750	February	16	Samuel Mourilyan, of Deal, & Susanna Longley, of St Lawrence in Thanet, by Licence
1750	March	3	Boys Pilcher and Judith Glandfield, both of St Mary's in Dover, by Licence
1750	March	23	Isaac Bargrave, of St Clements Danes, in Middlesex, Esq., & Sarah, the Daughter of Dr George Lynch, of the Precincts of this Church, by Licence (by the Dean)
1750	March	24	Wm Blackman & Mary Wellard, both of Town Sutton, by Licence
1751	March	31	John Cooper & Margaret Marks, both of St Lawrence in the Isle of Thannet, by Licence
1751	April	10	Francis Nepecker, of St George's, & Sarah Gosby, of the Precincts, by Banns

* In the original the name has been "Munns."

Year.	Month.	Day.	Names.
1751	May	21	Isaac Claypoole, of St James's, Westminster, & Sarah Hawker, of Dover, by Licence
1751	May	28	Robert Ladd & Elizabeth Brazier, both of St John's in the Isle of Thanet, by Licence
1751	May	30	James Hawkesly & Martha Roberts, both of St Laurence in the Isle of Thanet, by Licence (per R. L.)
1751	June	17	Henry Oliver, of Doddington, & Elizabeth Marden, of Wichling, by Licence
1751	July	13	Peter Factor, of Dover, and Mary Minet, of Eythorn, by Licence
1751	July	27	Thomas Wiatt, of Bridge, & Elizabeth Andrews, of Bishopsbourne, by Licence
1751	July	28	John Kingsford, of Deal, & Elizabeth Rose, of St James's in Dover, by Licence
1751	August	2	Thomas Rogers & Mary Scott, both of Molash, by Licence
1751	September	5	Charles Page, of Beaksbourn, & Elizabeth Stanley of Littlebourn, by Licence
1751	October	8	Robert Wisenden & Anne Turner, both of Hollingbourn, by Licence
1751	October	12	Thomas Christian & Margaret Cullen, both of Westbeer, by Licence
1751	October	14	Samuel Austen & Sarah Gray, both of Lympne, by Licence
1751	October	26	John North & Elizabeth Swan, both of Stockbury, by Licence
1751	November	4	Edward Trover & Mildred Fagg, both of Kennington, by Licence
1751	November	6	John Miller & Lucy Norwood, both of St Lawrence in the Isle of Thanet, by Licence
			Wm Broderip, Sacrist
1751	December	2	John Hodges, of Sheerness, & Elizabeth Weeks, of Iwade, by Licence
1751	December	25	Richard Terry, of Northgate, & Hester Wootton, of the Precincts of this Church, by Banns
1751	December	30	Thomas Moyne, of Beaksbourn, & Mary Munds, of Littlebourn, by Licence (by Mr Gostling)
1752	January	26	The Revd Mr Broderip, Minor Canon of this Church, and Mrs Jane Knowler, of St Andrew's Parish, wth Lic: by ye Dean
1752	February	6	James Buckhurst, of Sutton Vallance, & Ann German, of Chart-Sutton, by Lic.
1752	February	18	Thomas Hinde, & Sarah Large, both of Sittingbourn, by Lic.
1752	April	7	Henry Mempas, of St Peter's, Cant: & Mary Horne, of All S^ts^, Cant: by Lic (by Mr Leightonhouse)
1752	April	9	Samuel Milward, of St Andrew's, Holbourn, & Mary Luck, of St Andrew, Cant: by Lic.
1752	June	1	John Lamprey, of Holkam, Norfolk, & Mary Neame, of Gunston, by Lic.
1752	June	13	John Fairbread & Sarah Warren, both of Tonge, by Lic.
1752	June	27	Thomas Blackeyes and Elisabeth Bridge, both of All Saints, Canterbury, by Lic.
1752	July	7	William Blackmore & Eleanor Handcock, both of Tenterden, by Lic.
1752	July	25	Michael Stone & Hannah Bodkin, both of Marden, by Lic.
1752	August	27	John Reely & Sarah Smith, Widow, both of Brookland, by Lic.

Year.	Month.	Day.	Names.
1752	October	3	The Revd Mr Thomas Baker, Rector of Frinsted, & Mrs Elisabeth Wright, of Snave, by Lic.
1752	October	5	Richard Cook, of St Mary Northgate, & Mary Wiles, of ye Precincts of this Church, by Banns
1752	October	12	William Luckett, of Dymchurch, & Mary Bromley, of Folkestone, by Lic.
1752	October	27	Thomas Burgis & Elizabeth Pavis, both of Warehorn, by Lic.
1752	November	1	Nicolas Long & Mary Vane, both of Town-Sutton, by Lic.
			Tho: Lamprey, Sacrist
1753	January	31	William Knight & Anne Slatton, both of Ospringe, by Licence
1753	February	1	Isaac Barwick, of Woodnesborough, & Amy Court, of Preston, by Licence
1753	March	1	Joseph Rogers, of Shelwich, & Margaret Baker, of Molash, by Licence
1753	March	25	John Guerard, of St Mary, Northgate, & Mary Paran, of ye Precincts of this Church, by Banns
1753	April	8	Thomas Elliott, of St Dunstan's, & Florida Wellard, of St Mary Northgate, by Licence
1753	May	8	William Chalker & Judith Smith, both of Minst^{r} in Thanet, by Licence
1753	August	6	Thomas Giesbrook & Mary Martin, both of Tenterden, by Licence
1753	September	11	John Neame, of Birchington, & Martha Harrison, of St John's in Thanet, by Lic.
1753	September	16	Thomas Brown & Mary Oldfield, both of St Andrew's, by Licence
1753	October	12	Henry Johnson, of St Nicholas in Thanet, & Anne Haythorn, of the Precincts of this Church, by Bans
1753	November	15	Richard Bristow, of St Nicholas in Rochest^{r}, & Anne Perkins, of St Marg^{ts}, Cant^{bury}, by Lic.
			Richd Leightonhouse, Sacrist
1753	December	13	Richard Milton, Batchelor, & Sarah Bromley, Spinster, both of Folkstone, by Licence
1754	January	4	Thomas Sellinge, of Bredgar, Batchelor, and Elizabeth Weekes, of Boughton Malherb, Spinster, by Licence
1754	January	8	Stephen Idenden, of Kingsnoth, Batch^{r}, and Elizabeth Russell, of Shadoxherst, Spinster, by Licence
1754	February	12	William Blake, Batchelor, & Susanna Henneker, Spin^{r}: both of Doddington, by Licence
1754	February	26	Joseph Woolley, Batchelor, and Sarah Godden, Spin^{r}, both of Newnham, by Licence
			Fran: Gregory, Sacrist
			Here the New Marriage Act took place
1754	March	26	John Hooker, of Fordwich, & Elizabeth Robards, of the precinct of this Church, by Licence
1754	June	23	Isaac Blancher, of the precincts of this Church, and Dorothy Beverton, of the same place, by Licence
			Fr. Gregory, Sacrist
1754	December	30	William Branford, of the parish of Ash,* & Elizabeth Clark, of the Precincts of this Church, by Licence
			J^{n} Airson, Sacrist
1755	December	2	John Greet, of the Parish of St Mary Bredman,* and Mary Clark,† of the Precincts of this Church, by Licence

* "Bachelor" is added in the new Register. † "Spinster" is added in the new Register.

Year.	Month.	Day.	Names.
1755	December	18	The Revd Mr John Tucker of the Parish of St Mary, Northgate (under Master of the King's School), and Jane Gurney, of the Precinct of this Church, by Licence
1756	April	29	Edward Hayward, of St George's Parish, and Bridget Leightonhouse, of the Precinct of this Church, by Banns
1756	June	27	Jacob Blanchar and Judith Charrossin, both of the Precincts of this Church, by Banns
1756	July	28	George Culmer, of the Precinct of this Church, and Anne Botting, of St George's Parish in Canterbury, by Banns
1756	September	28	John Phillpot and Ann Whole, both of the Precinct of this Church, by Licence
1756	October	9	Adde Read and Sarah Arnold, both of the Precinct of this Church, by Licence

William Gostling, Sacrist

END OF THE MARRIAGES IN THE THIRD REGISTER.*

1757	January	11	Thos Dunn, of St Mildred's, and Pleasant Dadd, of the Precincts of this Church, by Banns
1757	January	25	Job Gambeer, of the Precincts of this Church, and Elizabeth Whitfeild, of the Parish of St George in Canterbury, by Licence
1757	April	11	George Sampson, of Shellness, Batchelor, and Thomazine Moore, of the Precincts of Xt Church, by Licence
1757	May	2	Francis Villiers, of St Alphage, and Martha West, of the Precincts of Xt Church, by Banns
1757	June	28	Stephen Roberts, of Bridge, and Martha Armstrong, of the Precincts of this Church, by Banns
1758	March	27	William Bailey, of Blean, and Sarah Saffery, of the Precincts of this Church, by Banns
1758	April	5	Leonard Wachers, of St Mary Bredin, and Elizabeth Stevens, of the Precinct of this Church, by Banns
1758	April	25	John Fox, of St Paul's, Canterbury, and Mary Penn, of the Precinct of this Church, by Licence
1758	August	3	The Revd Mr Thomas Hay, Rector of Wickhambreaux, and Ethelred Lynch, of the Precinct of this Church, by Licence
1759	January	15	Lewis Cage, Esquire, of Bersted, and Miss Annetta Coke, of the Precinct of this Church, by Licence
1759	April	1	John Neame, Batchelour, of the Precinct of this Church, and Catharine Wallsby, Spinster, of the same Precinct, by Licence
1759	July	5	Horton Crippen, of All Hallows, Barkin, London, and Anne La Garde, of the Precinct of this Church, by Licence
1760	February	14	Solgard Marshall, of the Precinct of this Church, Batchelor, and Mary Priscilla Hods, of the same, Spinster, by licence
1760	June	28	William Johnson, of the Precinct of this Church, Widower, and Hannah Francis, of the same, Spinster, by Licence

* At the end of the old Register, Mr. Leightonhouse, the then Sacrist, entered a selection of ten marriages from the years 1759, 1764 and 1769; as they are regularly inserted in the new Register in their chronological order they are omitted here. The last ten marriages in the old Register are entered again in the new Book.

Year.	Month.	Day.	Names.
1760	July	10	Edward Thompson, of the Precinct of this Church, Batchr, and Mary Maines, of the same Precinct, Spr, by Licence
1760	August	30	The Revd Mr John Nairn, of Wingham, Batchelor, and Miss Eliz. Hall, of the Precinct of this Church, Spinster, by Licence
1760	October	12	John Watwell, of St Mary's in Dover, and Bridget Ship, of the Precincts of this Church, by Licence
1760	October	22	William Court, of Mersham, Batchr, and Mary Goodsold, of the Precinct of this Church, Spr, by Banns
1761	June	25	George Saltwell, of the Precincts of the Old Castle, Extra Parochial, near St Mildred's, and Keziah Hawkley, of the Precincts of this Parish, Spinster, by Licence
1762	January	18	Thomas Pettit, of Goodnestone, and Anne Dale, of the Precincts of this Church, by Banns
1762	May	6	William Fairman, Widower, of Chislet, and Sarah Knowles, Spinster, of the Precinct of this Church, by Licence
1762	May	15	John Langley, of Ashford, Batchelor, and Elisabeth Pearce, of the Precinct of this Church, Spinster, by Licence
1762	October	9	Robert Palmer, of Chelsea, in ye County of Middlesex, Batchelour, and Mary Holdstock, of the Precincts of this Church, Spinster, by Licence
1763	January	11	Thos Sayers, of Harbledown, and Mary Laurence, of the Precincts of this Church, by Banns
1763	February	12	Richard Chambers, of the Precincts of this Church, and Anne Horne, of the same, by Banns
1763	March	5	John Howel, of the Precincts of this Church, and Mary File (?), of the same, by Licence
1763	March	21	Richard Halford, of St Margaret's, and Sarah Spencer, of the same Parish, by Special Licence
1763	July	18	Charles Prince, of Appledore, Clerk, Batchelour, and Margaret Munk, of the Precincts of Christ Church, Canterbury, Spinster, by License
1763	September	15	Thomas Steady, of Chartham, Widower, and Chesterton Harnett, of the Precincts of this Church, Spinster, by Licence
1763	October	13	Richard Lawrence, of Momghan (*sic*) Batchelor, and Elizth Lansfeild, of the Precincts of this Church, by Licence
1764	May	31	Stephen Warman, of the Precincts of this Church, Batchelour, and Elisabeth Denne* of Adisham, by Licence
1764	July	3	Bernard Egleson, Widower, of All Sts, Canterbury, and Anne Cook, of the Precinct of this Church, Spinster, by Licence
1764	July	31	Thomas Bailey,† of St Mary Northgate, and Anne Ore of the Precinct of this Parish, by Banns
1764	September	25	George Frend, of St Andrew, Widower, and Jane Kirby,‡ of the Precinct of this Church, by Licence
1764	November	25	Isaac Sladden, of the Precincts of this Church, Batchelor, and Sarah Staines, of Hearne, Spinster, by Licence
1764	December	24	James Bunce and Susannah Hunt, both of the Precinct of this Church, by Banns

* This is one of the selected marriages entered by the Sacrist at the end of the previous Register, where Elizabeth Denne is described as a spinster.

† Another of the selected entries, where Thomas Bailey is described as a Widower, and Ann Ore as a Spinster.

‡ Another of the selected entries, where St. Andrews is described as being in Canterbury, and Jane Kirby is described as Spinster.

Year.	Month.	Day.	Names.
1765	January	3	Henry Penton, Esq., of Winchester, & of St George's Hanover Square, in Middlesex, a Batchelor, and Anne Knowler, a Spinster, of the Precinct of this Church, by special licence from the Archbishop of Canterby
1765	July	11	Henry Mackeson, of Deal, Batchelor, and Elizabeth Hooper, of the Precinct of this Church, Widow, by Licence
1765	July	29	George Browning, of the Precinct of this Church, and Eliz: Silk, of St Alphege, by Banns
1765	August	29	Thomas Alcorn, of the Precinct of this Church, Batchelor, and Elizabeth Powell, of St Andrew, Spinster, by Licence
1766	January	25	John Culmer, of St Nicholas in the Isle of Thanet, Widower, and Margaret Harlow, of the Precinct of this Church, by Licence
1766	November	20	John Eager, of the Precincts of this Church, Batchelour, and Anne Baker, of the same, Spinster, by Licence
1767	April	20	Francis Lord and Isabella Harrison, both of the Archbishop's Palace, being extra-parochial, by Banns
1767	May	12	Daniel Savage, of the Precincts of this Church, Batchelor, and Elizabeth Burroughs, of St Dunstan's, Spinster, by Banns
1767	August	6	John Norris, of the Precincts of this Church, Batchelor, and Sarah Blanchard, of St George's in Canterbury, Spinster, by Licence
1767	August	23	Edward Lepine, of St Margaret's, Batchelor, and Sarah Hunt, of the Precincts of this Church, Spinster, by Banns
1767	December	24	Isaac Parker, of St George's, Canterbury, Batch., and Sarah Sole, of the Precincts of this Church, Spinster, by Licence
1768	April	5	Wm Dodson and Mary Seath, both of the Precincts of this Church, by Banns
1768	May	5	William Gostling, Esqr, Widower, of the Precincts of this Cathedral, and Captain in the Royal Regt of Artillery, and Mary Gurney, Spinster, of Sholden, in the diocese of Canterbury and County of Kent, by Licence
1768	July	5	William Belcher, Batchelor, of Ulcomb in Kent, and Charlott Thomson, Spinster, of the Precincts of the Cathedral Church of Christ, Canterbury, by Licence
1768	September	6	John Lawrence, a Batchelor, of the Precincts of this Church, and Sarah Pain, Spinster, of the same, by Licence
1769	January	28	John Preston, of the Precincts of this Church, Batchelour, and Martha Edwards, of the same, Widow, by Licence
1769	February	25	Jeremiah Hatton, of the Precincts of this Church, Batchelour, and Elisabeth Duddy, of St Mildred's, Spinster, by Licence
1769	November	6	James Lucas, of Sturry, and Sarah Burton, of the Precinct of ye Arch-Bishop's Palace, extra Parochial, by Banns
1771	May	11	Richard Beard, Batchelor, of the Precinct of this Church, and Ann Ginder, Spinster, of the same Precinct, by Licence
1771	November	18	John Paton, Esquire, of Grandhome in Aberdeenshire, Batchelor, and Mary Lance, Spinster, Daughter of William Lance, Esqr, of the Precincts of ye Church, by Licence
1771	November	30	John Smeed, of the Precinct of this Church, Batchelor, and Jane Pain, of Bishopsbourne, Spinster, by Licence

Year.	Month.	Day.	Names.
1772	July	15	John Whitehead, Batchelor, of Newport in Buckinghamshire, in the diocese of Lincoln, and Martha Stephens, Spinster, of the Precinct of this Church, by Licence
1773	February	16	Benjamin Skinner, Clerk, of the Parish of Purley, Berks, Batchelor, and Elizabeth Moore, of the Precincts of this Church, by Licence
1773	October	26	Robert Le Geyt, of the Precinct of the Archbishop's Palace, Widower, and Anna Maria Chandler, of St Mary Magdalene, Canterbury, Sp^{r}, by Licence
1774	January	13	John Royes, of St Mary Northgate in Canterbury, a Batchelor, and Sarah Hougham, of the Precincts of the Cathedral Church of X^{t}, Canterbury, a Spinster, by Licence
1774	November	22	Edward Dunn, of Lyminge, a Batchelor, and Ann Bromely, of the Precinct of this Church, Spinster, by Banns
1774	December	24	Jeremiah Hatton, of the Precinct of this Church, Widower, and Elizabeth Miller, of Bridge, Spinster, by Licence
1775	May	11	John White, of All Saints in this City, Batchelor, and Susanna Fielding, of the Precinct of this Church, Spinster, by Banns
1775	May	14	William Sothers, of Faversham, Widower, and Elizabeth Goodchild, of the Precinct of the Archbishop's Palace, Spinster, by Licence
1776	April	7	Thomas Cole, of St Mary Magdalen, and Elizabeth Dallydown, of the Precinct of this Church, by Banns
1777	February	4	Richard Jutson, of Whitstable, and Elizabeth Young, of the Precincts of this Church, by Banns
1777	March	30	John Illenden, of St George ye Martyr, Batchelor, and Elizabeth Sheafe, of the Precinct of this Church, by Licence
1777	April	5	Cornelius Hurst, of St Peter's in the Isle of Thanet, Batchelor, and Mary Bradly, of the Precinct of this Church, Spinster, by Licence
1777	April	10	Bartholomew Elvey, of the Precinct of this Church, Batchelor, and Mary Epps, of Northgate, by Banns
1777	October	19	William Pawson, of St Mary, Dover, Batchelor, and Susanna Hobbs, of the Precinct of this Church, a Spinster, by Licence
1777	October	27	The Honble Philip Leslie, of St Ann, Westminster, in ye County of Middlesex, and The Right Honble Lady Frances Manners, of the parish of St Mary Le Bone, in the same County, Daugh^{r} of ye late Marquis of Granby, by special Licence
1777	October	30	John Page, of St Mary Magdalen, Batchelor, and Lydia File, of the Precincts of this Church, Spinster, by Licence
1777	December	16	Eubulus Smith, of the Precinct of this Church, Batchelor, and Elizabeth Philpot, of ye Precinct of ye Archbishop's Palace adjoining, Spinster, by Licence
1778	April	5	Richard Mount, of Whitstable, Batchelor, and Hester Myland, of the Arch Bishop's Palace adjoining, and extra-parochial, Spinster, by Licence
1778	April	6	Thomas Edenden, of Sea Salter, a Widower, and Sarah Wooldrige, of the Precinct of this Church, Spinster, by Banns
1778	July	20	John Bounds, of St Mildred, Batchelor, and Elizabeth Norris, of the Precinct of this Church, Spinster, by Banns

Year.	Month.	Day.	Names.
1778	July	27	John Hawker, of St George's in this City, Batchelor, and Elizabeth Pilcher, of the Precinct of this Church, Spinster, by Banns
1780	January	8	Stephen Buley, of St Paul's, Batchelor, in the City of Canterbury, and Mary Jemmett, Spinster, of the Precincts of this Church, by Banns
1780	March	28	Jesse Sutton, of St Mary Magdalen, Bermondsey, Surrey, Batchelor, and Anne Gorely of the Precincts of this Church, Spinster, by Banns
1781	January	8	The Reverend Nicholas Simons, Rector of Hastingleigh, Kent, Batchelor, and Elizabeth Tucker, of the Precincts of the Cathedral Church of Christ, Canterbury, Spinster, by Licence
1781	September	29	John Millen, of Westwell, and Elizabeth Burton, of the Precincts of this Church, by Banns
1781	September	29	George Janeway, of Hothfield, and Elizabeth Millen, of the Precincts of this Church, by Licence
1782	April	2	William Jenkins, of St John's, Margate, Batchelor, and Sarah Wellard, of the Precinct of this Church, Spinster, by Banns
1783	July	18	William Hill, of Wye, Batchelor, and Elizabeth Slaughter, of the Precincts of this Church, Spinster, by Licence
1783	August	7	Thomas Hyde Page, Esqr, of St Margaret, Westminster, Widower, and Mary Albinia Woodward, of the Precincts of the Lord Archbishop's Palace, Spinster, by Licence
1784	August	2	John Baptist Emanuel Anthony Verstraeten, of this Parish, and Elizabeth Caroline Ffeast, of this Parish, by Banns
1784	September	12	Thomas Hymers, of the Borough of Staplegate, and Elizabeth Fletcher, of the Precinct of this Church, by Banns
1784	October	27	James Kettle, of the Precinct of this Church, Batchelor, and Sarah Paine, of the same, Spinster, by Banns
1784	December	12	Richard Mead, of Woodnesborough, and Hannah Bond, of the Precincts of this Church, by Licence
1785	February	7	William Andrews, of the Precincts of this Church, and Elizabeth Long, of the same, by Banns
1785	June	28	Thomas Miriams, of the district of Acol, in Birchington, and Susannah Justice, of the Archbishop's Palace, by Banns
1785	October	11	Richard Turrill, of St Mildred, and Mary Lonons, of the Precincts of this Church, by Banns
1786	January	3	William Wilds, of the Precincts of this Church, Batchelor, and Charlotte Gorely, of St Margaret's, by Licence
1787	January	11	John Mullens, of Portsmouth, in the County of Southampton, Esqr, Batchelor, and Jane Rebecca Trevor, Spinster, Minor, of Bridgewater, in Somerset, by special Licence of his Grace the Lord Archbishop of Cant^y
1787	May	27	James Little, of St Mary Breadman, Canterbury, and Sarah Read, of the Precincts of this Church, by Banns
1788	May	13	The Revd Willm Gregory, one of the Six Preachers, and of the Precincts of this Church, and Catharine Sayer, of the Precinct of this Church, by Licence
1788	August	24	John Wrightson, of this Parish, Batchelor, and Elizabeth Pemble, of the same, Widow, by Licence

Year.	Month.	Day.	Names.
1788	October	14	Champion Branfill, Esqr, of Upmenster, in ye County of Essex, Batchelor, and Charlotte Brydges, of the Precincts of this Church, Spinster, by Licence
1789	January	5	William Ansell, of the Archbishop's Palace, Widower, and Mary Ann Crouch, of St Andrew, Canterbury, Spinster, by Banns
1789	July	15	William Clements, of Wickhambreaux, a Batchelor, and Elizabeth Stoddard, of the Precinct of this Church, a Spinster, by Banns
1789	October	6	William Groombridge, of the Arch Bishop's Palace, a Widower, and Catherine Hayes, of St Paul's, Canterbury, a Spinster, by Licence
1789	October	20	William Johnson, of the Precinct of this Church, and Sarah Parker, of the same, by Banns
1790	February	14	William Young, of St Mary Bredman's, and Susanna Young, of the Precincts of this Church, by Banns
1790	July	5	Basil Hodges of St Lawrence in Thanet, and Sarah Cornwell, of the Precincts of this Church, by Licence
1790	October	25	William Vidgen and Mary Drayner, both of the Precincts of this Church, by Banns
1790	November	23	John Wigzell, of St Mary Bredin's in Canterbury, a Widower, and Margaret Jenkin, of the Precincts of this Church, a Spinster, by Licence
1791	April	17	Thomas Fordred, of St Paul's in Canterbury, Bachelor, and Frances Blackley, of the Precincts of this Church, Spinster, by Licence
1791	May	22	Francis Dunn, of the Precincts of this Church, and Sarah Hicks, of the same, by Licence
1791	June	28	James Mans, Batchelor, of the Precincts of this Church, and Susanna Sabben, of the same, by Banns
1791	September	7	Theadore Gardner, Batchelor, of St Mary Bredman's, and Elizabeth Sarah Murch, Spinster, of the Precincts of this Church, by Banns
1791	December	22	Christopher Cornelious, of St Mary the Virgin in Dover, Batchelor, & Elizabeth Loste, of the Precincts of this Church, Spinster, by Banns
1792	March	22	John Nairn, Rector of Kingston, a Widower, and Ann Jenkin, of the Precincts of this Church, a Spinster, by Licence
1792	October	30	William Noble, of Elham, a Batchelor, and Ann Rose, of the Precincts of this Church, a Spinster, by Licence
1793	January	30	Thomas Walton, of the Precincts of this Church, and Elizabeth Ifield, of St Margaret's, Canterbury, by Banns
1793	November	27	John Epps, of the Archbishop's Palace, a Batchelor, and Anne Wanstal, of the same, a Spinster, by Banns
1793	December	15	Walter Nash, of St George the Martyr, Canterbury, a Batchelor, and Elizabeth Golden, of the Precincts of this Church, a Spinster, by Licence
1794	January	6	William Finch, of the Arch Bishop's Palace, a Batchelor, and Ann Carter, of the Precincts of this Church, a Spinster & Minor, by Licence
1794	March	23	John Hogbin, of St Mildred's, a Batchelor, and Mary Monk, of the Precincts of this Church, Spinster, by Banns
1794	July	31	Brett Mercer, of St Mary Northgate, a Batchelor, and Elizabeth Gilham, of the Archbishop's Palace, a Spinster, by Banns

Year.	Month.	Day.	Names.
1794	September	22	Evan Evans, of the Precincts of this Church, a Batchelor, and Amy Deacon, of the same, a Spinster, by Licence
1794	October	9	John Baynes, of the Precincts of this Church, a Batchelor, and Mercy Eldridge, of St Margaret's in Canterbury, Widow, by Banns
1794	October	25	Isaac Burvill, of Littlebourne, a Batchelor, and Ann Elennor, of the Precinct of this Church, a Spinster, by Banns
1794	November	22	Abraham Pitt, of the Precinct of this Church, a Widower, and Hester Child, of the same, a Spinster, by Licence
1794	November	25	John Sanderson, of Holy Cross, Westgate, a Batchelor, and Ann Pildrem, of the Precincts of this Church, a Spinster, by Licence
1795	April	13	Richard Challcraft, of Nackington, and Ann Fryer, of the Precincts of this Church, by Banns
1795	April	28	Joseph Lunnis, of S[t] Paul's, and Ann Rouse, of the Precincts of this Church, by Banns
1795	June	4	William Wanstall, of Hearne, and Elizabeth Parker, of the Precincts of this Church, by Banns
1795	August	1	Valentine Smith, of S[t] Mildred's, and Sarah Reeves, of the Archbishop's Palace, by Banns
1795	August	11	Bernard Read, of S[t] Mildred's, and Elizabeth Pawson, of the Precincts of this Church, by Banns
1795	October	27	Joseph Daglish, of Kingston, and Mary Cobling, of the Precincts of this Church, by Banns
1795	November	24	Thomas Parnell, of the Precincts of this Church, and Catherine Wellard, of the same, by Banns
1795	December	17	John Pilcher, of Elmsted, and Catharine Dodd, of the Arch Bishop's Palace, by Banns
1796	July	10	Richard Wheeler, of S[t] George's, and Elizabeth Carpenter, of the Arch Bishop's Palace, by Banns
1796	August	14	William Powell, of S[t] Alphage, and Sarah Jackson, of the Precincts of this Church, by Banns
1796	November	29	John George Wood, of S[t] Mary le Bone, Westminster, and Margaretta Maria Freeman, of the Precincts of this Church, by Licence
1797	February	21	Joseph Spicer, of Folkstone, a Batchelor, with the consent of his Father, Kennett Spicer, being a minor, and Diana Southee, of the Palace of the Lord Archbishop of Canterbury, by Licence
1797	July	13	John Appleyard, a Batchelor, and Elizabeth Bromley, a Spinster, both of the Precincts of the Palace of the Lord Archbishop of Canterbury, an extra parochial place adjoining to this Church, by Licence
1797	August	31	John Mignot, a Batchelor, and Elizabeth Griffin, a Spinster, both of the Precincts of this Church, by Licence
1797	December	11	Thomas Thurston, of S[t] Margaret's, Canterbury, and Ann Spicer, Widow, of the Precincts of this Church, by Banns
1797	December	21	Stephen Holtum (or Holttum), of S[t] Mary's, Dover, Batch[r], and Ann Watts, Spinster, of the Precincts of the Arch Bishop's Palace, by Banns
1798	February	14	William Gibson, of S[t] Dunstan's, Batchelor, and Margaret Steele, of the Precincts of this Church, Spinster, by Banns
1798	March	6	William Preece, of S[t] Mildred's, Bachelor, and Hannah Marsh, Spinster, of the Precincts of this Church, by Banns

Year.	Month.	Day.	Names.
1798	May	16	Jacob Lawson, of Wickhambreaux, Bachelor, and Harriot Masters, of the Archbishop's Palace, Canterbury, by Banns
1798	November	6	William Surgent, of Bridge, and Elizabeth Shoveler, of the Precincts of this Church, by Banns
1798	November	18	Thomas Sladden, of the Precincts of this Church, Bachelor, and Elizabeth Parton, of Woodchurch, in the diocese of Canterbury, Widow, by Licence
1799	January	1	John Minet Henniker, of Lincoln's Inn, in the County of Middlesex, Bachelor, and Mary Chafy, Spinster, of the Precincts of this Church, by Licence
1799	October	26	Thomas Burch, of Brabourne, Batchelor, and Elizabeth Alcorn, of the Precincts of this Church, by Licence
1800	December	14	John Smeed, of St Paul's, Canterbury, Widower, and Jane Joyner, of the Precincts of this Church, Spinster, by Banns
1800	December	18	Charles Friend, of St Mary Magdalen's, Canterbury, Widower, and Sarah Price, of the Precincts of the Arch Bishop's Palace, Widow, by Licence
1801	April	9	Philip Le Geyt, of this Parish, Bachelor, and Jane Cairnes, of St Mildred's in Canterbury, Spinster, by Licence
1801	June	19	George Norley, of Hackington, alias St Stephen's, a Batchelor, and Mary Tevelein, of the Precincts of this Church, a Spinster, by Licence
1801	July	21	Philip Burrard, of St John's, Hackney, and Sarah Naylor, of this Precinct, by Licence
1801	August	16	Edward Woore, of the Precincts of this Church, Bachelor, and Elizabeth Mitchell, of the same, Spinster, by Licence
1801	November	14	Thomas Mitchell, of St George the Martyr, and Sarah Ann Porter, of the Precincts, by Licence
1801	November	21	Rigden Swain, of St Mary Magdalen, Bachelor, and Isabella Campbell, of the Precincts of this Church, Spinster, by Banns
1802	January	26	Henry Frederick Muller, of Walmer in this County, and Mary Anne Halliday, of the Precincts, by Banns
1802	July	20	William Bishop, of Harbledown, Batchelor, and Sarah Marsh, of the Precincts, by Banns
1803	April	10	George Sympson, of St Alphage, and Amy Millet, of this Parish, by Banns
1803	April	11	Robert Shin (or Shinn), of St Alphage, and Sarah Groves, of this Parish, by Banns
1803	April	16	Henry Pilcher, of St Paul's, and Ann Markes, of the Precincts of this Church, by Banns
1803	October	23	William Dean, of Northgate, and Mary Castle, of the Precincts of this Church, by Banns
1804	April	16	*James Saffery, Batchelor, of the Precincts of this Church, and Mary Anne Crothall, of St Paul's, Spinster, by Licence
1804	September	15	John Need, Esqr, of Sherwood Hall, in the County of Nottingham, Batchelor, and Mary Welfitt, of the Precincts of this Church, Spinster, by Licence
1805	January	8	William Cupee, of All Saints, Canterbury, and Millicent Admans, of the Precincts of this Church, by Banns

* This entry is partially overwritten in the original.

Year.	Month.	Day.	Names.
1805	April	23	John Hobday, of St Dunstan's, a Bachelor, and Sarah Fordred, of the Precincts of this Cathedral, by Licence
1806	June	28	Edmund Appleyard, of this Church, and Harriot Jenkins, of this Church, by Licence
1807	March	31	Thomas Wright, of the Precincts of this Church, a Bachelor, and Mary London, of the same, Spinster, by Banns
1807	August	20	George Lemar, of St Mary Magdalen's, a Widower, and Mary Cloke, of the Precincts of this Church, a Spinster, by Licence
1807	September	2	Thomas Barnett, Esqr, of St George's, Canterbury, and of the 96th Regim^{t} of Foot, Captain, and Mary Monins, of the Arch Bishop's Palace, a Minor, but wth the Consent of her Mother and Guardian, by Licence
1807	October	10	James Castle, of St Gregory's, an extra-parochial place in Northgate, and Frances Mason, of the Precincts of this Church, by Banns
1807	December	25	Isaac Wildash, of Boughton under Blean, a Bachelor, and Jane Rutherford, of the Precincts of this Church, a Spinster, by Banns
1808	June	3	Charles Allix, of Curlby, in the County of Lincoln, and Mary Hammond, of Nonington, Kent, by Licence
1808	August	7	Charles Williams, of Goodneston next Wingham, a Bachelor, and Mary Cox, of the Precincts of this Church, a Spinster, by Licence
1809	September	24	Charles Norley, Bachelor, of the Precincts of this Church, and Ann Tomsett, of the same, Spinster, by Banns
1810	February	12	William Gadesby, of St George the Martyr, and Ann Taysum, of the Precincts of this Church, by Licence
1810	February	20	Charles Tudor, of Hythe, in this County, and Elizth Moore, of the Precincts of this Church, both single persons, by Licence
1810	July	26	Richard Wells, of Petham, and Elizabeth Saffery, of the Precincts, of this Cathedral, by Banns

END OF THE FOURTH REGISTER OF MARRIAGES.

Being the Register first used after the passing of the Marriage Act. A period of nearly three years elapsed before another marriage was recorded.

1813	April	22	John Le Grand, of St Mary-le-bone, in the County of Middlesex, Batchelor, and Caroline Naylor, of this Parish, Spinster, by Licence
1815	June	7	Thomas Chattock, of Solihull, in the County of Warwick, a Bachelor, and Jane Prince, a Spinster, of the Precincts of Christ Church Cathedral, Canterbury, by Licence
1816	May	11	Thomas Jell, of the Precincts of this Cathedral, a Bachelor, and Susannah Price, of Elham, Kent, by Banns
1816	August	22	The Revd Charles Richard Handley, of this Parish, Bachelor, and Cassandra Hutchinson, of the same, Spinster, by Licence
1817	July	30	Henry Turner Dryden, of Adlestrop, in the County of Gloucester, Clerk, Bachelor, and Elizabeth Hutchinson, Spinster, of this Parish, by Licence

Year.	Month.	Day.	Names.
1817	October	23	The Revd James Halke, of Selling, in the County of Kent, Widower, and Mary Starr, of the Ville of Christ Church, Canterbury, Spinster, by Licence
1818	July	30	William Henry Baldwin, of Liverpool, in the County of Lancaster, and Mary Ann Hutchinson, of this Parish, by Licence
1818	July	30	The Revd William Grant Broughton, of Hartley Wespall, in the County of Southampton, a Bachelor, and Sarah Francis, of this Parish, a Spinster, by Licence
1818	December	17	Henry Anderson, of Dunbill, in the County of Kilkenny, in the Kingdom of Ireland, a Lieute^{t} in his Majesty's 69th Regiment of Foot, a Bachelor, and Lætitia Abbot, of the Precincts of the Cathedral Church of Christ in Canterbury, a Minor, by Licence, with consent of William Abbot, Esqr, the natural and lawful Father of the abovenamed Lætitia Abbot
1819	February	13	John Carter, Bachelor, of St Mary's Northgate, and Charlotte Vidgen, Spinster, of this Parish, by Banns
1819	February	13	James Williams, Bachelor, of Thanington, in this County, and Frances Chandler, Spinster, of this Parish, by Banns
1819	March	4	Henry Boxall, Bachelor, of St Paul's in this City, and Sophia Older, Spinster, of this Parish, by Banns
1819	May	7	John Marten, Widower, of this Precinct, and Sarah Taplin, Spinster, of the same, by Licence
1820	January	24	William Hubbard, a Bachelor, of Dartford, in Kent, and Elizabeth Munns, a Minor, of the Precincts of the Archbishop's Palace, an extra-parochial place, with the consent of Thomas Munns, the father of the abovenamed Elizabeth Munns, by Licence
1820	October	9	James Beckford Wildman, of Chilham Castle, in the County of Kent, and Mary Anne Lushington, of Norton Court, in the said County, a minor, by special licence, with consent of Stephen Rumbold Lushington, Esqr, the natural and lawful father of the said minor
1822	January	24	Samuel White, of St Alphege, a Minor, and Elizabeth Mary Hatton, a Minor, by licence, by consent of Daniel White & Charles Hatton, the respective and lawful Fathers of the abovenamed minors
1822	April	16	James Wright, of this Parish, a Widower, and Elizabeth Warren, of the same, a Spinster, by Licence
1822	June	13	Thomas John Dashwood, of St Mary Bredin's in Canterbury, Esquire, a Bachelor, and Susan Wodehouse, of this Parish, a Spinster, by License
1823	January	9	William Baines, a Bachelor, of St Alphege, and Catharine Restrick, a Spinster, of this Parish, by Banns
1824	August	10	John Mannings World, of St Luke's, Middlesex, and Elizabeth Burch, of this Parish, by Banns
1825	April	1	John Bilbe, of this Parish, a Bachelor, and Mary Munns, of the same, a Spinster, by Licence
1825	May	9	Richard Gibbons, of Deal in Kent, a Widower, and Mary Coleman, of this Parish, a Spinster, by Banns
1825	July	12	James Terry, of St Alphage, and Martha Baynes, of this Parish, by Banns
1825	August	16	John Smeed, of St Alphage in Canterbury, and Anne Hills, of this Parish, by Banns

Year.	Month.	Day.	Names.
1825	October	9	Benjamin Radford, of the Ville of St Gregory, and Sarah King, of this Parish, by Banns
1826	March	27	Richard Petts, of this Parish, Bachelor, and Hannah Pilcher, of the same, Spinster, by Banns
1827	March	19	Aaron Warlock, Bachelor, of Portsmouth, in the County of Southampton, and Harriet Holworthy, of this Parish, Spinster, by Licence
1827	April	17	Samuel Webb, Bachelor, of the Precincts of the Arch-Bp^s Palace, and Harriet Ratcliff, of the same, by Banns
1827	December	6	Charles Rose, of St Dunstan's, Canterb^y, a Bachelor, and Susan Court, of the Precincts of this Cathedral, by Banns
1828	February	23	William Keene, of St Mary's Northgate, and Mary Ann Stringer, of this Parish, by Banns
1828	April	7	Daniel Holttum, of Westbere, in this County, and Harriet Peirce, of this Parish, by Banns
1828	July	22	Stephen Folwell, of St Alphage, a Widower, and Mary Susanna Farris, of this Parish, a Spinster, by Licence
1828	November	11	George Castledon, of St Dunstan's, near Canterbury, a Bachelor, and Jane Packman Smith, of the Precincts of the Archbishop's Palace, an extra parochial place, &c., by Licence
1829	February	24	James Holland, of this Parish, a Bachelor, and Esther Richardson, a Spinster, of the Borough of Hoath, County of Kent, by Banns
1829	June	9	Adam Young, of Greenwich, in the County of Kent, Bachelor, and Anne Charity Bax, of this Parish, Spinster, by Licence
1830	July	29	George Oakes Miller, of Milton, otherwise Middleton Malzor, in the County of Northampton, Clerk, a Batchelor, and Jane Starr, of the Precincts of the Cathedral, Spinster, by Licence
1830	September	16	John Brampton, of Sturry, in the County of Kent, Bachelor, and Ann Chaney, of this Parish, Spinster & a Minor, by Licence
1830	December	25	John Bridgland, of Faversham, a Bachelor, and Mary Ann Small, of the Precincts of the Cathedral
1831	December	23	John Jackson Ward, of the Precincts of the Archbishop's Palace, and Ann Chadwick, of the same, by Banns
1832	August	4	George Grace, of St George the Martyr, and Frances Steddy, of this Parish, by Banns
1833	January	1	Richard Minter Mount, of St Mildred's, Canterbury, a Bachelor, and Isabel Mackeson, a Spinster, of the Precincts of this Cathedral, by Licence
1833	April	26	George Gillett, of this Parish, Bachelor, and Mary Ann Goodwin, of the same, Spinster, by Banns
1834	April	7	Josiah Fedarb, of the Precincts of the Archbishop's Palace, and Grace Avice Pursey, of the same, by Banns
1834	May	4	John Mount Simonds, of St Mildred's, Bachelor, and Mary Elizabeth Wattson, of the Precincts of the Archbishop's Palace, Spinster, by Licence
1834	November	7	James Gordon, of St Mary's Northgate, 93rd Reg^t, Bachelor, and Maria Carolina England, of the Precincts of the Archbishop's Palace, by Banns
1835	August	17	John Hubbard, of the Precincts of the Archbishop's Palace, and Sarah Caroline Skinner, of the same, by Banns

Year.	Month.	Day.	Names.
1835	November	23	Henry Stokes, of Barfreston, Kent, and Ann Whiting, of this Parish, by Banns
1836	June	7	Arthur Bastard Eastabrooke Holdsworth, of Townstall in Devon, Bachelor, and Ann Mervyn Baylay, Spinster, of this Parish, by Licence
1836	June	7	Edmund Telfer Yates, Bachelor, of Birchington in Kent, Clerk, and Mary Sophia Pollexfen Baylay, Spinster, of this Parish, by Licence
1837	May	30	Horatio Maunsell, Clerk, Bachelor, Rector of Drumbo in the County of Down in Ireland, and Louisa Anne Marriott, a Spinster, of this Parish, by Licence
1837	June	29	Robert Batley, a Bachelor, and Sophia Stokes, a Spinster, both of this Parish, by Banns
1837	July	25	John Penn, aged 26, Bachelor, Cabinet Maker, son of John Penn, and Maria Chaplin, aged 29, Spinster, both of St Mary Magdalen
1839	August	8	Alfred Boydell Lambe, aged 28, Bachelor, Wine Merchant, of New Bond Street, London, son of Alfred Lambe, & Mary Eliza Austin, aged 24, Spinster, daughter of George Austin
1839	August	26	William Nelson Hutchinson, of full age, Bachelor, Major 20th Regt, son of William Hutchinson, & Mary Russell, a Minor, Spinster, of the Precincts, daughter of John Russell, D.D., Prebendary of Canterbury
1840	May	23	William Harnett, Bachelor, of St George's, Canty, Butler, son of Benjamin Harnett, & Mary Wright, of the Precincts, Spinster, daughter of Thomas Wright
1840	July	6	Stephen West, Bachelor, of Wickham, Kent, Labourer, son of Stephen West, & Mary Ann Joad, Spinster, of the Precincts, a Servant, daughter of Thomas Joad
1841	May	6	George Gardner, Bachelor, a Minor, of Ickham, Gentleman, son of Robert Gardner, & Kate Austin, of the Ville of Archbishop's Palace, Spinster, daughter of George Austin
1841	October	7	Edward Allfree, Bachelor, of Cliffe, Kent, Clerk, Son of Edward Mott Allfree, & Charlotte Eleanor Bennett, of the Precincts, Spinster, daughter of Thomas Bennett
1842	October	29	Thomas Young, aged 34, Widower, of the Precincts, Professor of Music, son of Thomas Young, & Grace Mutton, aged 38, Widow, of St George's, Canty, daughter of John Griffery
1842	December	10	Frederick Robert Augustus Glover, Widower, of the Precincts, Clerk, son of John Glover, & Anne Starr, of the Precincts, Spinster, daughter of Thomas Starr
1843	December	27	Thomas Baker, Widower, of Wylye, Wilts, Surgeon, son of Gabriel Baker, & Sophia Jane Southey, of the Precincts, Spinster, daughter of Thomas Southey
1844	January	19	John Shrubsole Denne, Bachelor, of the Precincts, Musician, son of Benjamin Denne, & Harriet Jane Kelson, of the Precincts, Spinster, daughter of William Golightly Kelson
1844	February	19	George Johncock, Bachelor, of Minster, Labourer, son of Edward Johncock, & Hannah Downe, of the Precincts, Spinster, daughter of William Downe
1844	November	19	William Gardner, Bachelor, of Beaksbourne, Gentleman, son of William Gardner, & Jane Angelina Austin, Spinster, daughter of George Austin

Year.	Month.	Day.	Names.
1845	April	30	Thomas Nash, Bachelor, of Nonington, Kent, Builder, son of Thomas Nash, & Mary Martha Holtum, of the Precincts of St Augustine, Spinster, daughter of Richard Holtum
1845	June	12	Henry Russell, Widower, Carver & Gilder, son of James Russell, & Hannah Wright, Spinster, daughter of Thomas Wright, both of the Precincts
1845	December	17	Marmaduke Kelham, Bachelor, of Southwell, Notts, Solicitor, Son of Robert Kelham Kelham, & Julia Anne Christie, of the Precincts, Spinster, daughter of Robert Christie
1846	October	1	James Smith, Bachelor, of St Mary le Bone, Middlesex, Painter, Son of William Smith, & Sarah Philpot, of the Precincts, Spinster, Servant, daughter of John Philpot
1846	October	27	Henry Dunn Glasse, Bachelor, of Droxford, Hants, Assistant Surgeon Bombay Army, Son of Henry Glasse, & Sarah Louisa Southey, of the Precincts, Spinster, daughter of Thomas Southey
1847	January	12	John Keel, Bachelor, of Northgate, Baker, son of John Keel, & Amelia Scott, of the Precincts, Spinster, daughter of Thomas Scott
1847	March	15	George Woodruff, age 27, Bachelor, of the Ville of St Gregory, Joiner, son of Daniel Woodruff, & Elizabeth Terry, age 25, of the Ville of Christ Church, Spinster, a Servant, daughter of Isaac Terry
1848	January	19	Richard Stroud, Bachelor, of St Stephen's, Miller, son of William Stroud, & Mary Ann Holmans, of the Precincts, Spinster, daughter of William Holmans
1848	April	15	William Hawkes, age 29, Bachelor, of St George's, Servant, son of Joseph Hawkes, & Mary Amelia Sheppard, age 29, of the Precincts, Spinster, Servant, daughter of George Sheppard
1848	December	30	Lewis Victor Flatou, Widower, of the Precincts, Surgeon, son of Lewis Flatou, & Elizabeth Ann Simmonds, of Dover, Spinster, daughter of John Simmonds
1849	February	8	Francis Charles Drummond, Esquire, Bachelor, of Little Dunkeld, Perth, North Britain, Son of James, Viscount Strathallan, & Charlotte Mary Atholl Oakeley, of the Precincts, Spinster, daughter of Archdeacon Sir Herbert Oakeley, Bart.
1849	April	9	Ernest Edward Jacobs, Bachelor, of St Margaret's, Canterterbury, Jeweller, Son of Wolff Jacobs, and Jane Smith, of the Precincts, Widow, daughter of Edward Hatton
1849	August	9	William John Burvill, age 24, Bachelor, of the Ville of the Archbishop's Palace, Coal Merchant, Son of William Burvill, & Caroline Mount Stephens Chivers, age 24, Spinster, of the same, daughter of Henry Chivers
1850	May	28	Henry Dennett, Bachelor, of the Precincts, Servant, Son of Robert Dennett, & Susan Janet Hawley, of the same, Spinster, Servant, daughter of John Hawley
1850	June	11	Richard Pettman, age 30, Bachelor, of Whitstable, Baker, Son of Robert Pettman, & Mary Wells, age 24, of the Archbishop's Palace, Spinster, daughter of Blott Wells

Year.	Month.	Day.	Names.
1852	October	5	Thomas Evance Jones, Bachelor, of the Precincts, Professor of Music, Son of George Jones, and Maria Quested, of St Mildred's, Spinster, daughter of George Quested
1852	December	21	William Sneller, Bachelor, of Northgate, Grazier, son of John Sneller, & Ellen Wells, of Palace Street, Spinster, Milliner, daughter of Blott Wells
1853	May	3	William Prett, Widower, of St Alphage, Canty, Confectioner, Son of William Prett, deceased, & Sarah Ann Stokoe, of the Precincts, Spinster, Housekeeper, daughter of Thomas Stokoe
1853	June	13	Henry William Brown, Bachelor, of the Abp.'s Palace, Joiner, son of John Brown, & Caroline Thurston, of the same, Spinster, daughter of James Thurston
1853	June	13	John Homersham, Bachelor, of the Abp.'s Palace, Joiner, son of William Homersham, & Ann Elizabeth Margaret Martin, of the same, Spinster, daughter of Charles Martin
1856	September	16	Charles Frederick Jordan, age 24, Bachelor, Engineer in the Royal Navy, son of Hugh Jordan, and Mary Anne Chivers, age 25, Spinster, daughter of Henry Chivers, both of the Ville of the Abp.'s Palace
1857	December	26	John Goodliff, Bachelor, of St Mary, Haggerston, London, Carpenter, son of John Goodliff, & Mary Scrivens, of the Precincts, Spinster, Servant, daughter of James Scrivens
1859	January	25	Joshua Harrod, age 40, Widower, of the Cavalry Barracks, Army, son of John Harrod, & Eliza Ann Wells, of Palace Street, Spinster, Milliner, daughter of Blott Wells
1859	February	15	Edwin Butt, age 29, Bachelor, of the Precincts, Gardener, son of William Butt, & Ann Brooker, age 30, of Brompton, Spinster, daughter of William Brooker
1859	June	11	John Filmer,* age 23, Bachelor, of Broad Street, Printer, son of John Martin,* & Harriett Cook, age 23, of the Precincts of the Abp.'s Palace, Spinster, daughter of Stephen Cook
1859	June	30	John Fogarty, Widower, of Canterbury, Soldier, son of Michael Fogarty, and Mary Ann Kay, of the Cathedral Precincts, Widow, Servant, daughter of James Mills
1860	August	11	Robert Francis Obey, Bachelor, of the Precincts, Porter, son of William Obey, & Sarah Ann Clark, of Harbledown, Spinster, Servant, daughter of John Clark
1860	December	31	Alfred Peirce, age 21, Bachelor, of the Ville of Christ Church, Dairyman, son of William Walton Peirce, & Susan Allen Whale, age 20, of St Gregory's, Spinster, daughter of Ambrose Whale
1861	April	8	John Ellis Roalfe, age 24, Bachelor, of Chislett, Saddler, son of James Roalfe, & Elizabeth Caroline Blogg, age 28, of the Precincts of this Cathedral, Spinster, daughter of James Blogg
1861	April	11	William Orpin, age 25, of St Margts, near Rochester, Police Officer, son of John Orpin, & Esther Cooper, age 20, of the Precincts of this Cathedral, Spinster, daughter of George Cooper

* So in the original; the Register is signed John Filmer.

Year.	Month.	Day.	Names.
1862	June	25	Libert Chandler, age 25, Bachelor, of Goodrich, Canada West, Provincial Surveyor, son of William Berkeley Chandler, & Marian Holmes, age 19, of the Precincts of this Cathedral, Spinster, daughter of Marcus Holmes
1862	July	1	William Thomas Bullock, age 44, Bachelor, of Christ Church, St Mary le Bone, Middlesex, Clerk in Holy Orders, son of John Bullock, & Alice Oke Alford, age 25, of the Precincts of this Cathedral, Spinster, daughter of Henry Alford, Dean of this Cathedral
1862	July	19	Thomas Newing Bachelor, of the Ville of St Gregory, Baker, son of William Newing, & Fanny Ancle, of the Precincts of this Cathedral, Spinster, Servant, daughter of John Ancle
1862	October	27	Thomas Porter Petts, age 44, Widower, of St Andrew's Parish, Licensed Victualler, son of Thomas Petts, & Elizabeth Butcher, age 33, of the Precincts of this Cathedral, Spinster, daughter of Benjamin Butcher
1862	December	30	Ralph William Elliot Forster, Bachelor, of the District of St Gabriel, Pimlico, Barrister at Law, son of Ralph Forster, & Frances Joanna Stone, of the Ville of Christ Church, Canterbury, Spinster, daughter of William Stone, Canon of Canterbury
1863	January	18	William Samuel Grigg, Bachelor, of the Ville of the Archbishop's Palace, Greengrocer, son of William Grigg, & Louisa Sarah Wilson, of the same, Spinster, daughter of William Wilson
1863	March	5	George Edward Chapman, Bachelor, of Fontaine les Dijon, Côte d'Or, in the Empire of France, Gentleman, son of George Chapman, & Maria Jarvis, of the Precincts of this Cathedral, Spinster, daughter of William Jarvis
1863	July	8	Edward Bourne, Bachelor, of the Precincts of this Cathedral, Servant, son of William Bourne, & Ellen Frances Bishop, of the same, Spinster, Servant, daughter of Charles Bishop
1864	April	10	John Gartland, age 23, Bachelor, of the Barracks, Soldier in the Royal Horse Artillery, son of James Gartland, & Selina Fanny Jubb, age 21, of the Archbishop's Palace, Spinster, daughter of Joseph Jubb
1864	May	17	Edward Collier, age 29, Bachelor, of the Barracks, Sergeant in the Royal Horse Artillery, son of John Collier, & Jane Fanny Bates, age 20, of the Ville of the Arch Bishop's Palace, Spinster, daughter of George Bates
1864	July	9	William Trendall, age 28, Bachelor, of Maidstone, Printer, son of William Trendall, & Jane Winter, age 24, of the Ville of Christchurch, Spinster, daughter of John Winter
1864	August	31	Stephen Musgrave Hilton, Widower, of Bramling, in the Parish of Ickham, Kent, Esquire, son of Henry Hilton, & Emily Shuttleworth Stone, of this Ville of Christchurch, Spinster, daughter of William Stone, Canon of Canterbury
1864	September	8	Frederick Wright, age 32, Bachelor, of the Archbishop's Palace, Draper, son of William Wright, & Emma Austen, of the same, Spinster, daughter of Edward Austen

Year.	Month.	Day.	Names.
1864	October	3	Alfred Hunt, age 28, Batchelor, of All Saints, Poulterer, son of Edward Hunt, and Elizabeth Barnes, age 24, of Cathedral Precincts, Spinster, daughter of William Barnes
1864	October	7	Julian Marshall, Bachelor, of Duke Street, St James, London, Esquire, son of John Marshall, & Florence Ashton Thomas, of the Precincts of this Cathedral, Spinster, daughter of John Thomas, Canon of Canterbury
1864	November	26	William Aistrop, Bachelor, of St George's, Canterbury, servant, son of James Aistrop, and Elizabeth Blackman, of the Precincts of this Cathedral, Spinster, Servant, daughter of Thomas Blackman
1865	February	2	Edward Yard Brabant, age 25, Bachelor, of Herne Hill, Faversham, Lieutenant, C.M.R., son of John Thomas Brabant, and Mary Burnet Robertson, age 24, of the Precincts of this Cathedral, Spinster, daughter of James Craigie Robertson, Canon of this Cathedral
1865	June	1	Thomas Stuart Kennedy, age 24, Bachelor, of St John's Leeds, Machinist, son of Peter Kennedy, & Clara Thornton, age 24, of The Cathedral Precincts, Canterbury, Spinster, daughter of Henry George Thornton
1865	November	2	Isaac Moody, age 28, Bachelor, of Barham, Carpenter, son of William Moody, & Jane Willis, age 21, of the Precincts of this Cathedral, Spinster, daughter of James Willis
1866	October	2	George Wyver, age 18, Bachelor, of St Paul's, Canterbury, Painter, son of James Flowers Wyver, & Mary Sophia Bartlett, age 18, of the Precincts of the Archbishop's Palace, Spinster, daughter of Frederick Bartlett
1867	February	12	Henry Edmund Tilsley Cruso, age 24, Bachelor, of Canterbury, Clerk in Holy Orders, son of Edmund Cruso, & Frances Mary Oke Alford, age 28, of Canterbury, Spinster, daughter of Henry Alford, Dean of Canterbury
1867	July	30	Thomas Lewes Soley, age 36, Bachelor, of Tiverton, Devon, Clerk in Holy Orders, son of Thomas Ap-Rees Soley, & Harriet Fanny Austin, age 35, of the Precinct of this Cathedral, Spinster, daughter of George Austin
1867	September	11	Joseph Barton, Widower, of East Leigh, Havant, Hants, Clerk in Holy Orders, son of John Barton, and Susan Wilhelmina Sullivan, of the Precincts of this Cathedral, Spinster, daughter of James John Sullivan, Physician
1868	February	22	James Stupples, age 24, Bachelor, of Littlebourne, Butler, son of James Stupples, & Fanny Heathfield, age 27, of The Precincts, Spinster, daughter of Jesse Heathfield
1868	April	27	George West, age 28, Bachelor, of the Ville of Archbishop's Palace, Writer, son of George West, & Mary Thurston, age 25, of the same, Spinster, daughter of James Thurston
1868	October	22	Alfred Rawlings, age 30, Bachelor, of St Giles, Colchester, Serjeant, son of Christopher Rawlings, & Caroline Marshall Wells, age 23, of the Ville of Archbishop's Palace, Spinster, daughter of Blott Wells

Year	Month.	Day.	Names.
1869	January	24	Benjamin Brighurst, age 33, Widower, of the Ville of the Archbishop's Palace, Smith, son of Thomas Brighurst, & Elizabeth Strand, age 33, of the same, Spinster, daughter of Thomas Strand
1869	July	1	Henry William Chapman, age 35, Bachelor, of St Paul's, Canterbury, Gentleman, son of Henry Chapman, & Julia Elisabeth Robertson, age 27, of the Cathedral Precincts, Spinster, daughter of James Craigie Robertson, Canon of this Church
1869	November	4	Harry George Austin, Widower, of Cathedral Precincts, Surveyor, son of George Austin, & Georgiana Eliza Dowson, of Chartham, Widow, daugher of Lewis Hiram Smith, Gentleman
1870	February	3	Louis Henry Dugald Campbell, age 25, Bachelor, of the Archbishop's Palace, Baronet, son of John Eyton Campbell, Baronet, & Mary Ellen Edith Austin, age 20, of the same, Spinster, daughter of Harry George Austin
1870	April	26	James Standen, age 30, Bachelor, of the Cathedral Precincts, Grazier, son of Spencer Standen, & Mary Elizabeth Espenett, age 25, of St Mary Bredin, Spinster, daughter of Samuel Espenett
1870	November	9	Simon Stuart Maggs, age 29, Bachelor, of Cathedral Precincts, butler, son of John Maggs, & Mary Ann Baldwin, age 32, of Addington, Kent, Spinster, daughter of James Baldwin
1871	February	9	Edward John Lugard, age 26, Bachelor, of Aldershot, Lieutenant & Adjutant of the 4th Regiment of Foot, son of Henry Williamson Lugard, & Emmeline Elizabeth Hyder, age 21, of Cathedral Precincts, Spinster, daughter of William Augustine Hyder
1871	August	22	John William Boyd, age 30, Bachelor, of St Peter's, Canterbury, Clerk in Holy Orders, son of Alexander Pearson Boyd, Esquire, & Edith Louisa Leath Angel-Smith, age 25, of Cathedral Precincts, Spinster, daughter of Francis A. Angel-Smith
1871	September	11	Charles Chinery, Bachelor, of Holy Trinity, Blackheath, Tailor, son of Philip Chinery, & Emma Furner, of the Precincts, Canterbury, Spinster
1871	December	2	Edwin James Dixon, Widower, of Grove Ferry, Wickham Breux, Station Master, son of David Toomer Dixon, & Susanna Gibbs, of the Precincts of the Archbishop's Palace, Spinster, daughter of Thomas Gibbs
1872	May	18	Charles Russell, Bachelor, of Clifton, Yorks, Lieu^t Royal Artillery, son of David Russell, & Matilda Knight, of Cathedral Precincts, Spinster, daughter of Thomas John Knight, Barrister at Law
1873	February	18	Henry Sykes Thornton, age 25, Bachelor, of Cathedral Precincts, Canterbury, Gentleman, son of Watson Joseph Thornton, & Mary Louisa Rawlinson, age 23, of the same, Spinster, daughter of George Rawlinson, Canon of this Church
1873	June	4	Henry Stephen Swiney, age 28, Bachelor, of Cathedral Precincts, Canterbury, Captain in the 69th Reg^t, son of John Swiney, & Agnes Laura Lambert, age 23, of St George the Martyr, Canterbury, Spinster, daughter of Thomas Lambert

Year.	Month.	Day.	Names.
1873	July	3	Henry Curry, age 49, Widower, of Davington, Engineer, son of George Curry, and Jane Hollands, age 40, of Precincts, Widow, daughter of Edward Austen
1874	April	8	William Mansell, age 62, Widower, of the Precincts, Gentleman, son of William Mansell, & Mary Sarah Hudson, age 44, of Ramsgate, Spinster, daughter of Henry Hudson
1874	September	24	Charles Henry Drake, age 32, Bachelor, of the Precinct, Solicitor, son of Thomas Edward Drake, & Frances Elizabeth Page, age 24, of Sandgate, Widow, daughter of Joseph Clow
1875	January	28	James Innes, age 40, Bachelor, of St Cuthbert's, Edinburgh, Treasurer of Sarawak, son of Cosmo Innes, and Emily Anne Robertson, age 31, of the Cathedral Precincts, Canterbury, Spinster, daughter of James Craigie Robertson, Canon of this Church
1875	December	1	The ceremony of Marriage was performed between Joseph Norden & Caroline Louisa Hillersden Snowden, at their request, after previous marriage on the same day at the Registry Office for the District of Blean, in the County of Kent, as appears by the certificated Copy of the entry in that Register
(1876)*	January	11	Francis Foord Hilton, age 21, Bachelor, of Nackington House, Lieutenant in the Army, son of Thomas Hilton, and Marguerite Jane Rawlinson, age 23, of the Precincts, Spinster, daughter of George Rawlinson, Canon of this Cathedral
1876	February	20	George Pankhurst, age 32, Bachelor, of Canterbury, Butler, son of John Pankhurst, and Amy Weeks, age 37, of the same, Cook, Spinster, daughter of John Weeks
1876	June	10	Alfred Mellor Watkin, Bachelor, of Canterbury, gentleman, son of Edward William Watkin, Knight, and Catherine Elizabeth Payne-Smith, of the same, Spinster, daughter of Robert Payne-Smith, Dean
1876	August	29	Stephen Herbert Gatty, Bachelor, of the Vicarage, Ecclesfield, Barrister at law, son of Alfred Gatty, and Alice Georgiana Rawlinson, of the Precincts, Canterbury, Spinster, daughter of George Rawlinson, Canon of Canterbury
1876	September	12	John Henry Rogers, Bachelor, of the Precincts, Canterbury, Gentleman, son of John Hewst (?) Rogers, and Edith Bingham, of Hampstead, Spinster, daughter of Thomas Bingham
1876	October	12	John Fitzalan Cornwall, Bachelor, of Danbury, Essex, Clerk in Holy Orders, son of Alan Gardner Cornwall, and Louisa Harriet Young, of the Precincts, Cathedral, Spinster, daughter of George Augustus Young
1878	July	15	Walter Alfred Fetherstone, age 22, Bachelor, of the Ville of the Archbishop's Palace, Grocer, son of John Fetherstone, and Jemima Sutton Kate Hadley, age 22, of the Liberty of St Augustine's, Spinster, daughter of Henry Hadley
1878	August	15	George Ralph Prebble, Bachelor, of 2 Orchard Street, St Dunstan's, Gentleman, son of James Prebble, and Sarah Chiswell, of the Precincts of the Cathedral, Spinster, daughter of John Chiswell

* The year omitted in the original.

BURIALLS.

Year.	Month.	Day.	Names.
1571	June	8	Robert Pownoll
1586	October	21	Posthumus, the sonne of Robert Pownoll
1591	November	26	George, the sonne of John Nutt
1591	February	25	Richard Roberts
1592	April	24	The Ladie Hales, late Wyfe of Richard Lee, Esquire
1592	July	7	Pacience Birche
1592	July	18	Cisle Lundun
1599	December	20	Elizabeth, the daughter of Thomas Rooke
1599	January	15	William Heyman
1600	June	11	Margaret, the daughter of Richard Roger
1601	April	3	Anne, the daughter of Richarde Colfe
1601	November	5	Hope, the daughter of Richarde Byrde
1601	February	2	Agnies Tillden, servant to Mr Archdecon
1601	February	10	Mistris Gorly, wedow, in the graue of her first husband, Mr Dabbes
1602	April	30	Mistris Harte, wedow
1602	July	15	William hattof, one of ye quier
1602	September	16	Mistres Boyce, the wyfe of Mr Thomas Boyce
1602	October	18	Mistres hill, the wyfe of Mr Thomas hill
1602	October	23	Margeat, the daughter of Thomas Cawlldom
1602	October	24	Richard, sonne of ser William Lovles
1602	November	30	John Wood, sonne of Doctor Woode
1603	May	14	Robart Cowper
1603	August	14	Mistres Webb, the Wyfe of gorge Webb
1603	September	8	Mistres Butler
1603	September	12	Sanderes, the milner
1603	September	15	Melchesideck King
1603	November	1	Mr Odiam
1603	January	9*	M^trs^ Pownoll, widowe
1605	June	10	Hope, the Daughter of George Marson
1605	June	18	Mrs Carpenter Widdowe
1605	July	7	Mrs Robarts, the wife of Mr Robarts, at the Cheker
1605	December	15	Mrs Effell, the wife of Mr Effell
1605	January	7	Mr Winter, one of the worshipfull Prebendaries
1605	February	4	Katheren, the wife of Docter Sarauia, one of the worf': Prebendaries
1606	September	18	John, the sonne of Mr Masters
1606	January	16	Elzabeth Buck, seruante to Mr Byrdd
1606	January	18	George, the sonne of Docter Clarke
1606	December†	7	Mrs Gates, the wife of Mr Gates
1607	April	9	Charles the sonne of Mr Masters
1607	May	4	Mr William Nutt
1607	May	12	Mr George Clarke, Father of D. Clarke
1607	May	25	M^r^ J—— Masters

* Overwritten in the original.

† So in the original.

Year.	Month.	Day.	Names.
1607	September	28	Peludia, the daughter of Mr Byrde
1607	December	16	R——* Smithe, Carpenter, of St Peeter's
1607	December	26	A still borne Childe of D. Claks
1608	September	22	Thomas Marten, one of the laye Clarkes
1608	October	22	Cysly, the daughter of Docter Birde
1608	December	26	Mystris Parker, the Wife of Mr Nicholas Parker
1608	March	12	Mr Strugell Clarke, sometime pettecannon of this Church
1609	April	26	The Lady Thornehurst, Wife vnto Syrr Steene Thornhurst, Knight
1609	June	19	Doctor Byrde, one of the Worshipfull prebendaries
1609	July	27	Thomas, the sonne of Mr Doctor Masters, one of the Worshipfull prebendaryes
1609	July	31	Addam, the sonn of Mr Johnson
1609	September	15	Doctor Woode, one of the Worshipfull prebendaries
1609	September	22	M^{irs} Heuiseed, the Wife (of Mr Henry Heuiseed, one of the quire)
1609	November	18	Abraham Watson
1609	January	5	Jhethrow Foster
1609	January	10	John, the sonne of Goodman Shotwater
1609	February	4	Doctor Simpson, one of the Worshipfull prebendaries
1609	February	7	Margarett, the Daughter of Mr Doctor Masters
1609	February	16	Goodwife Shotwater
1610	April	9	Mrs Barnadina Justunion
1610	May	1	Mr George Smith
1610	July	9	John Cocke, one of the porters of the gattes
1610	October	10	Richard & Marye: ye sonne & daughter of Doctor fothersbye
1610	March	18	Cyslye, the daughter of Doctor Masters
1611	April	10	Roger, the sonne of William Warriner
1611	April	23	John Willdinge, Vergers debuty
1611	June	2	Marye, the daughter of Doctor Clarke
1611	July	18	Erasmus Fynche, Captaine of Deale Castle
1611	August	27	Thomas Baylye, one of the laye Clarkes of this Churche
1611	October	8	A still borne Childe of Mr John Sympson

Here at the foot of the page is an erasure of an entry

1611	October	17	Mr Thomas Cocks, Auditor of the Churche
1611	November	12	Goodman Lydde, subuerger
1611	November	18	Robarte, the sonne of Sir John Cullemr, Knighte
1612	April	10	William, the sonne of Mr Nicholas Sympsunne
1612	April	30	Henry forstall
1612	May	17	Kenburrowe, the daughter of Doctor Masters
1612	June	10	Mrs Marye Roger, the wife of Mr John Roger
1612	June	11	Thomas, the sonne of Mr Nicholas Parker
1612	September	1	John Elgar, seruante to Mr Houenden
1612	September	24	Syr John Boyce, Knight
1612	November	8	William, the Sonne of Doctor Clark
1612	January	2	Mr John Roger, Esqure
1612	January	19	Doctor Surauere (Saravia†), one of the worshipfull prebendaries
1612	March	13	Betteris, the Wife of Goodman Tibboll
1613	June	1	Mrs Tatnall, widdow
1613	July	23	Mrs Ann Rogers, widdow (sometime wife to the lord suffreean of douer)
1613	October	10	Doctor Colfe, one of the Worshipfull Prebendaries, & then Vicedeane

* So in the original.

† Saravia is written over this name in a later hand.

Year.	Month.	Day.	Names.
1613	December	18	William, the sonne of Doctor Clarke
1613	January	13	Doctor Langwoorth, one of the worshipfull Prebendaries
1613	March	21	Edward, the soonne of Mr John Warde
1614	May	18	Mr Edmund Denn
1614	June	14	Arter Shore
1614	August	11	Mychaell Ludde
1614	September	10	Mr Robartt Bartler
1614	October	9	Mr Alexander Neuell
1614	October	18	Mr John Sellers
1614	October	27	Henrye Stredick
1615	April	22	Roger Rauen, Scoolmaster of the kinge's Scoolle
1615	April	22	Mrs Susanna Brown
1615	February*	22	The Lady Edmondes was brought ouer ssees and buryed in or church
1615	May	7	Mr Docter Nevell, deane of this Church, and master of trenity coledg in cambrig
1615	August	28	John ffotherby, sonn of Mr John ffotherby
1615	September	1	Do: Abbutt, one of the worshipfull prebends of this church
1615	October	10	Thomas Shotwater
1615	November	5	John Miller
1615	December	26	John Seath, subporter of one of the gates
1615	December	26	William warriner, the sonn of william warriner
1615	January	15	Margarett, the daughter of William Warriner
1615	January	17	Rebecca Masters, the Daughter of Docter Masters
1616	May	11	John Baker: a gardener of Longdon, in Worster Sheer
1616	June	22	Thomas, the sonne of Mr Elye
1616	August	31	John, the sonne of Mr Nicholas Sympson
1616	October	16	Sirre Steeuen Thor'hirst, Knight
1616	December	11	Dudly, the sonne of Doctor Jacsone
1616	March	9	Goodwife Kidde, Widdow
1617	March	28	Mistris Simpson, the wife of Doctor Simpson
1617	April	14	Mistris Hide, widdowe
1617	April	15	Mistris Simpson the elder, the widdowe of Doctor Simpson
1617	April	25	George Master, the sonne of Doctor Master
1617	May	3	Master Nicholas Parker
1617	May	5	Elzabeth Marlow, seruante to Richard Fusser
1617	August	12	Thomas, the sonne of Mr Nicholas Simpson
1617	September	17	Mr John Warde, Petteeannon
1618†	March	22	Kathern, the daughter of Richard Filcock
1618	April	18	Mrs Robarts
1618	May	19	Mr John Allen
1618	June	30	Olde Mr Robarts
1618	July	31	Edward, the sonn of Michaell Boyle
1618	August	15	Jayne, the daughter of Doctor Masters
1618	September	24	Susan Ludd, widdow of Randall Ludd
1618	October	4	A still borne Childe of Mr Nicholas Sympson
1618	December	2	Mr Ford Brett, Son'e in law to Mr Ouenden
1618	December	20	Thomas Loes
1618	December	24	Mildred White, ye wife of Adam White
1618	February	25	Pelludia, the daughter of Richard Filcock
1618	February	25	Anne, the daughter of Mr Fleet
1619	April	5	Mr Charles Fotherby, Deane of this church
1619	May	3	Elisabeth Moyle, the daughter of Mr Robert Moyle
1619	May	14	Ms Frances Boyce, the daughter of Mr Thomas Boyce

* So in the original.

† So in the original; the figure 7 has been converted into 8.

Year.	Month.	Day.	Names.
1619	October	2	Tonstall Scott, the sonne of Mr Scott
1619	October	4	Penelope Fotherby, the daughter of Mr John Fotherby
1619	December	30	Mr Thomas Ouenden, ye Alderman
1619	January	19	Alice Warriner, ye wife of Mr Warriner
1619	March	21	Doctor Beacon, Phisitian
1619	March	21	Margeret Martin
1620	May	15	John, ye sonne of Doctor Clearke
1620	May	30	M^s * Barton
1620	May	31	Mr Robert Rose
1620	June	22	The Lady Thormx [or Thornix]
1620	July	30	Sir John Culmer
1620	September	17	John Martin, singingman
1620	October	8	Mistris Boyce, ye wife of Mr Thomas Boyce
1620	October	8	M^s Clarke, ye wife of Dr Clarke
1620	November	24	M^s Shepherd, ye wife of Mr John Shepherd
1620	November	24	James Archer
1621	August	2	Phillip Swallowe
1622	April	5	Alexander, the sonne of Rowland Vaham
1622	May	31	William, the sonn of Mr Slatter
1622	June	21	Mrs Katheren Drake, Mother to Doc^r Kyngeslye, Archdeacon of Canter'
1622	September	3	Dammariske, the Daughter of Doctor Masters
1622	November	8	Mr William Tonstall, Prebendary
1622	November	28	Mr Nicholas Tonstall
1622	January	7	Margaret Chrismas
1622	March	3	Mr Thomas Flood
1623	June	22	Kathern, the Wife of Adam Whit
1623	July	21	Marcye Spyce
1623	August	20	Susan, the daughter of Mr John Ludd
1623	October	22	Annise Teswell, seruante to Mr Bladwoorth
1623	December	26	Vincent fright, of St Thomas Hospitall, of Kings bridge
1623	January	4	Vincent fright, his widdowe
1623	March	23	Mrs Marye Musgraue, buryed at night
1624	May	25	William, the sonn of Doc^r Kingsle, Archdecon of Canterburye
1624	June	27	Richard sine, Almseman
1624	September	10	Richard the sonn of Doctor Clark
1624	November	8	Grace, the daughter of Mathe^w Washende'
1624	November	21	Mr James Bladworth, one of the 6 preachers
1624	December	2	Mrs Hoppe Winter
1624	December	22	Mattew, one of the Lord Woottons men
1624	February	25	Mrs Coult
1625	April	13	Thomas, the sonn of Doctor Challenor
1625	June	6	Orlando Gibbins
1625	June	22	Thomas, the sonn of Isack Raynard
1625	July	25	John, the sonne of Doctor Barger
1625	July	25	Henrye Lawes
1625	September	2	Mr Thomas Boyce, Esquire
1625	September	29	Elizabeth, the daughter of Edmond Brufe
1625	September	30	Mr John Boyce, Doctor in deuinity, and Deane of this Church
1625	October	4	M^r * Royden
1625	October	6	Sanford, the sonne of Mr John Ludd
1625	October	28	Mrs Bladworth
1625	October	29	Mr Neuell Whitgraue

* Blank in the original.

Year.	Month.	Day.	Names.
1625	November	28	Mr John Hammon
1625	December	3	Sara Bynge, Seruant to Mr Rauen
1625	December	11	Hester Clarke, Sister to Doctor Clarke
1625	January	5	Mrs Ann Sellers, Widdow
1625	February	25	John Hawkins
1625	February	17*	Gillian, the Wife of Edmond Brufe
1625	March	3	George, the sonn of Doctor Sea
1626	April	3	William Tonstall
1626	September	26	Cisly, the daughter of Mr Walter Mansel
1626	September	28	Angell Weston, of St John's hospitall, widdow
1626	November	18	Izack, the sonn of Doctor Barger, Deane of this Church
1626	December	8	Mr Frances Tucke
1626	December	27	Mr Robart Lawes
1626	January	20	Mrs Shore was buryed in the cloyster
1626	March	23	ffrances, the daughter of Mr William Watts, Buried in Doctor Sympsons the Elders grauе†
1627	April	8	William, the son of John Joyce†
1627	June	23	Mr John Denham, buryed, Cloysters†
1627	August	9	Phebe, the daughter of Mr Walter Mansell†
1627	August	22	William, the sone of Peeter Symons†
1627	November	30	Elzabeth Hamon†
1627	December	3	The Ladye Louelas†
1627	December	31	Doctor Cleuland†
1627	January	24	Mr William Haiman, buryed nere bell harry stepel doore†
1628	April	11	Katherne, the daughter of Mr Walter Mansell
1628	May	30	Doctor Masters
1628	July	11	Ellen Chapman
1628	July	13	Elizabeth, the daughter of Edward Kidder
1628	September	3	Mrs Sara Haymon, buried next bell harry stepll doore
1628	January	20	William, ye son'e of William Tunstall, one of ye Lay Clarks of this Church
1629	May	1	Mrs Cleyland, ye Widdow of Dor Cleyland
1629	May	24	Mr William Haymon, ye son'e of Sr Peter Haymon
1629	June	26	Mrs Rebecka Haymon, ye widdow of Mr Henry Haymon, of Sellinge
1629	July	4	Mary Spicer, a seruant of Do: Anyons, was buryed in ye Cloysters
1629	July	24	Mrs Crumpton, ye wife of Mr Tho: Crumpton
1629	July	30	Elizabeth, ye daughter of Isaack Rainard
1629	August	25	William, ye son'e of Isaack Rainard
1629	September	9	Do: Chapman, one of ye right worll prebends of this church
1629	September	26	Mr Sanforde, one of ye right worll prebends of this church
1629	January	15	Thomas Pamour, a brother of Eastbridge hospitall in Cant:
1629	February	3	Elizabeth Beacon, ye daughter of Doctor Beacon
1630	May	31	Dor Sympson, one of ye Right worll Prebends of this Church
1630	June	22	Sara and Dorathy, ye daughters of Do: Kingsly, Archdeacon of Cantr
1630	July	17	Mr Philemon Pownall, one of ye Peticanons of this Church
1630	July	23	Jane, ye daughter of Dor Bargroue Deane of this church
1630	October	24	Thomas, ye sonne of Thomas Jaruisse
1630	October	26	Roberte Owen
1631	May	21	Mrs Jane Hammon

* So in the original.
† Part of this entry is overwritten in the original.

Year.	Month.	Day.	Names.
1631	August	22	James, ye sone of Mr Causabone, one of ye wor^{ll} Prebends of this Church
1631	August	29	Mr Foxtone, minister
1631	September	6	Widdowe Miller, once wife of John Miller, one of ye lay Clarkes of this Churche
1631	February	5	Mr George Marson, once one of ye Peticanons of this churche, Master of the Choristers, and Organist alsoe of this Church
1631	March	22	Mr John Robarts*
1632	May	3	Elizabeth, ye wife of Mr Cartright, one of ye Vergerers of this church
1632	June	21	Mr Edwarde Robarts
1632	September	20	Lieutenante Colonell Proude was buryed in Somerset Chappell
1632	October	2	Mrs Katherin Spratling
1632	November	1	Mrs Ansell, widdow
1632	December	3	Mr John Smith
1632	January	17	Thomas Sturman
1632	January	24	Do^r Anyon, one of ye Prebends of this Church
1632	January	30	Mrs Mary Houlforde
1632	March	18	Vrsula Linger, seruant to Do: Jackson
1632†	April	3	Jone Norle
1633	April	10	Anne Hawkins
1633	June	24	Mr Thomas Robarts, Vsher of the free schoole
1633	June	25	Dorathy, ye wife of Thomas Wilks, one of ye Almesmen of this church
1633	August	5	Hester, ye daughter of Mr Horton Drayton
1633	January	22	Jone Tonge, seruant of Do: Kingsly
1633	February	17	John, ye sone of William Tunstall, one of ye Lay clarkes of this Church
1633	March	8	Edwarde Annisse, seruante of Do: Paske
1634	April	14	Isaack, ye son'e of Mr Causabone, of the Prebends of this church
1634	April	17	Mr Thomas Haymon
1634	April	17	Mr Steven Brett, buryed the same night
1634	May	14	Constance Hasarde, Mr Deane Bargroue his seruante, in ye Cloyster yarde
1634	June	12	William, ye sone of Robarte Lawes
1634	June	29	Edwarde Fox, one of ye Kings scholers of this schoole
1634	July	23	Edwarde Euans, one of the Lay Clarkes of this Church
1634	September	22	Thomas, ye sone of John Vincent, one of ye lay Clarkes of this Church
1634	September	29	Doctor Clarke
1634	October	27	Mrs Fothersby, ye widdowe of Mr Charles Fothersby, once Deane of this church
1634	December	2	Elisabeth Larryer
1634	December	17	Paule Latham (or Lathum)
1635	April	27	Sir John Wiles
1635	May	12	Mr William Harrison
1635	May	28	Mr John Edmunds
1635	July	15	Isaack Drayton, ye sonne of Horton
1635	August	25	M^s Anne Masters
1635	September	18	M^s Sarah Ouenden
1635	December	27	Margaret Lanslet
1635	January	28	Katherine Beames, daughter of John Beames

* Interlined in the original.

† So in the original, this entry has been interlined.

Year.	Month.	Day.	Names.
1635	March	3	Isaack Rayner, one of vesterers of this Church
1636	April	24	Elizabeth Swinford, daughter of Peter Swinford
1636	June	20	The Ladye ffotherby, the wife of Sr John ffothersby
1636	July	7	Mrs Whitgraue, the wife of Mr Edward Whitgraue
1636	September	15	Peter Swinford
1636	September	17	Mr Shepard, one of the Peticanons of this Church
1636	September	30	Thomas Midellton Seruant to Dr Warner
1636	November	18	Marye Warriner, daughter of Mr Mathew Warriner, Petticannon of this Church
1632	March	1	Rec^d of Do: Kingsly, Archdeacon of Cant., Six shillings & Eight pence to be distributed to ye poore w^thin ye p'cincte of this Church, wch he is to pay for a licence to eate flesh graunted to him and others by ye Arch-Bishop of Cant., his Dioccesan, & confirmed vnder ye broade Seale, by his Matie Mat: Wariner, Sacrist*
1636	December	16	Mrs Colfe, al's Haukins, widdowe
1636	December	31	Charles, ye sone of Richarde Gibbons, one of the lay Clarkes of this Church
1636	January	8	Henry, ye son'e of Do. Bargraue, Dean of this Church
1636	February	27	Susan Swinforde†
1637	April	16	Mrs Dukes
1637	May	3	Mr William Penn
1637	August	6	Mrs Masters, ye widdow of Do: Masters
1637	August	27	Elizabeth, ye daughter of Mr Jordan, one of ye Peticanons of this Church
1637	August	27	Elizabeth, ye daughter of John Beames, on of ye Substitutes of this Church
1637	September	11	Anne, ye daughter of John Ludlow
1637	September	13	Horton, ye sonn of Mr Horton Drayton
1637	September	15	Widdow Naylor
1637	September	15	Susan, ye wife of Edmunde Bruffe
1637	September	25	Margaret, ye daughter of John Vincent
1637	October	13	Widdow Bucke
1638	June	7	Mr Beniamin Jackson, sonne of Dr Jackson, one of the Prebendaries of this Church
1638	September	24	James Swinford, Sonne of John Swinford
1638	September	26	Joseph Longe, a ffranchman, of the Gray-ffriers
1638	October	14	Mrs Mary Haman
1638	November	21	John Painter, Sonne of Christopher Painter
1638	December	11	Mr Edward Whitgraue
1639	September	5	The Lady Thornix, ye late wife of Mr Anthony Sellinger
1639	September	27	The Reuerend Bishopp of Dunblaine, in Scotland, was buryed beside Dean Rogers tombestone
1639	October	7	Mr Francis Barton
1639	February	21	‡Damariske, ye Daughter of Mr Vincent, one of the Layclarks of this Church
1639	February	24	‡Mary, ye Daughter of Mr Vincent, one of the Layclarks of this Church
1640	June	6	‡Thomas, ye son of Jearomy (?) Hudson, one of ye Vesteres of this Church, and Joane his wife
1640	July	1	‡Jeane, ye Daughter of Frances Ansloe, and Clace (?) his wife

* The whole of this entry has been overwritten. † Interlined in the original.
‡ These entries have been overwritten in the original, at a later date.

Year.	Month.	Day.	Names.
1640	October	7	*Sibella, ye Daughter of Mr Bayliff, Petticannon, and Katherin his wife
1641	April	15	*John Cartwright, Vergerer of this Church
1641	May	8	*Rebecka, the daughter of Benjamen Jones
1641	June	10	William, the sone of Anthony Shorter?
1641	December	19	Thomas Fletcher, one of the Lay Clarks of this Church
1641	January	19	Phebe, the daughter Dan: Bollen, Petty Canon of this Ch:
1642	June	26	Margaret, the Wid: of Mr Nicholas Parker
1642	July	28	*Elizabeth, the daughter of Mr Horton Drayton, Auditor of this Church
1642	August	13	Mary, the daughter Dr Thomas Pashe, Prebend of this Church
1642	October	3	Thomas, the Sone of Dr Merick Casaubon, Prebend of this Church
1642	November	7	An', the daughter of Mr Will. Jourdan, Petty-canon of this Church
1642	November	16	Leonard, the son'e of Richard Gibbons, Lay Clark
†			John Somner, the sone of Mr John Somner, Buried tho
1642	January	25	The right Wor: Do: Bargraue Deane of Christ Church, Cant.
1643	April	1	Francis, the Son of John Vencent
1643	April	10	Iaack,‡ the sonne of DoMerick Casaubon, Prebend of this Church
1643	April	12	Susan, the dau' of John Shorter
1643	August	8	Peregrin Benson, the Sone of Richard Benson
1643	September	20	My Lady Mansfild
1643	November	3	Mr Thomas Boys
1643	November	13	As'tene (or Astew) Pising
1643	November	16	Mr Robart Hurtt
1643	November	22	Ruth, Mr Brownes Mayd
1643	December	19	Mary, the wife of Mr Richard Kinnad
1643	November§	29	Mathew, ye sonne of Richard Warriner
1644	November	1	Captaine Richard Benson
1644	February	17	Mrs Margaret‖ Hurst, wedow
1644	March	27¶	Ms Mary Haward, widow
1644	May	16	Elisabeth Lambe, ye daughter of James
1644	December	23	Sibella Dale
1644	January	29	Margaret Pising, ye daughter of Will:
1644	February	18	Lad Shorter
1644	February	25	Margaret Gibbons, ye daughter of Rich:
1645	August	28	Ellin Vale
1645	April ¶	13	John Vincent, ye sonne of John
1645	September	31	Mary Tunstall, ye wife of Mr Thomas Tunstall
1645	November	13	Ms Angela Boyce, widow
1645	December	17	Frances Drayton, ye daughter of Mr Horton Drayton
1643¶	January	10	Margaret, ye wife of Mr Mathew Warriner
1643¶	February	14	Mr Mathew Warriner
1646	August	8	Anthony Gibbs
1646	August	13	Grace Vaughan, ye daughter of Mr Thomas Vaughan
1646	November	2	Martha Razell
1646	November	13	Dr Jackson, one ye Prebends of this Church
1646	December	7	Ms Hales, ye wife of Mr William Hales
1646	December	12	Ms Angela Kingsly

* These entries have been overwritten in the original at a later date.
† No date to this entry in the original. ‡ So spelt in the original.
§ Interlined in the original. ‖ "Margaret" is interlined in another hand.
¶ So in the original; the dates of this period are irregular.

Year.	Month.	Day.	Names.
1647	June	2	Mr John Bayly
1647	June	8	Katherine, ye wife of Mr Bayly
1647	June	26	Anne Bayly, ye daughter of John
1647	June	26	Margaret Bayly, ye daughter of John
1647	February	2	Dr Kingsle, Archdeacon of Canterburie and Prebend of this Church
1648	April	7	William, ye sonne of Mr Robert Masters
1648	April	17	Martha Masters, thee daughter of Mr Robert Masters
1648	August	11	Sir Edward Masters
1648	January	6	Richard Gibbons
1648	June*	4	Mr William Tonstall, Minor Ca'non of this Church
1648	February	2	Lady Wild, wife of Sir John Wild
1648	February	3	Lady Haman
1648	June*	7	Ms Mary Simpson, ye wife of Mr Nicholas
1648	July*	22	Susan Ansloe, daughter of Francis
1649	March	28	Mr George Kingsly
1649	May	23	Mr Walter Knight
1649	May	28	Ms Mary Vincent
1649	June	6	Mr Horton Drayton
1649	August	20	Ms Masters, ye wife of Mr Robert Masters
1649	September	14	Mr John Ludd, schoolemaster
1649	November	20	(or 29) Mr Walter Knight, ye sonne of Walter
1649	December	18	Ms Shrubsall
1649	January	3	Mr Thomas Foach
1649	February	4	Thomas Simons
1649	March	18	Ms Does
1650	May	16	Mr George Kingsley
1650	February	2	John Shorter
1651	October	27	Mr Rowland Vaughan
1651	January	30	Anne Cheney, ye daughter of Richard
1652	September	28	Ms Margaret Vaughan
1653	February*	14	Thomas Weeks
1653	August	5	Mr Dudley Wiles
1653	March	15	†Mr Thomas Gould
1654	December	7	Robert Simons
1656	April	18	Mr Francis Taylor, preacher
1656	May	26	Mr Edmund Rouse
(1656)‡	July	12	John Cucko, sonn of Daniel & Elizabeth
(1656)‡	July	20	Jeremy Masterson, sonne of Jeremy & Afra
(1656)‡	August	20	Elizabeth Hamon, ye Daughter of Richard & Joane
(1656)‡	July	5	Elizabeth Croyden, daughter of Robert & Eliz.
(1656)‡	July	22	William Everden
(1656)‡	July	25	Ms Elizabeth Croyden
(1656)‡	July	23	Richard Croyden, sonne of Robert
(1656)‡	Septem.	21	William Best, sonn of Jonathan
(1656)‡	Septem.	22	Mr Thomas Morland
(1656)‡	October	5	William Nethersole dyed
(1656)‡	October	4	John Nethersole dyed
(1656)‡	October	15	Steven Monins dyed
(1656)‡	Novem.	28	Mrs Mary Man, Widdow
(1656)‡	December	1	Mr Elliot
(1656)‡	December	1	Alice Groues
(1656)‡	February	9	Jane, wife of John Terry

* So in the original. † Interlined in the original.

‡ The year is not given in the original, and several of these entries are out of chronological order.

Year.	Month.	Day.	Names.
1656	February	21	Mrs Magdalene Marson
1657	May	13	John, the sonne of Christopher Stonehouse
1657	May	17	Paule, the sonne of Mr Paule Barret
1657	June	12	Robert Hadds, sonne of Mr Mathew Hadds
1657	July	12	Anne Ingham, ye Daughter of Mr Edw. Ingham
1657	August	20	Mr Edward Roberts
1657	August	24	Mr John Banks
1657	August	24	Elizabeth Naze, daughter of Robert Naze
1657	August	29	Mr Richard Gibbons
1657	January	27	Mrs Elizabeth Jackson
1657	February	3	Anne Bayly, ye daughter of Thomas
1658	April	27	Mrs Susan'a Sumner, wife of Mr John Somner
1658	May	19	Martha Johnson, dyed 16:
1658	June	19	Ede, (?) wife of John Ludlow
1658	June	23	Dorathy, the wife of John Hopper
1658	July	22	Mr Edward Browne
1658	August	31	Mr William Somner, sonne of Mr John Somner
1658	August	26*	Ann Croyden, daughter of Robert
1658	October	6	Mrs Alice Roberts
1658	October	6	Dorathy Rablis
1658	December	2	Mr Thomas Kingsley
1658	December	5	Mrs Elizabeth Hauks (or Hanks), dyed
1658	December	15	Adwry, Lady Masters
1658	December	23	Mrs Anne Crispe, the wife of Thomas
1658	December	17*	Mrs Joane Masterson dyed
1658	January	14	Mr Thomas Broadnex dyed
1658	March	17	Mrs Elizabeth Turner dyed 14
1658	March	20	John Bayly, sonne of Thomas
1659	May	3	Thomazine Pemble, died May 1
1659	May	9	Anne Popillion, daughter of Thomas & Jane
1659	May	18	John Wray
1659	June	30	Mary Nayre, ye daughter of William and Mary
1659	August	26	Anne Croyden, daughter of Robert
1659	August	31	Robert Bargraue, ye sonne of Mr Robert Bargraue
1659	October	19	Elizabeth Walton
1659	September	24	Judith De New, the daughter of John
1659	January	18	Mrs Katherine Langworth, dyed January 13th
1660	April	23	Mr Thomas Gey
1660	April	27	Mr Robert Doocs
1660	May	4	Mary Harrison, daughter of Henry
1660	May	5	Charles Kingsley, sonn of Mr William
1660	May	22	Elizabeth Harrison, daughter of Henry
1660	May	21*	John Jacob, sonne of Mr John Jacob, dyed May 18
1660	June	13	Mrs Ann Huffam, dyed 9th
1660	July	11	Rebecca, ye daughter of Jonathan Best
1660	August	10	ffrancis, the sonne of Jonathan Best
1660	August	27	Susanna De New, daughter of John De New
1660	October	3	Elizabeth Mummery
1660	November	8	Ann Line, Widdow, dyed ye 4th
1660	November	5*	Jehostiaphat Star
1660	December	6	Mr John Player, dyed December 2
1660	January	19	Barbara Tuckerman
1660	March	11	Mary Allen
1661	June	4	Thomas Cucko, sonne of Thomas
1661	June	21	Mr Robert Croyden

* So in the original.

Year.	Month.	Day.	Names.
1661	July	14	Clasen Onslow, ye daughter of ffrancis
1661	September	15	Mr William Jarvis
1661	September	22	Mrs Gibbon
1661	September	28	Thomas, the sonne of Dr Peirce, one of the Worp^{ll} Prebens
1661	October	29	Mr James Lambe, one of the Pettie Cannons of this Church, dyed October the 26th
1661	November	5	Jane Russell, the wife of James Russell
1661	January	23	Frances Crane (alias Elliot), ye late wife of Mr John Crane, Towne-Clarke of ye Citty of Canterbury
1662	May	25	Peter, ye son of Mr Thomas Hardres, ye Councellor, and Philadelphia his wife
1662	June	5	Jane, ye daughter of Mr John Parris, Schoolemaster of ye Kings free schoole in Christ Church, and Jane his wife
1662	June	14	Hester, ye Daughter of Dr Edward Wilford and Elisabeth his wife
1662	July	15	Frances Ansloe
1662	August	20	Charles, ye Son of Captayne William Kingsly and Margaret his wife
1662	January	11	Sarah, ye Daughter of Daniell Chilton and Sarah his wife
1662	January	27	Henry Hunniwood, Gent., sometimes a Collonell under that Grand Rebell Olliuer Cromwell
1662	March	19	*Mary, ye wife of Mr William Nayer, in the Cloystrs
1663	May	20	*Mr Richard Cheyny, dijng in St George's Parish in the City of Canterbury, was Buried in the Cloyster of Christchurch, Canterbury
1663	June	9	*Annis Heyword, a seruant to old M^{ris} Sabin
1663	July	13	*Isaac, ye Son of Mr Robert Bargraue and Elisabeth his wife
1663	November	9	*Ann, ye Daughter of Dr Edward Willford and Elisabeth his wife
1663	November	10	*Thomas, ye Son of Mr Richard Langham (one of ye Minor Cannons of this Church) and Frances his wife
1663	December	3	*William, ye Son of Thomas Mathews, one of ye Substitutes of this Church, & Mary his wife
1664	May	4	*John Vincent, one of ye Lay Clerkes of this Church
1664	May	27	*ffrancis, ye Son of Mr William Somner, Auditor of this Church and Barbarie his wife
1664	August	9	*Thomas, ye Son of Mr Thomas Gibs, Organist, and Mary his wife
1664	October	24	*Elisabeth, ye wife of Mr Daniell Cucko, in ye Cloysters
1664	March	6	*Mr James Cawsabone, Brother to ye right Wor^{ll} Dr Merick Cawsabone, Prebend of this Church
1665	April	13	*Mr Elias Juxon, one of ye Six Preachers
1665	June	17	*Frances, ye Daughter of Dr Edward Willford and Elisabeth his wife
1665	June	27	*Elisabeth, ye Daughter of Mr Richard Langham, a minor Cannon of this Church, and Frances his wife
1665	August	28	*Ann Constance, a mayd seruant to Mr Burnill (or Buruill), was Buryd in the South side of the Church, where not any before by the space of forty yeares at the least haue bin buried
1665	December	29	*George Johnson, a prisoner, was buryed in ye South side of the Churchyard
1665	January	9	*Ellen Admans, maid to Mr Spratlin, was buried in ye South-side of ye Churchyard

* These entries are overwritten in the original.

Year.	Month.	Day.	Names.
1666	March	28	*Sr John Fothersby
1666	August†	19	*John Bamfeild, son to Thomas Bamfeild, member of this Church
1666	May	27	*Mr James Hudson, member of this Church, was buryed in the Cloysters
1666	May	20‡	*Mr Chilton, member of the Church, was buryed in the Cloyster
1666	November	14	*John Walter, a poore prisoner
1666	January	18	Martin, ye Son of Mr Thomas Fothersby and Elisabeth his wife
1666	February	23	Mris Jane Buck, wife of Mr John Buck, minister
1667	June	29	Mris Elisabeth Bargraue, ye relict widow of the Reuerend Deane Bargraue
1667	August	27	Mrs Jane Weames, the relict widow of Doctor Lodowick Weames, sometymes prebend of Westminster
1667	September	6	Robert Mills, one of the Lay-Clarks of this Church, in ye Cloysters
1667	October	23	Mr Richard Kennard, one of the Lay-Clarks of Christ Church, Canterbury
1667	December	16	Peter Frampton, one of the Porters of the Church
1668	July	15	Mris Mabella Cullimore, dijng at Dr Hardess his house, was Buried in the Cloyster of Christchurch, Canterbury
1668	July	18	Peter, ye Son of Mr William Courtop, of Stadmarsh
1668	November	24	Gregory, ye Son of Mris Jane Parker, widdow
1669	March	28§	Elizabeth, ye Daughter of Mr Edmund Burges, a minor Canon of this Church, & ffrances his wife
1669	April	2	Mr Willm Sumner, Auditor of this Church, was buried at St Margaret's
1669	April	11	Anne Ludlow
1669	May	27	Elizabeth, ye Daughter of Mr Willm Kingsley, & Priscilla his wife
1669	July	5	Dorothy, ye wife of Mr Willm Jordan, one of ye Minor Canons of this Church
1669	October	20	Tho: Barber, one of ye Ley-Clerkes of this Church
1669	December	28	Charles, the son of Doctor William Kingsley, some time Archdeacon and prebend of Christ-church, Canterbury
1670	September	23	‖Gregory Hennam, a Prisoner
1670	January	30	‖Mr Elisha Robinson, a Minor Canon, Buried in St George's
1670	February	23	George Essex, an old Prisoner
1671	July	21	Dr Mericke Cassawbon, one of ye Prebendaries of this Church
1671	July	25	Henry, the Son of Dr Willm Belke, A Prebend of this Church
1671	October	18	Mr Abraham Vander Heyden, of this p'ecincts
1671	November	4	Mr Leonard Browne, Auditor of this Church, & an Alderman of ye City of Caut: Buried at St Margaret's
1672	April	24	Richard, ye son of Mr Edmund Burges and Francis his wife
1672	August	22	James Johnson, one of ye Lay Clerkes of this Church
1672	September	4	John, ye Son of Mr Edmund Burges (one of ye Minor Canons of this Church) and Francis his wife

* These entries are overwritten in the original.
† The month is August in the original, probably it should be April.
‡ So in the original.
§ The date has been overwritten in the original, and is very indistinct.
‖ Both interlined in the original.

Year.	Month.	Day.	Names.
1672	October	17	Dr Thomas Turner, the Reverend Deane of Canterbury
1672	December	12	William Morden (or Marden), a little child, dyng at Mris Hudson's house
1672	March	21	Thomas, a little child of Dr John Castillion and Margaret his wife
1673	June	4	George Nuttall, a Gentleman Trooper, com'ing to an untimely death was Buried in ye Cloysters
1673	June	10	Thomas, ye son of Mr Thomas Knowler, Alderman of ye Citty of Canterbury, was Buried in ye Cloysters
1673	July	16	Mr Edward Aldee (?), Prebend of Christ Church, Canterbury, departed this Life the 12th day of July, and was Buried in St Andrew's Church
1673	September	12	Mr Silas Johnson was Buried in the Cloysters
1673	September	25	Mris Margaret Hadds, Widow, Dijng in Christ Church, Canterbury, was Buried in the Parish of St Alphage
1673	October	3	Thomas Mathers (?), one of the Lay Clarks of this Church
1673	November	12	James Frale, Ensigne to one of his Maiesties foote Company, com'ing to an untimely end was Buried in the Cloysters
1673	November	18	Symon Man, one of the Vesterers of Christ Church, Cant., was Buried in the Cloysters
1673	December	6	ffrances, ye wife of Mr Richard Langham, A Minor Canon of this Church
1673	February	8	Mr John Atkinson, a Gentleman of his Majesties Troop, was buried in ye Cloyster
1673	February	13	Abigaill, ye Daughter of Mr Ri: Langham, A Minor Canon of this Church
1674	April	11	William, ye Son of Thomas and Ester Turner, a little Child
1674	May	8	Mr Willm Hawkins, Buried at St Margaret's
1674	May	20	William, ye Son of Tho: Bamfeild
1674	July	18	Mary, ye Relict Widow of James Johnson, was Buried in ye Cloyster
1674	December	1	Mr Thomas Fothirby
1675	May	11	William Pane, sometime Coachman to Dr Dumolleyn, dijng of the small Pox
1675	July	6	*Richard Pising, a Lay Clarke, dyng in Christchurch July the 4th, was Buried in St Pauls Church
1675	July	23	*Mris Elisabeth Sargenson departed this Life the 20th day of July, '75, and was Buried at St Georges parish
1675	August	20	*Robert, ye son of Mr Henry Hughs, a Minor Cannon of this Church, and Catherine his wife
1675	August	28	*Elisabeth Pennill, made seruant unto Mrs Aldee
1675	September	29	*Mr Richard Langham, a Minor Cannon of this Church
1675	December	8	Mr Robert Spratling, Son to Mr Robert Spratling
1675	December	18	Mrs ——— Cullin, wife to Mr Cullin, Vsher to the Kings Schoole
1675	March	3	Mrs Engham buried in St Margarets
1675	March	20	Mrs Jane Hardres, of St George Parish, was buried in the Martyrdome
1676	April	2	————† Reading, grandchild to Prebend Reading, and apprentice to Mr Canon, Watchmaker
1676	———	—†	Mrs Anslow, of St Elfrids Parish
1676	August	15	Dr Belke, Prebendary of this Church
1676	August	21	Catherine, the Daughter of Mr May, one of the 6 Preachers
1676	February	2	Robert Hale, the Arch-Deacons servant

* Overwritten in the original. † Blank in the original.

Year.	Month.	Day.	Names.
1677	May	23	Elizabeth, ye wife John Cooke, of St Mary, Norgate, was Buryed in Christ Church yard
1677	April*	5	Mr John Trusser, of ye Precincts of Christ Church, was buryed in Chapell Churchyeard
1677	June	16	Daniell, ye Son of Daniel Wood, Vesterer
1677	July	19	Jane, ye Daughter of Mr Thomas Knowler, Alderman of Canterbury, in ye Cloysters
1677	August	12	William, ye Sonn of Thomas Bamfield, Lay Clerk
1677	October	28	Ambrose Bedford, a Beadsman
1677	January	4	Elizabeth, ye Daughter of Mr Thomas Knowler, Alderman of Canterbury
1677	January	22	Sarah, ye Daughter of Peter Screvener
1677	March	21	Mrs Sarah, ye Widd' of Dr Grifith
1678	April	21	Mr ——— Ginder
1678	May	19	Mr William Clappam, marchant, ye son'e of George Clappam, Esqr of Bethemsley, in Yorkshire
1678	June	22	Fothrby, ye Son of Mr Will' Kingsley
1678	July	15	Dr Peter Hardres, Canon of Christ Church
1678	September	5	Margaret, ye wife of William Sanders, of Chislett
1678	September	15	James Burleigh, Soldier
1678	November	1	Mrs Damaris Kinsley, ye Widd' of Arch Deacon Kingsley
1678	November	2	Mr Bartholomew Lamb
1678	January	11	Mr Robert Dalechampe, Curate to Dr De-Moulin, in the Cloysters
1678	January	31	Mrs Elizabeth Brome, Widd', in the Deanes Chappell
1679	July	15	Daniell Picard, an infant, in the Cloysters
1679	August	19	Mr Simon Bayly, one the Six preachers of this Church, in the Boddy of the Church
1679	September	2	Mrs Mary Drayton, widdow, in the body of the Church
1679	September	6	Mrs Lucie Hirst, wife of Mr Martin Hirst, Register of the Arch Bishops Court, in the body of the Church
1679	September	30	Elizabeth Friend, an infant
1679	October	2	Elizabeth Cheesman, A Servant maid
1679	October	12	John Farthing, Jorniman to Mr Sampson
1679	October	14	William, Son of Thomas Banfeildt†
1679	November	27	Elinor Cooke
1679	December	1	James Wicks of ye Bishops palace liberty‡
1679	March	4	George, ye Son of Mr William Kingsley
1679	March	18	James, ye Son of James Pont, of St Andrews Parish
1679	January*	10	Mis: Elizabeth Claver, widdow
1680	April	2	Mr Martin Hirst,§ ye Register, in ye Body of ye Church
1680	May	13	Dr John Bargrave, one of ye Prebendaries of this Church
1680	July	23	Tho: Scrivener, an Infant
1680	August	21	Mr William Jordan, Minor Canon of or Church
1680	August	25	Nicholas Sympson, of Milton, Gentleman
1680	October	19	Wm Paine, an Infant‖
1680	September	21	Mis Clark, in ye Cloyster yard
1680	December	1	Old widow Wicks, of ye Bishops Palace, buried Dec: 1 Her husband exactly a yeer before

* So in the original.

† In the Register of Affidavits of Burials in woollen this entry does not appear, but under the same date is the following: 1679, October 14th Elizabeth Banfield buried in woollen Affidavit brought the 21st.

‡ In the Register of Affidavits he is described as James Bickes, an Almsman of this Church; in the Register of burial the letter B has been overwritten with W.

§ Described in the Register of Affidavits as "the elder."

‖ Interpolated at the foot of a page.

Year.	Month.	Day.	Names.
1680	December	17*	Mrs Kath : Quested, of ye Bishop's Pallace
1680	December	23	Mary, Daughter of Mrs Priscilla Johnson, of the Bishop's Pallace, in the Cloysters
1680	January	7	Charles Hills, an Infant
1680	January	19	Ann, Wife of ye Reverend Dr Pet : De-mouline, one of the Prebendarys of this Church
1680	January	29	Stephen Manou, Servant of Dr De L'Angle
1680	January	29	Joseph Banfield, an Infant
1680	February	4	Merick, Son of Mr John Causabon
1681	April	30	Mr Edmund Burgesse, Minor Canon of this Church
1681	May	26	Mr John Vander Heyden, Minor Canon of this Church, in ye Cloysters
1681	June	28	Elizabeth, the wife of John Carter†
1681	August	12	Frances, the wife of John Bathan
1681	October	14	John, the Son of Mr Basil Drayton, Rector of Little Charte
1681	November	12	Silas, Son of Mr Tho : Johnson, Minor Canon of this Church (Tho : Johnson was Sacrist this year)
1681	January	12	William Nayer, of St Andrew's Parish, in ye Cloyster
1681	February	5	Rebecca, ye daughter of Dr Parker, Archdeacon
1682	June	22	Richard Wall, an Infant
1682	August	8	Anne Jordan, a young Girle
1682	August	20	Charles Hill, an Infant
1682	August	28	Frances Kingsley, daughter‡ of Mr William Kingsley
1682	September	14	Thomas, Son of Mr Tho : Johnson
1682	September	14	Ursula Horsmondon, an Infant
1682	September	19	Doctor Crawforth, D.D., of Northamptonshire
1682	October	1	Edward Jacob
1682	November	5	Dr Herault
1682	November	24	Thomas Jacob, An Infant
1682	January	11	Charles Henry, Earle of Bellomont and Baron of Wotton, was buried on Thursday
1682	January	18	Mary, the wife of Dr Thorpe, one of the Prebendarys of this Church
1682	February	22	Mrs Mary Blechenden
1683	June	26§	Mr William Marsh, in the Cloysters
1683	August	10	Priscilla, the wife of William Kingsley, Esqr, was buried in the passage to the Dean's Chappell
1683	October	11	Mr Inward Ansloe
1683	October	17	William Nayer, an Infant
1683	November	16	Mrs Hudson,‖ widdow, of the Bishop's Pallace
1683	March	6	Willm Pysin, a membr of ye Choire, in ye Cloysters
1684	May	6¶	Ms Ann Drayton, of ye Precincts of this Church, in the body of ye Church
1684	May	28**	Mr ffrances Onslow, of ye parish of St Margaret virgin, in ye Cloyster yard
1684	August	10	Mary Janeway, an infant, in ye Cloyster Yard
1684	September	22	Ham'ond Goatly, of ye Precincts of this Church, in Cloyster yard
1684	October	13	Dr Du-moulin, one of ye Prebendarys of this Ch :
1685	April	6	Thomas, son of Mr Tho : Johnson

* In the Register of Affidavits it is December 14th.
† In the Register of Affidavits described as of the Precincts.
‡ In the Register of Affidavits described as "an Infant."
§ In the Register of Affidavits the date of burial is June 22.
‖ In the Register of Affidavits described as Joanna Hudson.
¶ In the Register of Affidavits it is May 12.
** In the Register of Affidavits it is May 31.

Year.	Month.	Day.	Names.
1685	May	..	The wife of Mr Tho. Best, in the Cloysters
1685	July	15	Mr Robert Knowler, in the Cloysters
1685	July	24	Elizabeth Hammond, in the Cloyster yard
1685	August	6	Margarett, daughter of Mr James Williams, in the Cloysters
1685	August	27	Cavelliero Knowler, son of Mr Robt Knowler, in the Cloysters
1685	September	4	Mrs Frances Walsall, in the Cloyster
1685	October	22	The Wife of Edw Clynch, in Cloysters
1685	December	5	Mary, ye wife of Mr Jonathan Rogers, in ye Cloyster yd*
1685	December	6	Mr Valentine Parker, of St George's parish, in ye body of Xt Church
1685	December	12	Dr John Bradford,† one of ye Prebendaries of ys Ch:
1685	December	22	Mary, ye Daughter of Mr Will' Pizing, in ye Cloysters
1685	February	19	Sarah, ye daughter of Mr Willm Nayer, of Sr Andrew's Parish, in ye Cloysters
1685	March	16	Mr Thoresby Hardresse, in ye sout cross of Xt Church
1686	April	25	Thomas, ye son of Tho: ffriend, in ye Cloyster yard
1686	June	22	Susana Pont, in ye Cloyster yard
1686	August	26	Mrs Bargrave, ye Relict of Dr Bargrave, formerly Pr'b'nd of ys Church, in ye body of ye Church
1686	September	26	Mrs Frances Burges, in ye Cloysters
1686	October	21	Mrs Catherine Stephens, in ye Cloysters
1686	February	1	Sarah Ellis, an Infant, in the Cloyster yard
1687	April	10	Mary Palmer, an Infant, in the Cloyster
1687	August	19	Elizabeth Buckewell, an Infant, in the Cloyster yard
1687	August	30	William Upton, an Infant, in the Cloyster yard
1687	September	13	Mr Robt Palmer, in the Cloyster
			Charles Kilburne, Sachrist
1687	November	30	Mrs Margarett Jordan, relict of Mr William Jordan, late Minor Canon of this Church, in the North Isle of the body of the Church

END OF THE BURIALS IN THE FIRST BOOK.

1687	November	30	Margarett Lamb, widdow‡
1688	February	1	Robert Spratling, gent., in the North Isle of the body of the Church
1688	July	5	Rebecca, the wife of Jonathan Best, one of the Porters of Christ Church, in the Cloysters
1688	August	12	Mary, daughter of James Pout, in the Cloyster yard
1688	August	18	Ann, daughter of Mr Tho: Johnson, Minor Canon of this Church, in the Cloyster
1688	August	19	Ann, daughter of Edward Kibblewhite, in the Cloyster yard
1688	September	7§	Elizabeth, daughter of Edw: Kibblewhite, in the Cloyster yard
1688	October	17	Mary, daughter of Edw: Kibblewhite, in the Cloyster yard

* In the Register of Affidavits is added "bury'd in Linen for wch (ym selves Informing), 2l 10s was paid to ye Treasurerer."

† In the Register of Affidavits it is entered December 13, with the addition of "Wrapt in Searcloth, for whom noe affidavit was or could be brought."

‡ From the Register of Affidavits it is omitted in the Register of Burials.

§ In the Register of Affidavits the date is September 1st.

Year.	Month.	Day.	Names.
1688	October	25	The Reverend John Castilion, D.D., Dean of Rochester, and one of the Prebendarys of this Church
			Tho. Johnson, Sac[t]
1688	December	14	Elizabeth, Daughter of Herbert Randolph, Esq[r], & Mary his wife, in y[e] South Isle of y[e] body of y[e] Church
168$\frac{8}{9}$*	December	31	Tufton, Daughter of y[e] Rev[d] D[r] Jeffryes,† Prebendary of this Church, & Margaret his wife, in y[e] North side of the Church
168$\frac{8}{9}$	January	15	Elizabeth, Daughter of M[r] William Kingsley & Priscilla his wife, in the South-crosse-Isle of the Church
168$\frac{8}{9}$	February	24	M[r] Humphrey Dicas, late of S[t] Margaret's in Canterbury, in y[e] Cloysters
1689	May	17	M[r] John Neesbitt, Lievtenant in Coll. Coliares Regiment, in y[e] South side of y[e] body of y[e] Church
1689	September	6	The Reverend D[r] James Jeffryes, Prebendary of y[e] Church, in y[e] North Cross Isl.
1689	October	11	M[r] John Harrison, in y[e] Cloyster yard
1689	April‡	17	Margaret Nayer, in y[e] Cloyster
1689	October	23	Martha Hayward, in y[e] Cloyster yard
1689	October	30	John Lewsly, Stonecutter, in y[e] Cloyster yard
168$\frac{9}{90}$	January	22	M[r] Peter Smythwick, keeper of y[e] Library of S[t] Peter's College, Westminster, in y[e] Cloysters of this Church
1690	April	13	Mary, y[e] wife of Robert Gilpen (or Tilpen), of S[t] Mildred's Parish, in y[e] Cloysters
1690	April	15	The Lady Hardresse,§ late of S[t] George's Parish in Canterbury, in y[e] South-cross-Isl of y[e] Church
1690	September	16	M[r] Daniel Cuckow, clerk, in the Cloysters
1690	September	21	Elizabeth, y[e] wife of John Elvey, in y[e] Cloysters
1690	August‖	23	John, son of M[r] Robert Scudder, an infant, in y[e] Cloysters
			S. D'Evereux, Sacrist
1690	November	26	Ann Harris,¶ in the Cloyster yard
1691	March	27	Jone** Best, a Porter of this Church, in the Cloysters
1691	April	16	Martha Knowler, of S[t] Andrews Parish, in the Cloysters
1691	June	21	The Lady Rebecca Parker, widdow, within the first Iron Grate in the South Ile
1691	July	14	Richard Harris, Gole Keeper in this Church, in the Cloyster yard
1691	July	30	John, Sone of Herbert Randolph, Esq[r], in the Body of the Church
1691	August	19	——†† Daughter of Maurice and Susanna Horner, in the Cloyster yard
1691	September	28	M[r] Robet Wren,‡‡ Organist of this Church, in the Cloyster
1691	October	21	Elizbeth Cumberland, widdow, in the Cloyster yard
1691	October	24	James Williams, formerly Upholsterer in this Church, in the Cloyster
			Charles Kilburne, Sachrist

* So in the original.
† In the Register of Affidavits described as Dr. James Jeffryes.
‡ At the foot of the page, evidently omitted from its proper place.
§ In the Register of Affidavits described as Dame Philadelphia Hardres.
‖ So in the original.
¶ In the original the name is overwritten, but in the Register of Affidavits she is described as Ann, y[e] wife of Richard Harrison.
** In the original this name has also been overwritten, but in the Register of Affidavits it is entered as Jonathan Best.
†† In the Register of Affidavits the entry is "Susan Horner."
‡‡ In the Register of Affidavits d scribed as Robert Wrenn.

Year.	Month.	Day.	Names.
1691	December	20	James,* Son of Mr Charles Dodd, in the Cloyster yard
1691	†January	14	Sammuell Brewster, in the Body of the Church
1691	†January	22	Herbert, Son of Herbert Randolph, Esqr, in the South Isle of the Body of this Church
1691	†March	5	Mary Gold, in the Cloyster Yard
1692	May	4	Peter, Son of Peter Trouillart, Clerke, agd 17 days, in the Cloyster yard
1692	August	4	Jacob, the son of William Eaton, in the Cloysters
1692	August	10	Danniell, Son of Peter Troüillart, in ye Cloyster yard
1692	August	29	Thomas, Son of Robert Buckwell, in ye Cloyster yard
1692	September	4	Ann, daughter of Robert Buckwell, in ye Cloyster yard
1692	November	20	St John Goard, Porter of the fore Gate of this Church, in the Cloyster
			Tho: Johnson, Sacrist
1692	November	26	Margaret, the Daughter of Herbert Randolph, Esq., and Mary his wife, in the South Isle of the Body of the Church
1692	January	15	Thomas Banfeild, a Singing man of this Church, in the Cloyster
1692	February	19	Mr John Causabon, in the South Crosse Ile of the Church
1693	March	26	Mary Paine, of St Andrew's Parish, in the Cloyster yard
1693	June	7	Margaret Buckwell, an Infant, in the Cloyster yard
1693	June	13	Susan: Waddell, in the Cloyster yard
1693	July‡	25	Catherine, the daughter of Dr Aucher, Prebendarie of this Church, in the Body of the Church
1693	August	24	George Renn,§ an Infant, in the Cloyster
1693	August	29	Matthew Johnson, in the Cloyster yard
1693	September	7	Mr James Craford,‖ Leuent, in the Cloyster
1693	September	28	Susan Horner, in the Cloyster yard
1693	October	24	Ms Sarah Edwardes,¶ in the Body of the Church
1623	October	28	Joh Hull, in the Cloyster yard
1693	November	15	Ann Janeway, an Infant, in the Cloyster yard
			Charles Kilburne, Sacrist
1693	December	2	Anne, Daughter Mr Anthony Belk & Elizabeth his wife, in the body of ye Church
1693	January	11	Mr Isaac Jordan, in the Cloyster yard
1693	February	5	Mary, ye Daughter of Daniel White, Esqr, & Anne his wife, in ye body of ye Church
1693	February	6	John Carter, Choir-man of this Church, in ye Cloyster yard
1693	February	16	William Urmeston, ye son of Thomas Urmeston, of London, in y Cloysters
1693	February	21	Peter, Son of Peter Troüillart, and Susanna his wife, in ye Cloister yard
1694	September	6	Jane, ye wife of Thomas Knowler, Alderman of Canterbury, in ye Cloysters
			S. D'Evereux, Sacrist
1694	December	20	Rebecca Spracling, daughter of Mr Adam Sprackling, in the North Isle of the Body of the Church

* This entry has been overwritten, and James is probably an error; in the Register of Affidavits the entry is John, the son of Charles Dodd.

† Overwritten in the original.

‡ In the Register of Affidavits the date of Burial is June 25th; the affidavit was brought July 13th.

§ In the Register of Affidavits spelt Wren.

‖ In the Register of Affidavits spelt "*Crayford*."

¶ She was buried "in lining pd 50s to the poore of the Church."

Year.	Month.	Day.	Names.
1694	December	30	Robert, Son of Daniell Wood, in the Cloysters
1695	April	30	Charles Pont, an Infant
1695	May	18	Ann Impitt, widdow, in the Cloyster yard
1695	August	8	George Knowler, in the Cloysters
			Tho: Johnson, Sacrist
1696	April	4	Mrs Sarah Cooke, Widdow, in ye Cloyster Yard
1696	April	8	Mary Wemsted, in ye Cloyster Yard
1696	June	5	Robert Pain, in ye Cloyster yard
1696	September	18	Edward, Son of Edward Burges, in ye Cloysters
1696	September	22	Mr —— Du Faij, in ye Cloyster yard
1696	November	13	Vincent, Son of Vincent & Ann Lad, in ye Cloyster yard
			R. Cumberland, Sacrist
1696	December	8	William, the Sone of Ms Mary Eaton, Widdow, in the Cloyster
1696	December	16	Thomas, Sone of Mrs Mary Eaton, Widdow, in the Cloyster
1696	January	30	Rebecca, daughter of Morrice and Susan* Horner, in the Cloyster yard
1696	February	17	Mary, the wife of Edw Burges, in the Cloyster
1696	March	24	Ann, the daughter of Herbert Randolph, Esqr, in the South Isle of the Body of this Church
1697	April	16	Ms Elizabeth Randolph, Widdow, in the South Isle of the Body of this Church†
1697	May	14	Richard Pembrook, in the Cloyster yard
1697	May	26	Robert Carlesse, Porter of this Church, in the Cloyster of Christ Church
1697	July	7‡	Jane, the Daughter of Mr Alderman Knowler, in the Cloyster of Christ Church
1697	August	18	Elizabeth, the Wife of Mr Wil: Shottwater, in the Cloyster of Christ Church of Canterb:
1697	October	6	Mary Ann Missabinn,§ in the Cloyster yard of Cht Church
1697	October	29	Margaret, the Daughter of Mr Gilbert Burough‖ and Margt his wife, in the North isle of the Church, near the Font
1697	November	1	Susan: Carde, in the Cloyster of Chrt Church, Cant:
1697	November	17	¶Christopher Drayton, one of the Singing men of Ch: Church, in the Cloyster
			Ch: Kilburne, Sacrist
1697	November	29	Priscilla Quested, in the Cloyster yard
1697	January	7	Margarett, Daughter of Mr Wm Nayer, in the Cloyster
1697	January	20	Katherine, wife of Mr Wm Bettys, in the Cloyster
1697	January	20	Anthony Belke,** Auditor of this Church, in the South Ile of the body
1697	January	31	Mary, wife of Herbert Randolph, Esqr, in the South Crosse
1697	January	22††	Mrs Elizabeth Courthop, widdow, in the South Ile of the body of the Church
1697	February	3	Dorothy, daughter of Herbert Randolph, Esqr, in the graue with her mother
1697	March	16	Sarah‡‡ Drayton, widdow, in the Cloyster

* In the Register of Affidavits "Susannah."

† She was *not* buried in woollen.

‡ In the Register of Affidavits July 14, but probably an error, as the affidavit was produced the same day.

§ In the Register of Affidavits spelt "Missawbin."

‖ In the Register of Affidavits spelt "Buroughs."

¶ Overwritten in the original.

** In the Register of Affidavits styled "Mr."

†† So in the original.

‡‡ In the Register of Affidavits "Mary Drayton."

Year.	Month.	Day.	Names.
1698	April	6	William, Son of M[r] William Nayer, in the Cloyster
1698	April	14	M[rs] Catherine Belke, in the South Ile of the body of the Church
1698	May	26	Mary Gerant, in the Cloyster yard
1698	July	14	John, Son of M[r] Jacob Janneway, in the Cloyster Yard
1698	September	15	Mary, daughter of Morris Horner, in the Cloyster yard
1698	October	3	Ann Dodd, Servant to the Dean, in the Cloyster yard
			Tho: Johnson, Sacrist
1698	December	20	Mary, wife of Robert Buckwell, in y[e] Cloyster yard
1698	January	27	Thomas, son of M[r] Gilbert Burroughs & Margaret his wife, in y[e] North Isle of y[e] Body of y[e] Church
1698	February	15	Mary, Daughter of Charles Beeson, in y[e] Cloyster yard
1698	March	3	Thomas Irons, in y[e] Cloyster
1699	March	26	Robert Wild, in y[e] Cloyster
1699	April	7	Elizabeth Peroe, in y[e] Cloyster Yard
1699	June	5	Francis, son of y[e] Reverend D[r] Isham, one of y[e] Prebendaryes of this Church, in y[e] North Crosse Isle*
1699	July	4	Frances, wife of John Trepsack, Clerke, in y[e] North Isle of y[e] body of y[e] Church
1699	November	19	Christopher Goatly, in y[e] Cloyster yard
			Rob: Cumberland, Sacrist
1699	February	29†	James Famouts,‡ a French Gentleman, in y[e] Cloyster yard
1699	February	29†	Robert Horner, an infant, in y[e] Cloyster yard
1699	March	7	M[r] Edward Vaughan,§ in y[e] South Cross Isl of y[e] Church
1700	March	30	Catharine Burrough, an infant, in y[e] body of y[e] Church
1700	April	10	Susan Horner, an infant, in the Cloyster yard
1700	April	19	M[r] Nicholas Wootton, late Organist of this Church, in y[e] body of it
1700	May	1	Elizabeth Friend, in the Cloyster yard
1700	June	23	James Pount, one of y[e] town Serjeants, in y[e] cloyster yard
1700	July	2	Elizabeth Nethersole, in the cloyster yard
1700	July	18	John, son of George Knowler, in y[e] cloysters
1700	July	19	Thomas Stokes, an infant, in y[e] cloyster yard
1700	August	7	Elizabeth, wife of James Wishart, in y[e] cloyster yard
1700	September	1	Jacob Buckwell, in the cloyster yard
1700	September	1	Ann Lowe, an infant, in the cloyster yard
1700	September	27	M[r] Thomas Atkyn, Master of the King's Schole within y[e] Precincts of this Church, in y[e] body of y[e] same
1700	October	14	The Reverend M[r] John Clark, in y[e] North cross Isl of y[e] Church
			S. D'Evereux, Sacrist
1700	December	8	Sarah Ekins, a servant, in y[e] Cloyster yard
1700	January	24	Mary, Daughter of y[e] Widdow Pout, in y[e] Cloyster yard
1700	March	15	The Reverend D[r] John Aucher, one of y[e] Prebendaries of this Church, in y[e] North Isle of y[e] Body of it
1701	April	1	William Kingsley, Esq[r], in y[e] South Crosse Isle
1701	July	2	Elizabeth Cartault, in y[e] Cloyster yard
1701	July	16	M[r] Peter Bossatran, in y[e] Cloyster yard
1701	September	6	M[r] William Belke, in y[e] South Isle of y[e] body of y[e] Church
			Robert Cumberland, Sac[st]

* Not entered in the Register of Affidavits.
† So in the original.
‡ In the Register of Affidavits spelt "Famouse."
§ In the Register of Affidavits is added, "brought from beyond seas, wrapp'd in sear cloth, & putt in a leaden coffin, was buried, but no affidavit brought."

Year.	Month.	Day.	Names.
1701	December	19	Thomas Curteis, a Tayler, in the Cloyster yard
1701	December	23	Ms Elizb Belke, the wid: of the Reverd Dr Belke, one of the Prebendaries of this Church, in the South Ile
1701	January	1	Mary Lewsley, wid: in the Cloyster yard
1701	January	18	Capt John Hunt, of the Bishop's Palace, in the North Ile of the body of Christ Church
1701	February	1	Charles Beeson, Golekeeper, in the Cloyster yard
1701	March	22	John Wodwell, one of the Porters of this Church, in the Cloyster yard
1702	March	29	Ms Elizabeth Dods-worth, in the North Ile of the Body of the Church
1702	March	29	William, Son of William Stokes, in the Cloyster yard
1702	April	13	Ms Margarit Geraud, in the Cloystery yard
1702	April	20	Elizabeth, daughter of John Mahew, Porter of this Church, in the Cloyster
1702	June	22	John Moore, Coachman to Dr Belke, in the Cloyster yard
1702	June	25	John Martyn, Coachman to Dean Hooper, in the Cloyster
1702	July	23	George, sone of Herbert Randolph, Esqr, in the South Ile of Christ Church
1702	September	17	Ms Aphra Reynals,* in the Cloyster
1702	October	14	Ellen Harris, in the Cloyster yard
1702	October	15	Mr George Hale, in the Cloyster
			Charles Kilburne, Sacrist
1703	April	18	Mr William Nayers,† in the Cloyster
1703	May	26	Patience Bix, widdow, in the Cloyster
1703	August‡	7	Mrs D'Prez, in the South Ile of the body of this Church
			Tho: Johnson, Sacrist
1703	February	9	William, Son of John Mahew, in the Cloyster of Xst Church
1704	April	2	Mr Nicholas Hunt, in the North Ile of the Body of this Church
1704	May	14	Mary Allen, in the Cloyster yard
1704	June	24	Elizabeth Horner, an Infant, in the Cloyster yard
1704	August	29	Priscilla, daughter of Mr Thomas & Ann Johnson, in the Cloyster§
1704	September	13	Elizabeth, daughtr of Elizabeth Belke, widow, in the South Ile of the Body of the Church
1704	November	21	Mr Tho: Knowler, in the Cloysters
1704	November	24	Mrs Judith Hunt, in the North Ile of the body of this Church
			James Henstridge, Sacrist
1704	January	14	Hannah, Daughter of Robert Buckwell, in ye Cloyster yard
1705	April	3	Mr Thomas Knowler, late Alderman of ye citty, in ye Cloysters
1705	August	22	Ursula Langham, Widdow, of St Margaret's, Cant: in ye Cloysters
			Robert Cumberland, Sacrist
1705	November	30	Mrs Sarah Nayers, Widd', in the Cloysters
1705	December	14	Robert, son of Vincent Ladd & Ann his wife, in ye Cloyster yard‖

* In the Register of Affidavits spelt "Renalls."
† In the Register of Affidavits spelt "Nayer," and described as a "Goldsmith."
‡ In the Register of Affidavits it is entered October 7.
§ Not entered in the Register of Affidavits.
‖ Not entered in the Register of Affidavits.

Year.	Month.	Day.	Names.
1706	April	2	M^{s} Rebecca Sprakling, in the North Isle of the Body of this Church
1706	April	24	Mildred Banfeild, of St Alphage, Cant: Widow, in the Cloysters
1706	April	25	Margaret Horner, an Infant, in the Cloyster yard
1706	April	27	Robert Buckwell, in the Cloyster yard
1706	June	4	Mrs Birmie, Widow, in the Cloyster yard*
1706	August	5	Elizabeth Randolph, an Infant, in the South Isle of ye body of the Church†
1706	October	24	Mrs Cotton, in the Cloysters
1706	November	1	John Pinger, in the Cloyster Yard
			James Henstridge, Sacrist
1707	April	17	Wm Piseing, one of the Singing men of this Church, in the Cloyster
1707	April	24	Mary, the daught. of Mr Thomas Bean and Auis his wife, in the Cloysters
1707	October	28	Mary, the Daughter of John Mayhew and Elizab: his wife, in the Cloyster
1707	October	31	Judeth, the Daughter of Herbert Randolph, Esqr, and Grace his wife, in the North Ile of Ch^{t} Church
1707	November	24	M^{s} Elizabeth Bookey, Wid., in the Cloyster of Christ Church, Cant.
			Ch. Kilburne, Sacrist
1708	September	12	Morris Horner, in the Cloyster yard
1708	October	14	The Reverend John Battely, D.D., Arch-Deacon of the Diocesse of Canterbury, and one of the Prebendarys of this Church
1708	October	15	Margarett, Daughter of John Mahew, in the Cloyster
1708	November	8	Mrs Priscilla Johnson, Widdow, in the back Cloyster
			Tho: Johnson, Sacrist
1708	December	23	M^{rs} ffransse Murgeuse,‡ in ye Cloyster yard
1708	January	5	Charles Dodd, one of ye Vesterers of this Church, in ye Cloyster yard
1708	February	25	Mrs Ann Knowler, of St Andrew's, Cant:, in ye Cloysters
1708	March	16	Mr Peter Nowell, in ye North Isle of ye Body of X^{t} Church
1708	March	23	Mrs Sarah Knowler, in ye Cloyster
1709	May	11	Widow Oxenbridge, in the Cloyster yard§
1709	September	7	Ann Ladd, an Infant, in the Cloyster yard
			Ja. Henstridge, Sa^{t}
1709	February	9	Martha, Daughter of John Mahew, in ye Cloysters
1709	February	23	William Bryan, of East Bridge Hospital, in ye Cloyster yard
1710	April	2	Joseph, Son of John Pysing, in ye Cloysters
1710	May	27	Peter Horner, in ye Cloyster yard
1710	June	14	Charlotte, Daughter of ye Revd Dr Thomas Green, Prebendary of this Church and Arch Deacon, in ye North Isle of ye Body of ye Church
1710	September	17	Ann, Daughter of Robert Lowe, in ye Cloyster yard
1710	October	25	Elizabeth, Daughter of Robert Lowe, in ye Cloyster yard
1710	November	2	Thomas Fotherby, Gent: in ye North Crosse Isle
			Rob: Cumberland, Sacrist
1710	January	4	Sarah Pedenden, in the Cloyster yard

* In the original this entry is overwritten; it is not entered in the Register of Affidavits.

† Not entered in the Register of Affidavits.

‡ In the Register of Affidavits spelt "Murgote."

§ In the Register of Affidavits is added, "no affidavit brought, this certifyed to ye Chapt^{r} May ye 30th."

Year.	Month.	Day.	Names.
1710	January	10	Mary Jordan, wid., in the Cloysters
1710	February	1	Thomas, son of John Friend, in the Cloyster yard
1711	March	25	Charles, Sone of Uincent Lad, in the Cloyster yard
1711	April	11	Ann, the wife of Mr Thomas Johnson, Minor Canon of this Church, in the Cloyster
1711	August	28	Henry, Son of Henry Rigden and . . . ., in the Cloyster yard
1711	October	15	M^{s} Jane Arnaud, in the Cloysters
1711	October	21	Joseph, Son of John Piseing, in the Cloyster
			Ch: Kilburne, Sacrist
1711	November	29	Thomas Nowell, Gent: in the North Isle of the body of the Church
1711	January	15	John Kibblewhite, in the Cloyster yard
1711	February	7	Margarett, wife of Mr Gilbert Burroughs, in the North Isle of the body of the Church
1711	February	24	The Lady Anne* Head, in the lower South Crosse neer the steps of the Door
1711	March	20	Mrs Frances Best, in the Cloyster yard
1712	April	8	Peter Scriuener, in the Cloyster yard
1712	July	22	Peter Lemastre† from the Arch Bishop's pallace, in the Cloyster yard
1712	September	11	The Lady Montague, in the Martyrdome‡
1712	September	20	The Revd Dr Belke, one of the Prebendarys of this Church, in the South Crosse
1712	October	9	The Honble Francis Godfrey, Esq,§ in St Michael's Chappell within this Church
			Tho. Johnson, Sacrist
1712	December	7	The Widow Pysing, in ye Cloysters
1712	January	14	The Wife of Mr Chirpenter,‖ in ye Cloysters
1713	April	30	Ann, Daught: of John Pysing, in ye Cloysters
1713	June	16	Ann Horner, in the Cloyster Yard
1713	September	6	The widow Pont, in ye Cloyster yard
1713	November	8	Bennet, Daught^{r} of John Pysing, in ye Cloysters
			Ja: Henstridge, Sacrist
1713	December	17	Elizabeth, wife of Edward Kibblewhite, in ye Cloyster yard
1713	January	26	Mr Gregory Knowler, (Alderman of ye City), in ye Cloysters
1714	April	1	Elizabeth, Daughter of John Brice, in ye Cloyster yard
1714	May	6	Mary Bryan, of Eastbridge Hospitall, in ye Cloyster yard
1714	May	23	William Baker, of All Saints, Cant: in ye Cloyster yard
1714	October	25	Mrs Mary De La Serpaudrie, Widow, in ye Cloysters
			Robt Cumberland, Sacrist
1714	December	21	The Widow Austin, in the Cloysters
1714	December	29	M^{s} Ann Mills, eldest daughter of Samuell Mills, Esqr, in St Michael's Chappell in the South Ile
1714	January	24	Mary, Daughter of the Revd Dr Thomas Green, Prebendary of this Church and Arch-Deacon, in the North Isle of the Body of the Church

* In the original the entry has been The Lady Damaris Head, but Damaris has been crossed out and Anne written over it.

† In the Register of Affidavits spelt "Lematre."

‡ In the Register of Affidavits is added, "was upon information buried in a velvett coffin, and for wch fifty shillings was paid to the poor of this church."

§ In the Register of Affidavits is added, "was upon affidavit buried in linnen and fiue pound p^{d} to the poor, according to the Act of Parliament in that case prouided."

‖ In the Register of Affidavits described as "Francess Carpenter."

Year.	Month.	Day.	Names.
1714	February	1	George, Son of John Piseing, in the Cloysters
1715	April	21*	Ms Henstrige, the wife of Mr Henstrige, organist of this Church, in the South Ile of the Body of the Church
1715	May	31	Thomas Clarke, one of the Bellringers of this Church, aged 80 yeares, in the Cloyster yard
1715	June	14	William, Son of William Smithson, an Infant, in the Cloyster yard
1715	July	16	(Thomas†) Pope, in the Cloyster yard
1715	August	29	The Reuerend Dr James Depree, in the body of the Church
1715	September	15	Mr Lardo, a frenchman, in the Cloyster
1715	October	22	Daniel Wood, one of the Uesterers of this Church, Aged Eighty fower yeares, in the Cloyster
1715	November	20	Widdow Scriuener
			Ch: Kilburne, Sacrist
1715	December	11	Mrs Marquevel, widdow
1715	December	22	Mrs Homersham, widdow
1715	January	2	Mr William Johnson, Proctor in the Arch Bishop's Court, in the Cloyster
1716	April	7	Mr Robert Wrentmore, at the upper end of the North Cloyster
1716	April	13	Hester, Daughter of Mrs Knowler, wid: in the Cloyster
1716	August	25	Margarett Castillion, Relict of the Revd Dr Castillion, late Dean of Rochester and Prebendary of this Church, in the South Crosse
1716	November	16	Susanna, daughter of Mrs Knowler, wid: in the Cloyster
			Tho: Johnson, Sacrist
1716	December	30	Nathaniel Hering, Esqr, in ye body near ye South Isle of this Church‡
1717	April	28	James Bodar, a ffrenchman, in ye Cloyster Yard
1717	May	30	Thomas ffriend, in the Cloyster yard
			Jam: Henstridge, Sacrist
1717	December	31	Elizabeth Wood, widow, in ye Cloysters
1717	January	13	Thomas Battely, Gent: in ye Body of ye Church
1717	January	19	Edward Kibblewhite, one of ye Vergerers, in ye Cloyster yard
1717	February	7	The Reverend Mr John Smith, Master of ye King's School, in ye Body of the Church
1717	March	8	The Reverend Mr George Wren, Minou Canon of Rochester, in ye Cloysters
1718	May	12	Lancelot, Son of Samuel Head, in ye Cloyster yard
1718	May	28	Thomas, Son of John Brice, in ye Cloyster yard
1718	June	12	John Pattinoe, in ye Cloyster yard
1718	October	6	Jonathan Horner, in ye Cloyster yard
1718	October	11	Mrs Ann De Pres, in ye South Isle of ye Body of ye Church
			Rob' Cumberland, Sacrist
1718	March	14	John, Son of Samuel Head, in the Cloyster yard
1719	May	4	Mr Le Cassel, in the South Ile in the Body of the Church
1719	June	24	Ann, daughter of John Pising, in the Cloyster
1719	July	13	Thomas, Son of The Reuerend Dr Rolph Blomer, Prebendary of this Church, in the Body of the Church
1719	July	19	John, Son of John Friend, in the Cloyster yard
1719	September	4	Mr Jacob Janeway, in the Cloyster yard

* In the Register of Affidavits the date is entered April 2, and the affidavit brought April 10.

† In the original there is a blank for the Christian name and Thomas has been written in pencil. In the Register of Affidavits the entry has been overwritten "Wm." Query if correct?

‡ Not entered in the Register of Affidavits.

Year.	Month.	Day.	Names.
1719	October	4*	Anna Maria Philpott, in the Cloyster yard
			Ch: Kilburne, Sacrist
1719	November	28	The Reverend & Hospitable George Thorp, D.D., and one of the Prebendarys of this Church, in the South Crosse
1719	January†	13	Mary, wife of Dudly Soan, in the Back Cloyster
1720	April	20	Mrs Francis (?) Gotier, in the Cloyster yard
1720	April	26	James Wood, in the back Cloyster
1720	July	17	Ann, wife of Vincent Ladd, in the Cloyster yard
1720	July	21	Mary, daughter of Vincent Ladd, in the Cloyster yard
1720	August	4	Œlizab: Wife the Revd Mr Bushnell, Clerke, in the North Cloyster
1720	August	17	John Alban, in the Cloyster yard
1720	November	2	Edward Tadd, an Infant, in the Cloyster yard
1720	December	10	The Reverend Dr Turner,‡ on of ye Prebendarys, in ye North Isle of ye body of this Church
1720	February	18	Francess, ye daughter of ye Revd Mr Richard Marsh, Vicar of St Marg^{ts} Clift, in ye Cloysters
1720	March	2	John, ye Son of Robert Lowe, in ye Cloyster yard
1720	March	2	Susanna, ye daughter of Mrs Frances Titus, in ye Cloyster yard
1721	April	4	Mr Henry Noakes,§ Student of Xst Church in Oxford, in ye Cloysters
1721	April	11	Henry Moon, a Prisoner in ye Church Goal, in ye Cloyster yard
1721	April	15	Jacob, ye Son of Mr John Hudson, in ye Cloyster yard
1721	June	14	Mary, ye Daughter of Stephen Philpott, in ye Cloyster yard
1721	June	16	Elizabeth, ye Daughter of George Friend, in ye Cloyster yard
1721	July	7	Mary Knott, in the Cloyster yard
1721	July	16	Mrs Mary Hunt, in ye North Isle of ye body of Xst Church
1721	July	25‖	Anthony Peyden (or Pegden), in ye Cloysters
1721	August	13‖	Ellen, the wife of Henry Smith, & a Sister of St John's Hospital, in ye Cloyster Yard
1721	August	28	Sarah Steward, in ye Cloyster Yard
1721	September	15	Mr Thomas Nayers, of St Andrew, Cant: in ye Cloysters
1721	September	23	Mrs Sardeau (?), a french woman, in ye Cloysters
1721	November	24	The Reverend Charles Elstob, D.D., & one of ye Prebendarys of this Church, in North Crosse Isle
			Ja: Henstridge, Sacrist
1721	November	28	Mary Green, in ye Cloyster Yard
1721	January	6	Sarah Vorrall, in ye Cloyster Yard
1721	January	31	Ann Pattinoe, widow, in ye Cloyster Yard
1721	February	25	Joyce, ye wife of John Sherwood, in the Cloyster Yard
1721	March	12	Elizabeth, Daughter of Sr William Boys, Knight, in ye Body of ye Church
1722	July	24	Susanna Burges, in ye Cloysters
1722	August	31	Squire, Son of John Pysing, in ye Cloysters
1722	October	21	Henry Knowler, Gent: in ye Cloysters
			Rob': Cumberland, Sacrist

* In the original the figure 4 has been overwritten with the figure 9; it is clearly an error, as in the Register of Affidavits it is entered under October 4th.

† In the Register of Affidavits the date of burial is February 13.

‡ In the Register of Affidavits described as Dr. John Turner.

§ In the Register of Affidavits described as Mr. Henry Noakes, gent.

‖ Overwritten in the original.

Year.	Month.	Day.	Names.
1723	August	18	Robert de Noon, Infant
1723	August	30	Elizabeth, daughter of James & Elizabeth Turner
1723	September	21	Mrs Margaret Jeffries, Widow, in the North Cross Ile
1723	September	22	Margaret, daughter of George Friend & Elizabeth his wife, in ye Cloyster yard
			John Gostling, Sacrist
1723	November	28	Mr William Nayer, in ye Cloyster
1723	December	20	Hannah Green-Court, in ye Cloyster Yard
1723	February	8	Elizabeth Emes, in the Cloyster Yard
1723	February	9	Mr Humphrey Nayer, in the Cloister
1724	April	5	Mr Jacob Janeway, in the Cloyster Yard
1724	June	19	Mrs Catharine Bossatran, in the Cloyster Yard
1724	August	4	Mr John Cotton, Rectr of Swalecliff, in the Cloyster
1724	August	4	John Ladd, in the Cloyster Yard
1724	October	5	Mrs Ann Barrett, in the Body of the Church
			Simn D'Evereux, Sacrist
1724	March	14	*Thomas Atwell, one of the Bellringers of this Church, in the Cloyster, Aged 86 years
1725	April	7	Frances the wife of the Revd Dr Holcomb, in the South Ile
1725	July	9	Mr John Cotton, Son of Mr John Cotton, Rect of Swalecliff, in the Cloyster
1725	September	8	John, Son of Herbert Randolph, Esqr, in the South Isle of the body of the Church
1725	October	3	Mr Fletcher, Wine Marchant, in the Cloyster
1725	November	20	Mrs Jane, daughter of Herbert Randolph, Esqr, in the South Isle of the Body of the Church, in her brother's graue
			Ch: Kilburne, Sacrist
1725	November	29	† . . . Clark, Widdow, in the Cloyster yard
1725	December	17	† . . . Mills, Widdow, in the North Cloyster
1725	February	6	Mrs Dodd, Widdow, in the Cloyster Yard
1725	February	6	The wife of John Crispe, of All Saints, in the Cloyster yard
1725	March	19	Herbert Randolph, Esqr, late Recorder of the Neighbouring City, in the South Isle of the body of Christ Church
1726	April	1	Sarah, relict of the Revd Dr John Turner, late Prebendary of this Church, in the North Isle of the body in her husband's Graue
1726	May	25	Ann, daughter of William Gostling, Clerk, in the West Cloyster
1726	June	2	Mr Julines Herring, in his ffather's graue, in the Body of Christ Church
			Tho: Johnson, Sacrist
1726	December	6	Bennett, wife of John Pysing, in the Cloysters
1726	January	11	Dorothy, Daughter of the Revd Dr Edward Tenison, Prebendary of this Church, in the body of the Church
1726	February	11	Sophia, Daughter of the Revd Dr Edward Tenison, Prebendary of this Church, in the Body of the Church
1727	August	19	Matilda, Daughter of Mr Tho. Hill, in the body of ye Church
1727	October	12	Mr John Chirpenter, Minister of ye ffrench Congregation, in ye Cloysters
1727	October	15	John, the Son of John Mahew, in ye Cloysters

* Overwritten in the original.

† In the original both these entries have a blank space preceding the names, but in the Register of Affidavits they are described "Mrs."

Year.	Month.	Day.	Names.
1727	November	11	Mr Thomas Johnson, one of the Minor Canons of this Church, in ye Cloysters
1727	November	23	Ann Margarett, Daughter of Mr William Gosling, in ye Cloysters
1727	January	10	Mary, Daughter of Michael Ladd, in ye Cloyster Yard
1727	January	22	Adam Sprakeling, Gent., in ye Body of ye Church
1727	February	22	Cranmer Herris, Gent., in ye Cloysters
1727	March	21	Margaret Friend, Widow, in ye Cloyster Yard
1728	May	19	James, son of James Turner, in ye Cloyster Yard
1728	June	18	Elizabeth Fletcher,* Widow, in ye Cloysters
1728	August	16	William, son of ye Revd Mr William Gostling, in ye Cloysters
1728	November	20	Sarah de Cassel, widow, in ye Body of ye Church
			Rob' Cumberland, Sacrist
1728	January	2	Edward Kibblewhite,† in the Cloyster Yard
1728	January	14	Robert Wood,‡ in the Cloysters
1729	April	14	Ralph,§ son of the Revnd Ralph Blomer, Prebendary of this Church, in the Body of the Church
1729	April	15	Elizabeth, Wife of Michael Lade, in ye Cloyster Yard
1729	April	18	John Dolly, Bell-Ringer of ye Church, in ye Cloyster Yard
1729	April	30	John, Son of Thomas Rowse, in ye Cloyster
1729	May	27	Thomas, Son of the Revnd Mr Willm Gostling, in the Cloysters
1729	June	8	Ann, daughter of John Pysin ye Elder, in the Cloysters
1729	July	3	Margaret, daughter of George Friend, in ye Cloyster Yard
1729	July	9	Elizabeth, Wife of the Revnd Mr John L'Hunt, Master of the King's School, in ye Body of the Church
1729	July	10	Thomas, son of George Friend, in the Cloyster Yard
1729	July	29	Thomas Lade, from Burgate, in the Cloyster Yard
1729	July	31	Edward, son of Edward Keet, Vesterer of the Church, in ye Cloyster Yard
1729	August	7	James, son of John Pysin, Junr, in the Cloysters
1729	August	21	John,‖ son of Roger Kenett, of Feversham, in the Cloysters
1729	August	28	Parry, son of John Pysin ye elder, in the Cloysters
1729	October	14	Sarah, Wife of John Brice, of the A. Bishop's Palace, in ye Cloyster Yard
1729	November	19	Susan Horner, Widow, in the Cloyster Yard
			S: D'Evereux, Sacrist
1730	March	27	Vincent Lade, from Burgate, in the Cloyster Yard
1730	April	5	Elisabeth Wren, in the Cloyster Yard
1730	April	17	Elisabeth, daughter of Michael Lade, of Burgate, in the Cloyster Yard
1730	May	10	Mary, the Wife of Henry Rigden, in ye Cloyster Yard
1730	May	22	Ann Wren, Widow, in the Cloyster Yard
1730	June	28	Abraham, Son of Abraham Maynar,¶ of the burrough of Staplegate, in the Cloyster Yard
1730	July	8	Edward, Son of Stephen Philpot, in the Cloyster Yard
1730	July	19	Elisabeth, the wife of John Mayhew, in the Cloyster
			William Gostling, Sacrist
1730	December	23	Martha, Wife of Edward Burges, in ye Cloysters
1730	January	29	**Mrs Badenhope, a frenchwoman, in ye Cloyster Yard

* In the Register of Affidavits described as Mrs Elizabeth Fletcher.
† In the Register of Affidavits described as Virgerer of this Church.
‡ In the Register of Affidavits described as Mr Robert Wood.
§ In the Register of Affidavits described as Mr Ralph Blomer.
‖ In the Register of Affidavits described as John Kennett, Gent.
¶ In the Register of Affidavits spelt Maynard.
** Overwritten in the original.

Year.	Month.	Day.	Names.
1730	February	19	Mrs Dorothy Nixon, relict of Dr Thomas Nixon, formerly Prebendary of this Church, in ye South Isle of ye body of this Church
1730	February	21	George Smith, a Servant to the Rev Dr Tenison,* in ye Cloyster Yard
1730	February	23	Mrs †Knowler, Widow, in the Cloyster
1731	April	24	Mrs Lyttleton,‡ Daughter of ye Revd Dr Edward Tenison, one of ye prebendarys of this Church, in ye body of ye Church
1731	May	21	Mrs Janaway,§ Widow, in ye Cloyster Yard
1731	June	14	Mrs Taylor, a Gentlewoman from St Stephen's, in the Body of ye Church
1731	June	27	Dudley Soane, from St Alphage, in ye Cloysters
1731	July	9	John Webster, a Servant of ye Revd Dr Lisle, one of ye Prebendarys & Arch Deacon, in ye Cloyster Yard
1731	August	23	Millesent Johnson, from St Andrew's, Cant: in ye Cloysters
1731	September	5	Margarett, daughter of George Frend, in ye Cloyster Yard
1731	November	12	Mrs Damaris Smith, Widow, from St Peter's, Cant., in ye body of ye Church
			James Henstridge, Sacrist
1731	March	8	Mr Jeremiah Harteup, in ye Body of ye Church
1732	April	6	The Revd Dr Ralph Blomer, Prebendary of this Church, in ye Body of ye Church
1732	April	30	Mrs Esther Susanna Demondesir, in ye Cloyster Yard
1732	June	26	William, son of ye Revd Dr Thomas Gooch, in ye South Cross Isl
1732	September	19	Thomas, Son of John Phillmore, in ye Cloyster Yard
1732	November	11	The Revd Dr Edward Wake, Prebendary of this Church, in the South Cross Isl
			Rob' Cumberland, Sacrist
1732	January	5	Catherine Simpon (an Infant), in ye Body of ye Church
1732	January	16	Ann Pembroke (Widow), in ye Cloystor Yard
1732	January	31	Mrs Mary Knowler (Widow), in ye Cloysters
1732	March	14	William, son of ye Revd Dr Egerton, Prebendary of this Church, in ye South Cross Isle of ye Church
1732	March	18	Elizabeth, Wife of James Webb, in ye Cloyster Yard
1733	April	1	Mrs Judith Hunt (Widow), in ye North Isle of ye Body of ye Church
1733	April	5	John, son of Francis Whitfield, in ye Cloysters
1733	April	19	Mr James Laveaure, in ye Cloyster Yard
1733	July	10	The Revd Mr Simeon D'Evereux, Minor Canon of this Church, in ye Cloysters
1733	July	21	The Revd Mr John Gostling, Minor Canon of this Church, in ye Cloysters
1733	September	1	Sarah, Daughter of Robert Cumberland, Minor Canon of this Church, in ye Cloysters
1733	October	3	Mrs Ann Belke, Widow of ye Revd Dr Thomas Belke, late Prebendary of this Church, in ye South Cross Ile of ye Church
			Rob: Cumberland, Sacrist

END OF SECOND REGISTER OF BURIALS.

* The original has been overwritten Benison.
† In the Register of Affidavits described as Mrs Elizabeth Knowler.
‡ In the Register of Affidavits described as Mrs Lyttleton Tenison.
§ In the Register of Affidavits described as Francess Janeway.

Year.	Month.	Day.	Names.
1733	January	19	Mary, Daughter of the Revd Mr Thomas Clendon, and Elisabeth his wife, in the Cloyster Yard
1733	March	7	Mary, Daughter of John and Mary Lade, in the Cloyster Yard
1734	March	27	John, Son of John and Mary Lade, in the Cloyster Yard
1734	April	17	Mary, daughter of Mr John Sympson, of St Stephen's, and Mary his Wife, in the body of the Church
1734	August	8	The Revd Mr John Frances, Master of the King's School, in the Cloyster
1734	September	3	James Web, in the Cloyster Yard
1734	November	12	The Revd Mr Robert Cumberland, Minor Canon of this Church, in the Cloyster
			William Gostling, Sacrist
1734	January	3	*Elizabeth, ye daughter of George Friend & Eliz: his Wife, in ye Cloyster Yard
1734	January	19	*John, Son of Francis Whitfeild, in ye Cloysters
1735	March	28	*Ann, Wife of Robert Lowe, in the Cloyster Yard
1735	April	3	Thomas Hill, Esqr,† in ye North Cross Isle of the Church
1735	May	19	*Henry, a Black, from London, in ye Cloysters
1735	June	29	Elizabeth Castle, Widow, in the Cloyster Yard
			James Henstridge, Sacrist
1735	February	15	Sarah, Daughter of John Philpott & Margaret his Wife
1736	June	4	Mr Daniel Henstridge, Organist of this Church
1736	November	17	Hannah, Daughter of the Revd Mr James Evans, Under-Master of the King's School, & Hannah his Wife, in ye Cloyster
			Tho: Buttonshaw, Sacrist
1737	January	30	*Mr Tho: Frances, in the Cloyster
1737	March	10	*Mrs Sarah Janeway, in the Cloyster Yard
‡	May	28	Tho: Lade, in ye Cloyster Yard
‡	July	5	Mich: Lade
‡	June	20	Tho: Parker, in ye Cloyster Yd
1737	July	19	John Lade, in ye Cloyster Yard
‡	June	24	James, ye son of John Phillmore and Alidia his Wife
‡	August	13	Dr John Gray
‡	September	15	Mrs Soon (or Soan)
‡	October	15	Mr Legrond
‡	October	16	Wm Halsey
			Robt Jenkin, Sacrist
1737	December	10	Herriot, Daughtr of ye Revd Mr Thomas Clendon, Vicar of Sturry, & Eliz: his wife, in the Cloyster yard
1737	December	10	Joyce, Wife of ye Revd Mr James Henstridge, in ye Cloysters
1737	December	27	Elizabeth Cornwall, Widw, in The Cloysters
173$\frac{7}{8}$	January	17	Elizabeth, Wife of the Revd Mr Thomas Clendon, Vicar of Sturry, in the Cloysters
173$\frac{7}{8}$	February	3	Thomas, Son of Edward & Mary Keet, in ye Cloyster yard
			Peter Vallavine
1738	December	16	The Revd Mr Ed: Wake, one of the Prebends of this Church, was buried in the South Isle by the Revd ye Dean
1738	December	17	William, Son of Richd Allsay, in the church yard

* Overwritten in the original.

† In the Register of Affidavits is added, "was buried in linnen; information whereof was given to ye overseers Apr. 4th." In the Burial Register the entry is overwritten.

‡ The year omitted.

Year.	Month.	Day.	Names.
1738	March	5	Mrs Elizabeth Gosling, in the Cloysters, Affidavit brought ye 9th
1739	April	3	Mr Charles Knowler, in the Cloysters
1739	September	24	Joseph Sutherland, in the Cloysters
1739	July*	6	Mrs Matilda Elstob, in the North Cross Isle
1739	November*	16	Elizabeth, wife of James Turner, in ye Cloyster Yard
1739	June*	15	Mary, Daughter of the Revd Mr Wm Gostling & Hester his wife, in ye Cloysters
			William Broderip, Sacrist
1739	March	5	Judith Horn, of the Arch-Bishop's Palace, in the Cloyster Yard
1740	March	26	Mrs Elisabeth Elliot (Widow), in the Body of the Church
1740	May	11	Robert Lowe (aged 94), in the Cloyster Yard
1740	June	8	Mary Gentil (a child), in the Cloyster
1740	July	18	Margaret Woolcott (a child), in the Cloyster Yard
1740	August	20	Daniel Villiers (Porter of the Green Court Gate), in the Cloyster Yard
1740	September	28	Mrs Susanna Wren (Widow), in the West Cloyster
			William Gostling, Sacrist
1740	January	11	Mr Edward Burgess, one of the Lay Clerks of this Church, in ye Cloyster Yard
1740	February†	23	John (an Infant), Son of Henry Despain & Mary his Wife, in ye Cloyster Yard
1740	March	13	Anne, an Infant, Daughter of Mr John Phillmore & Alicia his Wife
1740	March	22	George Goree, from London, who boarded at Mr Evans's, was buried in ye Cloysters
1741	April	1	Mr Thomas Geery, Distiller, of the Arch-Bishop's Palace, in ye Cloysters
1741	April	26	William, Son of the Revd Mr William Broderip, Minor Canon of this Church, & Elizabeth his Wife, in ye Cloysters
1741 (or 1740)	January	14	Charles, Son of the Revd Mr James Evans, Under Master of the King's School, & Hannah his Wife, in ye Cloysters
1741	July	15	Catherine, the Wife of ye Revd Mr Herbert Randolph, one of ye Six Preachers of this Church, & Minster of Deal, in ye South Cross Isle of the Church
1741	October	31	Mary Bartram, a child of a wayfaring woman, in ye Cloyster Yard
			James Henstridge, Sact, from Midsummer
1741	December	1	Evan Loyd, a young Gentleman from Deal, in ye Cloysters
174½	February	2	John, the Son of ye Revd Dr Tenison, Prebendary of this Church, & Mary his Wife, in ye Body of the Church
1742	April	11	Tho: Fraine, from Norgeam‡ in Sussex, who boarded at Mr Monins's, was buried in ye Cloysters
1742	April	23	Mastr Steph Hall, in ye Cloyster
1742	April	24	Henry, ye Son of Robert Jenkin, a Minor Canon of this Church, & Catherine his Wife, in ye Cloyster
1742	May	15	The Revd Dr Tho: Tenison, a Prebendary of this Church, in ye Body of ye Church
1742	June	13	John Mayhoe (Porter of ye Ch. Yd Gate), in ye Cloyster
1742	July	30	Eliz: Wood, in ye Cloyster
			Robt Jenkin, Sacrist
1742	November	28	Mary Gilbert, Widow, in the Cloysters

* So in the original. † Overwritten in the original. ‡ Northiam?

Year.	Month.	Day.	Names.
1742	December	9	Henry Rigden, in the Cloyster Yard
1742	January	18	John Coates, One of the Vergers of this Church, in ye Cloyst^r^ yard
1743	April	28	Ann Carpenter, in the Cloysters
1743	June	6	John Pysing, One of the Lay Clerks of This Church, in the Cloysters
			Peter Vallavine, Sacrist to Midsummer
1743	August	18	John Clarke, in the Cloyster Yard
*	October	8	The Revd Mr James Evans, Under Master of the King's School, in the Cloysters
			Jam: Henstridge, Sac^st^ from Midsum^r^
*	December	16	James Turner, Vesterer of this Church, in the Cloyster Yard, affidavit made ye 17th
*	February	18	—— Hyde, in the Cloysters
1744	April	20	James, Son of the Revd Wm Broderip, in the Cloysters
*	August	4	Sir Wm Bois, in the body of the Church
*	October	22	Mary, daughter of J. & Mary Ager, in the Cloyster Yard. Affidavit brought ye 24th
			Wm Broderip, Sacrist
1744	December	24	Mary, the Wife of James Agar, in the Cloyster-Yard
1745	April	4	Margaret, the Wife of John Philpot, in the Cloyster Yard
1745	August	2	Mary, the Wife of Edward Keet, in the Cloyster Yard
1745	August	13	George Frend, in the Cloyster Yard
			Tho: Lamprey, Sacrist
1745	December	6	Elizabeth, Wife of John Blonchard, in the Cloyster Yard
1745	December	13	The Revd Mr James Henstridge, Minor Canon of this Church, in the Cloyster
1745	December	15	John Blonchard, in the Cloyster Yard
1745	January	23	John, Son of the Revd Dr Potter (Prebendary of y^s^ Church), & Martha his Wife, in ye Body of the Church
1745	January	24	The Revd Dr Edward Donne (Prebendary of this Church), in the North-Cross-Isle of the Church
1746	April	27	Mary Dodd, in the Cloyster Yard
1746	November	6	John Smith, Servant to Dr Ayerst, in the Cloyster Yard
1746	November	26	Herbert-Frend, Son of ye Revd Mr Richd Marsh (Minor Canon of this Church), & Elisabeth his Wife, in ye Cloysters
			Richd Leightonhouse, Sacrist
1746	March	8	Amy Hatton, Spinster, of ye Precincts of ye Arch-Bishop's Palace, in ye Cloyster Yard
1747	July†	19	George Turner Putland, in the Cloyster Yard
1747	June	2	Susanna Broderip, Daughter of the Revd Mr Wm Broderip, Minor Canon of this Church, & Elisabeth his Wife, in the Cloysters
			Fran: Gregory, Sacrist
1747	December	21	Elizabeth Bentham, of Sheerness, in the Chancell
1747	January	19	Isabella Buckwell, in the Cloyster Yard
1747	January	25	Mrs Mary Norris, in the Body
1747	March	16	Ester Selwyn, in ye Cloyster Yard
1748	April	1	Mary Gregory, Daughter of the Revd Mr Francis GreGory, Minor Canon of this Church, & Elisabeth his Wife, in the Cloysters
1748	June	14	John SimpSon, Esqr, in the Body of the Church

* No year given in the original. † So in the original.

Year.	Month.	Day.	Names.
1748	August	21	Robert Wright, in the Body of the Church
			Robt. Ayerst, Sacrist
1749	May	27	Mrs Tennison, Widow of the Revd Dr Thomas Tennison, late Prebendary of this Church, in the Body of the Church
1749	September	19	Mrs Anne Henstridge, in the Cloyster Yard
1749	October	22	Mr Thomas Knowler, in the Cloysters
			Fran: Gregory, Sacrist
1749	December	7	Thomas Pope, of St Gregory's, in the Cloyster Yard
1749	December	12	Mrs Elisabeth Cumberland, Widow of the Revd Mr Robt Cumberland, late Minor Canon of this Church, in the Cloysters
1749	January	16	Susannah Pope, of St Gregory's, Widow, in the Cloyster Yard
1750	April	19	Mrs Anne Tenison, Widow of Edward, late Lord Bishop of Ossory, in the Body of the Church*
1750	August	3	Mrs Grace Randolph, Widow† of the late Recorder Randolph, in the Body of the Church
			William Gostling, Sacrist
1750	January	6	Charles Pembroke, in the Cloysters
1751	April	25	Elisabeth, Wife of ye Revd Mr Will: Broderip, Minor Canon of this Church, in ye Cloysters, by R.L.
1751	July	7	Richard Pembroke, in the Cloysters
1751	July	9	Wm, Son of George Wolcot, in the Cloyster Yard
1751	August	11	Mary, Daughter of Mrs Pembroke, in the Cloysters
1751	November	17	Dina‡ Dod, in the Cloyster Yard
			Wm Broderip, Sacrist
1751	December	13	Hester, Daughter of Mary Pembroke, Widow, in the Cloysters
1751	December	22	Alice Buckwell, Widow, in the Cloyster Yard
1752	March	18	Mrs Mary Knowler, of St Andrew's Parish, in the Cloysters
1752	April	28	Mrs Jane Frances, Widow from St Margaret's, in the Cloysters
1752	October	26	Ann Coates, Widow, in the Cloyster Yard
			Tho: Lamprey, Sacrist
1753	January	22	Samuel Norris (Auditor of this Church 37 Years), in the Body of the Church
1753	February	2	Lady Anne Boys, Relict of Sr Wm Boys, in the Body of the Church
1753	June	4	Mary Norris, Spinster, in the Body of the Church
1753	September	16	The Revd Mr Richd Hughes, Chaplain to the Old Buffs, was buried in the Cloysters
			Richard Leightonhouse, Sacrist
1753	December	2	Vincent, Son of John & Rebecca Saffary, in the Cloyster Yard
1754	January	19	John, Son of the Revd Mr John Airson, (Minor Canon of this Church) and Anne his Wife, in the Cloysters
1754	January	20	John, Son of George Frend and Catherine his Wife, in the Cloyster Yard
1754	February	26	Richard May, Esq , in the Body of the Church, from Northgate parish
1754	July	12	Elizabeth, the Wife of the Revd Mr Gregory, Minor Canon of this Church, in the Cloysters

* In the Register of Affidavits is added, "was buried in Linnen of wch Information was given & fifty shillings paid to Mr Vanbrug (Overseer), Ap. 27."

† From Oxford. Register of Affidavits.

‡ In the original the name is written Diana, a line being drawn through the first *a*.

Year	Month.	Day.	Names.
1754	July	20	Dr Samuel Shuckford, late Prebendary of this Church, in the Body of the Church
1754	September	23	Mr Isaac Terry, in the Cloysters
1754	October	22	Elizabeth, Daughter of George & Mary Turner, in the Cloyster-yard
			Fran: Gregory, Sacrist
1754	December	26	Mary, the Wife of John Lade, of the Parish of St Alphage, in the Cloyster yard
1755	March	9	Mrs Frances Pysing, in the Cloysters
1755	March	13	Mr Thomas Perronet, in the Cloysters
1755	April	2	John Hill, Esqr, in the North-Cross Isle of the Church
1755	April	4	Mrs Margaret Cotton, in the Cloysters
1755	April	9	Richard, Son of Richard & Mary Halsey, in the Cloyster yard
1755	July	15	Martha Taylor, in the Cloyster-yard
1755	September	8	The Revd Mr Herbert Randolph, one of the Six Preachers of this Church, & Rector of Upper Deal, in the South Cross Isle of this Church
1755	October	7	Mrs Mary Knowler, of the Parish of St Andrew, Widow, in the Cloysters
			Jn Airson, Sacrist
1755	December	6	Mrs Mary Atkins, Widow, in the Body of the Church
1755	December	12	John Airson (an Infant), Son of the Revd Mr Airson, Minor Canon of this Church, in the North Cloyster
1755	December	14	Rebecca Saffory (an Infant) Daughter of John and Rebecca Saffory, in the Cloyster Yard
1756	February	15	Stephen Philpot, one of the Bell Ringers, in the Cloyster Yard
1756	February	27	Susanna, Wife of the Revd Mr Thomas Ibbot, in the grave of Dr Gray, her former Husband, in the Body of the Church
1756	March	5	John Rogers, in the Cloyster Yard
1756	March	12	Mr Edward Roberts, of St Thomas's Hill, in the South Cross Isle
1756	July	16	Mr John Hodges, Excise Officer (of Ashford), in the Cloyster Yard
1756	September	24	Mrs Ann Bridge, in the Cloyster Yard
			William Gostling, Sacrist
1757	April	5*	Edward, Son of the Revd Mr Francis Gregory (Minor Canon of this Church) and Elizabeth his wife, in the Cloysters
1757	June	27	David Egelson, in the Cloysters
1757	November	11	Anne, daughter of Richd Pembroke, in the Cloysters
1757	November	13	Anne, daughter of Thomas Hill Esqr, and Matilda his wife, in the North Cross Isle
			Wm Broderip, Sacrist
1757	November	27	Mrs Elizabeth Hatton, Widow (of the Precinct of ye A. Bp's Palace), in the Cloyster Yard
1758	April	22	Ann-Frances, Dr of Captain John Flemming, in ye Cloysters
1758	September	19	Mrs Elisabeth Knowler (from Burgate), in the Cloysters
1758	October	16	Mr George Vanburgh, in the Cloyster Yard
			Tho: Lamprey, Sacrist
1758	December	18	Frances, ye Wife of ye Revd Mr Thos Lamprey, Min: Can: of this Church, in ye Cloysters

* In the Register of Affidavits the date is April 1st

Year.	Month.	Day.	Names.
1759	June	10	Elisabeth, Wife of William Johnson, in the Cloyster-Yard Richd Leightonhouse, Sacrist
1759	November	29	William, Son of the Revd Mr John Tucker (Under Master of the King's School) and Jane his wife, in ye Cloysters
1759	December	23	—— Clarke, Widow, in the Cloyster Yard, from Harble-Down Hospital
1760	March	3	Mrs Esther Gostling, Wife of the Revd Mr William Gostling (Minor Canon of this Church), in the Cloysters
1760	May	14	James, Son of George & Catherine Frend (an Infant), in the Cloyster Yard
1760	September	5	The Revd Mr Thomas Lamprey, Minor Canon of this Church, in the Cloysters
1760	October	29	Elizabeth Churchman, Widow, in the Cloyster Yard Fran: Gregory, Sacrist
1761	March	1	Richard Halsey, in the Cloyster Yard
1761	March	11	William, Son of George & Margaret Legrand, in the Cloysters
1761	March	17	John, Son of George & Catherine Frend, in ye Cloyster Yard
1761	April	7	Dr Samuel Holcombe, late Prebendary of this Church, aged 95, in the South Isle of the Church
1761	June	28	Edward Keet, in the Cloyster yard
1761	October	11	Matilda, Daughter of the Revd Mr John Airson (Minor Canon of this Church) & Ann his Wife, in the Cloysters
1761	November	23	Mrs Blomer, Widow of the Revd Dr Blomer, late Prebendary of this Church, in the Body of the Church J. Airson, Sacrist
1761	December	1	Mr John Buckwell, of the Archbishop's Palace, in the Cloyster Yard
1761	December	5	Mrs Gertrude Johnson (Widow from London), in her Husband's Grave, in the North Cloyter
1761	December	31	Mrs Mary Maynar, Widow, of St John's Hospital, in the Cloyster Yard
1762	September	30	Alice Dorothy, Infant Daughter of the Revd Mr John Tucker (under Master of the King's School) and Jane his Wife, in the West Cloyster
1762	November	20	Jane, Daughter of the Revd Mr Osmund Beauvoir (Master of the King's School), in the West Cloyster William Gostling, Sacrist
1763	January	28	John Kemp, Servant to Dr Geekie, in the Cloyster yard
1763	February	6	The Widow Philpot, in the Cloyster yard
1763	February	7	Mrs Frend and her Son, an Infant, in the Cloyster yard
1763	February	11	Mrs Elizabeth May, in the body of the Church
1763	May	18	*Chaworth Brabazon, Earl of Meath, in the South Isle of the body of the Church
1763	April	26†	Samuel Dandy, of the precincts
1763	June	11	Anne, daughter of George & Margaret Legrand, in the Cloysters
1763	June	14	Hannah Steers, in the Cloyster yard
1763	June	26	Mrs Hannah Webb, of St George's Parish, in the West Cloysters
1763	July	26	Mr James Webb, in the West Cloyster, from St George's Parish

* In the original this entry has been overwritten; it is probable the entry should be March.
† So in the original.

Year.	Month.	Day.	Names.
1763	October	12	Mr Francis Whitfilde, of the parish of St Andrew, in the North Isle of the Cloysters, by me,
			William Broderip, Sacrist
1764	February	26	Margaret, Wife of Mr George Legrand, of St Andrew's Parish, in the Cloysters
1764	March	11	Benjamin, Son of Mr George Legrand aforesaid, in the Cloysters
1764	March	28	Eliz: Anne,* Daughtr of ye Revd Mr Thomas Freeman (M: C: of this Church) & Margaret his Wife, in ye Cloyst.
1764	March	29	John Porter, Esquire, of St Mary Bredin Parish, in the Body of the Church
1764	April	23	The Revd Mr Wm Broderip, Minr Canon of this Church, in ye North Isle of ye Cloysters
			Richd Leightonhouse, Sacrist
1765	February	8	Sarah Bedingfield Fairman, in the Cloysters
1765	March	27	Elizabeth Cotton, in the Cloysters
1765	April	24	Sarah, Wife of James Eager, in the Cloyster Yard
1765	May	15	The Revd Dr William Ayerst, Prebendary of this Church, in the Body of the Church
			Fran: Gregory, Sacrist
1766	January	20	Elizabeth, the Wife of John Frend, of the Precinct of this Church, in the Cloyster Yard
1766	February	15	The Revd Dr John Davis, Prebendary of this Church, in the Body of the Church
1766	March	18	Mr John Lade (Alderman), of the Parish of St Alphage, in the Cloyster Yard
1766	March	28	Samuel, Son of Mr Samuel Porter, Organist, & Sarah his Wife, in the Cloysters
1766	March	28	Mr William Jordan, of the Arch-Bishop's Palace, in the Cloyster Yard
1766	June	23	Mary, the Daughter of the Revd Mr William Taswell (Minor Canon of this Church) & Hannah his wife, in the Cloysters
1766	October	8	Elizabeth, Daughter of Mr George Legrand, of St Andrew's Parish, in the Cloysters
1766	October	9	William, Son of the Revd Mr John Tucker (Under Master of the King's School) & Jane his Wife, in the Cloysters
1766	November	17	John Frend, of the Precinct of this Church, in the Cloyster-yard
			John Airson, Sacrist
			†Dr Freind, Dean of this Church, died Novr 26th, 1766, Aged 82. Buried at Witney in Oxfordshire
1767	January	7	Hannah-Mary, Daughter of John & Ann Philpot
1767	January	21	Ann, Daughter of Martha Dandy, of the Precincts of this Church
1767	January	31	Ann, Wife of John Philpot, in ye Cloyster-yard
1767	March	16	Margt Lushington, Daughter of Mr George Legrand, of St Andrew's Parish, in the Cloysters
1767	March	20	The Revd Mr Isaac Johnson, Vicar of St Dunstan's, in the Cloysters
1767	May	2	Sarah, Daughter of John & Ann Philpot, in ye Cloyster-yard

* In the Register of Affidavits described as Anne Freeman.

† Inserted in the margin.

Year.	Month.	Day.	Names.
1767	August	5	(or 8) Henry, Son of the Revd Mr Francis Gregory, Minor Canon of this Church, & Eliz: his Wife, in the Cloysters
1767	September	8	Daniel Church, one of the Vergers of this Church, in the Cloyster yard
			Tho. Freeman, Sacrist
1768	March	6	James Agar, one of the Porters of this Church, in the Cloyster yard
1768	June	16	Ann, Daughter of the late Revnd Dr John Davis, Prebendary of this Church, in the Body of the Church
1768	June	13*	Joseph Prince, Esqr, a Captain upon half Pay, of the Archbishop's Palace, in the Cloysters
1768	August	17	George, Son of the Revnd Mr Benson, Prebendary of this Church, and Susannah his Wife, in the Cloysters
1768	November	12	Martha, Wife of the Revnd Mr Leightonhouse, Minor Canon of this Church, in the Cloysters
1768	November	18	Mary, Wife of George Turner, in the Cloyster yard
			W. Taswell, Sacrist
1769	March	19	George Turner (Wood Reeve of this Church), in ye Cloyster yard
1769	April	5	Mrs Jane Usteson (fro' St Alphege), in ye Cloyst^{r} y^{d}
1769	April	23	Anna-Maria, Daught^{r} of George & Sarah Philpot (of ye A: Bp's Palace), in ye West Cloyst^{r}
1769	May	19	Magdalen Villiers, fro' Northgate, in ye Cloyst^{r} y^{d}
1769	June	7	Mrs Hannah Evans, Widow of the Revd Mr Evans, late Under Master of ye King's Schole, in ye Cloysters
1769	September	27	Jeremiah Hatton (an Infant), Son of Jeremiah & Elizabeth Hatton, in ye Cloyst^{r} y^{d}
1769	October	12	Thomas Scamell (one of ye Vesterers of this Church), in the Cloyster-Yard
1769	November	2	Elizabeth, Wife of Jeremiah Hatton, in ye Cloyster-Yard
1769	November	10	Adde Read, House Keep^{r}, in ye Cloyst^{r} Y^{d}
			Richd Leightonhouse, Sacrist
1770	May	15	John Philpot, in ye Cloyster-Yard
1770	May	30	Mr George Philpot, of the Archbishop's Palace, in ye Cloysters
1770	June	7	Mr William Broderip, Organist, of Lemster in Herefordshire; in the Cloysters
1770	June	15	Mrs Damaris Cumberland, in the Cloysters
1770	August	28	William Walker, Son of the Revd Mr William Taswell, Minor Canon of this Church, and Hannah his Wife, in the Cloysters
1770	September	19	The Revd Mr Richard Leightonhouse, Minor Canon of this Church, in the Cloysters
1770	September	27	The Revd Dr John Potter, Dean of this Church, in the Dean's Chapel
1770	November	16	Elizabeth, the Wife of Captain Andrew Lyon,† in the Body of the Church
			Fran: Gregory, Sacrist
1771	February	21	Francis, Son of the Revd Mr Francis Gregory, Minor Canon of this Church, and Elizabeth his wife, in the Cloysters
1771	April	10	Mrs Ann‡ Knowler (from Burgate), in the Cloysters

* So in the original.

† In the Register of Affidavits is added, "was buried in Linnen, of which Information was given, and the Penalty of fifty shillings paid to Mr Hatton, Overseer."

‡ In the original Mary has been obliterated and Ann written over.

Year.	Month.	Day.	Names.
1771	April	17	William Hart, Servant to Dr Tatten, in the Cloyster-Yard
1771	April	19	Ann, Daughter of Thomas & Elizabeth Alcorn, in the Cloyst^r Y^d
1771	May	24	William Crowter, in the Cloyster Yard
1771	August	24	Catharine, Daughter of the Revd Mr William Taswell, Minor Canon of this Church, & Hannah his wife, in the Cloysters
1771	November	21	Ann-Betty, Daughter of the Revd Mr Thomas Freeman (Minor Canon of this Church) & Margaret his wife, in the Cloysters
			J. Airson, Sacrist
1772	February	22	Miss Lance, in the Body of the Church
			T. Freeman, Sacrist
1773	February	20*	Martha Dandy
1773	August	14	Deborah Lee, in the Cloyster Yard
1773	August	26	—— Lowe, in the Cloyster Yard
1773	September	6	Willm Hannah, in the Cloysters
1773	October	10	Sarah Rogers, in the Cloyster Yard
1773	November	15	Ann, Dau^r of the Rev^nd Wm Taswell, one of the Minor Canons of this Church, & Hannah his Wife, in ye Cloysters
1773	February	28*	George Wolcot
1773	May	22*	John Philpot
			Wm Taswell, Sacrist
1774	January	12	Hester Pembrook, died Jany 5th, & was buried in the Cloysters, Jan. 12th, aged 80
1774	May	28	Matilda Knowler (of Chelsea), in the South Cross of the Cathedral
1774	August	14	Elizabeth Broderip (from St Andrew's Parish), in the Cloysters
1774	August	25	George Marshall (from Northgate Parish), in the Cloyster Yard
1774	September	17	Mary, Barbara, Bennett, Hasted, Infant, in the Cloysters
1774	November	7	Harriot, Daughter of the Revd Mr Taswell, one of the Minor Canons of this Church, & Hannah his Wife, in ye Cloysters†
			J. Dix, Sacrist
1775	February	11	William, Son of the Right Revd John, Lord Bishop of Bangor & Catharine his Wife; in the Dean's Chapel
1775	March	9	Mrs Martha Potter, Relict of the Revd Dr John Potter, late Dean of this Church, in the Dean's Chapel
1775	March	17	Mrs Martha Marshall, Relict of the late Mr George Marshall, in the Cloyster Yard
1775	April	3	William Dodson, in the Cloyster Yard
1775	April	17	George Robert, Son of the Revd Dr George Berkeley, Prebendary of this Church, and Elizabeth his Wife, in the Body of the Church
1775	May	19	Mrs Elizabeth Whitfield, Relict of the late Mr Francis Whitfield, of St Andrew's Parish, in the Cloysters
1775	September	11	Mrs Ann Le Grand, Relict of the late Mr Benjamin Le Grand, in the Cloysters, from All Saints
			Fran: Gregory, Sacrist
1775	November	30	Mr John Venner, from St Alphage, in the Cloysters

* Omitted to be inserted by the Sacrist in their proper places.
† In another hand is added "an infant."

Year.	Month.	Day.	Names.
1775	December	11	Alice, Daughter of Thomas & Elizabeth Alcorn, in the Cloyster Yard
1776	April	12	The honourable Henry Digby, Son of the right honourable Henry Lord Digby & Mary his Wife, in the north Isle of the body of the Church
1776	August	16	Mr Charles Perronet, in the Cloyster Yard
			John Airson, Sacrist
1777	March	15	The Revd Mr William Gostling, a Minor Canon of this Church, in the Cloysters
1777	March	27	Mrs Elizabeth Knowler, from Burgate, in the Cloysters
1777	July	27	Thomas Leutton, in the Cloyster Yard
1777	August	10	Elizabeth Pearce, in the Cloyster Yard
1777	August	17	Lydia* Royse, in the Cloyster Yard
			Tho. Freeman, Sacrist
1778	May	3	Miss Isabella Lethieullier, in the North Aisle of the Body of the Church, and wrapped in Linen
1778	August	14	Jane Broderip, in the Cloysters
1778	October	16	Elizabeth Frend (from St Margaret's), in ye Cloyster Yard
			J. Dix, Sacrist
1779	February	18	Mrs Rant (?) Benson, in the Cloysters
1779	May	26	Matilda Hill, in the Dean's Chapel
1779	August	1	Mrs Sympson (from St George's Parish), in the Body of the Church
1779	October	20	Mrs Elizh Cumberland; in ye Cloysters
			James Ford, Sacrist
1779	December	20	Mrs Ann Le Grand (from the Parish of St George's), in the Cloyster
1780	January	15	Mr Charles Hill (from Chelsea, Middlesex), in the Martyrdom
1780	January	24	Mrs Susanna Wren, in the Cloysters, and wrapped in Woollen
1780	February	15	Elizabeth, Daughter of the Revd Mr John Airson (Minor Canon of this Church), and Ann his Wife, in the Cloysters
1780	March	13	Joseph Highmore, Esqr, in the Body of the Church, and wrapped in Sheeps-Wool
1780	March	17	Sarah Gay, in the Cloyster-Yard
1780	May	7	Mary Buckwell, in the Cloyster Yard, and wrapped in Woollen
1780	July	23	Lancelott Lade (from the Parish of St Mary Magdalene), in the Cloyster Yard
1780	July	27	Ann Lade (from the Parish of St Mary Magdalene), in the Cloyster Yard
1780	September	2	William Batt, in the Cloyster Yard
			William Chafy, Sacrist
1780	December	20	Charles Rogers, one of the Vergers of this Church, in ye Cloyster Yard
1781	March	20	Eleanor Woolcot, Widow of George Woolcot (late Lay-Clerk of this Church), in the Cloyster Yard
1781	April	13	Charles Whitfield, an Infant from the Parish of St Andrew, in the Cloysters
1781	April	22	Ann Jager (a Child), in the Cloyster Yard
1781	May	10	William, Son of the Revd James Ford (Minor Canon of this Church) and Dorothy his Wife, in the Cloysters
1781	May	10	Mrs Ann Cumberland, in the Cloysters

* The name Rebecca has been erased, and Lydia written over it.

Year.	Month.	Day.	Names.
1781	May	29	John Venner (an Infant), Son of Captain John Venner & Elizabeth his Wife, in the Cloysters
1781	August	12	Henry, Son of John & Hannah Jager
1781	November	16	Mrs Mary Cumberland, in the Cloysters
1781	November	21	Mr Francis Whitfield, of St Andrew's Parish, in the Cloysters
			Fran: Gregory, Sacrist
1781	December	9	John, the Son of Francis Whitfield & Elizabeth his wife, of St Andrew's Parish, in the Cloysters
1782	September	25	Mary, Daughter of John Springall & Mary his wife, in the Cloyster yard
			John Airson, Sacrist
1783	January	16	Mrs Hannah Johnson, from St Paul's, in the Cloyster Yard
1783	April	13	Elizabeth Jarman, in the Cloyster Yard
1783	May	15	Henry, Son of John & Ruth Simmonds, in the Cloyster yard
1783	September	20	Charles Fitzgerald (from Margate), in the Cloysters
			Tho: Freeman, Sacrist
1784	February	11	Mrs Caroline Wren (aged 77), in the Cloysters
1784	August	14	William Batt, Son of Benjamin & Mary Batt, in the Cloyster Yard
			J. Dix, Sacrist
1785	January	9	Catharine, Daughter of John & Christophor* Krugelstine, in the Cloyster Yard
1785	January	28	Elizabeth, Wife of the Revd Francis Gregory (Minor Canon of this Church), in the Cloysters
1785	February	18	George, Son of John & Hannah Jager, in the Cloyster Yard
1785	February	22	John Abbott, in the Cloyster Yard
1785	October	30	Randolph Greenway, Esqr (brought from France), in the Cloysters
			J. Ford, Sacrist
1786	February	2	Thomas Taylor (from the Parish of Westgate), in the Cloyster-yard
1786	February	21	John, Son of John and Hannah Jager,† in the Cloyster yard
1786	March	29	Ann, Daughter of Bartholomew and Mary Elvey,† in the Cloyster yard
1786	August	27	Thomas, Son of John and Martha Preston, in the Cloyster yard
1786	November	20	Ann, Wife of the Revd John Airson, Minor Canon of this Church, in the Cloysters
			William Chafy, Sacrist
1786	November	25	Richard Cope Hopton, Esq., in the South Aile of the Body of the Church
1787	April	8	John Preston, one of the Vesterers of this Church, in the Cloyster Yard
			Fran: Gregory, Sacrist
1787	December	18	The Revd Mr John Airson, a Minor Canon of this Cathedral, in the Cloysters
1788	January	13	Michael & John Wootton, Sons of Thos & Mary Lade, from St George's, in the Cloyster yard, in one Grave
1788	January	15	William, Son of Bartholomew & Mary Elvy, in the Cloyster yard

* So in the original.

† In the Register of Affidavits described as an Infant.

Year.	Month.	Day.	Names.
1788	March	3	John, Son of Jeremiah & Elizabeth Hatton, in the Cloyster yard
1788	September	18	Mrs Ann Lade, fm Burgate
1788	November	24	Edward, base-born Son of Ann Marsh
			Tho. Freeman, Sacrist
1788	December	19	Henry, Son of Henry & Ann Gee, infant, in the Cloyster Yard
1789	May	8	Christopher Lethieleur,* Esqr, in the Cloysters
1789	June	16	Charles Abbott, Infant, in the Cloyster Yard
1789	November	18	Elizabeth Smith, from the Arch Bps. Palace, in the Cloysters
			Joshua Dix, Sacrist
1789	December	24	George Frend (from the Parish of St George), in the Cloyster Yard
1790	May	8	Sarah,† Daughter of Wm & Sarah Green, in ye Cloyster Yard
1790	June	23	Harriott†, Daughter of William & Ann Welby, in the Cloyster Yard
1790	July	16	Jane Frend (from the Parish of St George), in the Cloyster Yard
1790	July	27	Eliza, Daughter of the Revd John Francis (Second Master of the King's School) and Mary his Wife, in the Cloysters
1790	August	14	Charlotte, Daughter of John & Ruth Simmonds, in the Cloyster Yard
1790	December	19	Mary, Wife of Thomas Lade (from the Parish of St Mary Magdalen), in the Cloyster yard
1790	December	22	Mary Lethieullier, Widow, (from the Parish of St Mary Bredin), in the Cloysters
1791	February	7	Mary Simmonds, of the Precincts of this Church, in the Cloyster-yard
1791	March	10	Ann Hasted, Widow, of the Precincts of this Church, in the Cloysters
1791	April	21	Mary Sutton, of the Precincts of this Church, in the Cloyster-yard
1791	May	11	Mary Panton, of the Precincts of this Church, in the Cloyster yard
1791	July	12	Mary Ustinson, of the Parish of St Alphage, Canterbury, in the Cloyster-yard
1791	October	25	Montague Booth, Esqr, from Boulogne, France, in the Cloysters
			William Chafy, Sacrist
1791	December	11	James Springall, a Child, Son of John & Mary Springall
1792	January	8	Mr Edwd Perronett, in the Cloisters
1792	March	4	Mrs Elizabeth Hannah, of the parish of St Alphege, in the Cloisters
1792	March	13	Sarah Knowler, of the parish of St Alphege, in the Cloister yard
1792	April	15	Mr Robert Le Geyt, Junr, of the Archbishop's Palace, in the Cloysters
1792	June	12	Mr Henry Gregory, B.A., of Emanuel College, Camb: and Son of the Revd Fran: Gregory, Minor Canon of this Church, in the Cloysters
			Fran: Gregory, Sacrist
1793	January	9	Celia Abbott, from St Mary Magdalen, in woollen

* In the Register of Affidavits spelt Lethieullier.

† In the Register of Affidavits described as an Infant.

Year.	Month.	Day.	Names.
1793	January	24	James Cornfoot, of the Precincts, in woollen
1793	February	8	Mrs Davis, Relict of Dr John Davis, late Prebendary of this Church, in the Chancel, aged 82
1793	April	2	Mr Charles Topping, in the Cloyster yard
1793	April	14	Mrs Alice Abbott, in the Cloyster-yard
1793	August	17	Sarah, Daughter of the Revd James Merest and Sarah his Wife, of Wortham, in the County of Suffolk, in the Cloysters, aged 11 years & 10 Months
1793	October	1	Captain Thomas Piercy, in the North Chancel or Martyrdom
			Tho. Freeman, Sacrist

Note.—There has been no Burial during the whole Year 1794*

J. Dix, Sacrist

1794	December	14	Sarah Halsey (from St John's Hospital), in the Cloyster-yard
1794	December	26	John Smith (Servant to the Dean), in the Cloysters
1795	February	12	Richard Edwards, Esqr (Admiral of the Blue), in the South Cross Isle
1795	March	4	Mary Johnson (from St George's), in the Cloysters
1795	April	22	Maria, Daughter of Mr Robert Le Geyt (of the Archbishop's Palace), in the Cloysters
1795	December	30	Sarah Fekins (from the Kentish and Canterbury-Hospital), in the Cloyster Yard
1796	September	23	Robert, S. of Richard and Ann Frend (from the Parish of St Paul's), in the Cloyster Yard
1796	October	15	Thomas Shepherd, in the Cloyster-Yard
			William Chafy, Sacrist
1797	February	8	Mary Le Geyt (from the Black friars), in the Cloysters
1797	February	18	Thomas Young (Servant to the Archdeacon), in the Cloysters
1797	February	22	Mr Edwin Legrand (from St George's), in the Cloysters
1797	July	6	Thomas Tiddeman, an Infant, in the Cloyster-Yard
			Henry John Todd, Sacrist
1797	November	26	Elizabeth London, a Child, from ye Archbishop's Palace, in the Cloister-Yard
1798	February	22	Mrs Sarah Francis, relict of the Revd John Francis, M. A., Vicar of Soham in the County of Cambridge; in the east Cloister
1798	March	5	Edwina Legrand, an infant, from the Precincts of Eastbridge Hospital, in the West Cloister
1798	March	7	Mrs Hannah Walsby, in the Sermon House, alias Chapter House
1798	June	14	John, Son of John and Hannah Jager (a Child), in the Cloister-yard
1798	July	3	Mrs Hester Gostling, in the West-Cloister
1798	October	1	Mr Robert Le Geyt, of the Archbishop's Palace, in the West Cloister
1798	October	18	Mrs Ann Fitzgerald, Widow, from Duke Street, Portland Place, London, in the South Cloister of this Church (near the North Door of the said Church, leading into what is call'd the Martyrdom).
			Fran: Gregory, Sacrist
1799	April	28	Francis Charles D'Villars, French Priest & Emigrant, of the Archbishop's Palace

* In the Register of Affidavits the note reads, "Not one Burial during the whole year *of the Sacrist's Office for* 1794;" it is important to note the words in italics, because the two following burials took place in 1794.

Year.	Month.	Day.	Names.
1799	May	2	Elizabeth Adams
1799	May	31	Mr Edward Carlos Gregory, from Lemon Street, Goodman's Fields, London, in the North Cloyster, Son of the Rev. Francis Gregory, Minor Canon of this Church
1799	June	23	Maria, Daughter of William & Mary Vidgen, in the Cloyster Yard
1799	September	14	Hester Gregory, Spinster, Daughter of the Revd Francis Gregory, Minor Canon of this Cathedral, in the North Cloyster
1799	December	30	Harriot Burt, Inhabitant of the Precincts, in the Sermon House
1800	April	3	Sarah Munns, of the Arch Bishop's Palace, in the Cloyster Yard
			J. Dix, Sacrist
1800	April	28	The Revd Thos Lamprey, in the Cloysters
1800	April	28	Bartholomew Elvy, in the Cloyster Yard
1800	May	19	Elizabeth Harding, of the Archbishop's Palace, Infant, in ye Cloyster Yard
1800	September	19	Diana Ustinson, Aged 80, in the Cloyster Yard
1800	October	24	Susanna Jenkin, Aged 58, in the Cloysters, North side
1800	October	25	Sarah Porter, Aged 66, in the West Cloyster
1800	October	30	Elizabeth Rede, in the Sermon House
			Joshua Dix, Sacrist
1801	January	5	Captn John Bentham, of the Royal Artillery, in the Sermon House
1801	January	15	Richard, Son of Richard and Ann Frend (from the Parish of St Paul's), in the Cloyster-Yard
1801	February	13	Reuben Jackson, of the Arch Bishop's Palace, in the Cloyster-Yard
1801	April	4	The Revd Francis Gregory, upwards of fifty-four years a Minor-Canon of this Church, and having nearly completed the eightieth year of his age; in the Cloysters
1801	June	17	William Webster, of the Arch Bishop's Palace, in the Cloyster-yard
1801	July	21	Ann Lade, from Burgate Street, Canterby; in the Cloyster yard
1801	August	27	Harriot, Daughter of Thomas and Catherine Parnell, in the Cloyster-yard
			William Chafy, Sacrist
1801	August	27	William, Son of John and Elizabeth Fryer, of the Arch Bishop's Palace, in the Cloyster yard
1801	September	10	William Powell, from the Arch Bishop's Palace, in the Cloyster yard
1801	October	24	Elizabeth, Daughter of Thomas and Catherine Parnell, in the Cloyster-yard
			William Chafy, Sacrist
1801	December	30	Sarah, Daughter of Richard & Susannah Harding, an infant, of the Arch Bishop's Palace, in the Cloyster-yard
1802	February	3	Lucy Legassick, a servant of the Dean, aged 42 years; in the Cloyster yard
1802	February	11	Mary Hart, Widow, of the precincts of the Church, aged 77 Years, in the Cloyster-yard
1802	March	14	Mary Catherine, daur of Edward & Sarah Smith, of the Archbishop's Palace, in the Cloyster-yard, aged 2 years
1802	June	18	Mary Ann, daur of William & Ann Hacker, an infant, of the Archbishop's Palace in the Cloyster yard

Year.	Month.	Day.	Names.
1802	July	14	John Simmonds, of the Precincts, aged 29 years, in the Cloyster yard
1802	July	19	Ann Ismay, aged 74 years (brought from Dover), in the Cloyster-yard
1802	October	8	The Revd Thomas Johnson, Curate of Whitstable; in the Cloysters
1802	November	25	William, Son of Rigden & Isabella Swain, in the Cloyster yard
			William Bennett, Sacrist
1803	January	5	Mary Elvy, Widow, Aged 57 Years, in the Cloyster-Yard
1803	February	7	The Revd Wm Gregory, Rector of St Andrews, with St Mary Bredman, in Canterbury, & Vicar of Blean, in the Cloysters, aged 43
1803	March	10	The Revd William Lardner, Minor Canon of this Church, in the Cloysters, aged 33
1803	March	11	Mr John Venner, in the Cloysters
1803	April	11	Mr Alderman Frend's Child, in the Cloyster yard, in a Vault
1803	April	17	Mr Thos Lade, in the Cloyster yard
1803	September	10	—— Elliott, in the Cloyster yard, Aged 79
1804	May	31	The Revd John Gostling, in the Cloysters, Aged 79
1804	August	29	Thomas Allcorn, in the Cloyster yard
1804	September	9	Mrs Webb, from St George's Parish, in the Cloysters
1804	November	5	Captn William Gostling, R.A., in the Cloysters, aged 74
1804	September	2	The Child of R. Frend, Esqr (Mayor of Canterbury), in a Vault in the Cloyster Yard
1804	September	3	Dr Benson, Prebendary of this Church, in the Sermon House
			* The two last Names were neglected to be registered in their proper places.
			T. A. Mutlow, Sacrist
1805	January	5	Sarah Topping, Aged 72, in the Cloyster Yard
1805	May	24	Thomas Simmonds, in the Cloyster Yard, Aged 30 Years
1805	June	5	Thomas Tiddeman, in ye Cloyster Yard, Aged 4 Years
			J. Dix, Sacrist
1806	January	18	Ann, Wife of Mr Richard Frend, from St Paul's, in the Cloyster Yard
1806	April	26	John, Son of John Need, Esqr, of Sherwood Hall, in the County of Nottingham, & Mary his Wife, in the Sermon House
1806	August	25	Mrs Piercy, Relict of Captain Thomas Piercy, in the North Chancel
1806	September	4	Mrs Gostling, Relict of Captain William Gostling, in the Cloysters
1806	September	10	Ann Jones, in the Church Yard
1806	November	7	Robert Barret, of Swindon in Wiltshire, in the Cloysters, age 20 years
			Tho. Freeman, Sacrist
1806	December	1	Elizabeth Longley, of the Precincts, in the Cloyster-Yard. Aged 71 Years
1806	December	29	John Emery, of the Precincts, in the South Cloyster. Aged 67
1806	October	31	Jane Clowse, in the Cloyster yard, Aged 17 years
			N.B.—This was omitted to be inserted in its place above. J. Dix
1807	January	30	Mary Dodson, from St John's Hospital, in ye Cloyster Yard. Aged 82
1807	March	6	George Le Grand, from Watling Street, in the Cloysters Aged 77

Year.	Month.	Day.	Names.
1807	July	25	The Revd Thomas Freeman, one of the Minor Canons of this Church, aged 82 Years, in the Cloysters J. Dix, Sacrist
1808	February	5	Henrietta-Mary, daughter of the Revd Henry-William Champneys and Lucy his Wife, of the Precinct of this Church, in the Sermon House
1808	July	5	Mary, Wife of John Springall, of the Precinct of this Church, in the Cloyster Yard. Aged 62 years Jno Yeates, Sacrist
1808	December	21	John Jager, one of the Lay Clerks of this Cathedral, in the Cloyster Yard T. A. Mutlow, Sacrist
1809	May	21	Henry Jay Stammers, an Infant, in the Cloyster Yard
1809	October	7	The very Revd Dr Thomas Powys, Dean of this Cathedral, in the Dean's Chapel. Aged 73
1810	January	14	Susanna Starr, in the Cloysters. Aged 10 Years
1810	January	23	Mary Ann Naylor, in the Cloysters. Aged 29 yrs John Radcliffe, Sacrist
1810	October	15	Thomas Greene, in the Cloysters
1810	October	26	Mary Ann Simmonds, an Infant, in a vault in the Cloyster Green J. Radcliffe, Sacrist
1810	December	18	Samuel Porter, late Organist of this Church, in the Cloysters. aged 77 years
1811	February	7	Martha Sutton, in the Cloyster Yard
1811	March	5	Mary Spearman, in the Cloysters. aged 67 Years
1811	June	13	Findlater Grant, Esqr, aged 21 years, in the Cloysters, brought from St Paul's Parish in Canterbury
1811	June	27	William Greene, in the Cloysters, in the 17 year of his Age
1811	July	21	Susannah London, in the Cloyster Yard. aged 63 years W. Bennett, Sact
1812	January	18	James Lamotte, Esqr, A Captain in His Majesty's 1st Regt or Royal Dragoons, was brought from St Paul's Parish, & buried in the Sermon House, with military Honours
1812	May	14	Mrs Betty Elsley, from St Margaret's Parish, in the Sermon House. Aged 60 W. Bennett, Sacrist

End of Burials in the Third Register.

1813	July	12	Jane Simmonds, of St Mary, Northgate. Age 9 months
1813	December	2	George Le-gassick, of St John's Hospital, Northgate. Age 73 Years
1814	April	6	George Prince, of the Precincts. Age 22 Years
1814	December	3	John Simmonds, of St Mary Bredin's, Canterbury. Age 17 months
1815	January	9	Elizabeth Simmonds, of St Peter's, Canterbury. Age 8 months
1815	March	24	Eliza Frend, of St Andrew's, Canterbury. Age 19 years
1815	April	30	Margaret Jones, of the Precincts. Age 24 years
1815	May	16	Martha Wright, of the Precincts. Age 2 years
1815	June	14	The Revd Edward Walsby, D.D., Prebendary of this Cathedral. Age 64 years
1815	October	1	Charlotte Julian Bennett, of the Precincts. Age 5 weeks

Year.	Month.	Day.	Names.
1815	December	12	Henrietta Walsby, Widow of the late Revd Edward Walsby, D.D., late of the Precincts. Died in Burgate Parish. Age not mentioned
1816	January	20	Catherine Gregory, of the Precincts. Age 59 Years
1816	April	13	The Revd Thomas Spencer, A.B., of the Precincts, Sacrist, Minor Canon of this Cathedral. Age 58 years
1816	April	18	The Reverend Christopher Naylor, A.M., of the Mint Yard, Head Master of the King's School. Aged 78 years
1816	July	*	Stephen Bayden Simmonds, of Northgate. Age 14 months
1816	December	4	Ann Jager, of the Precincts. Age 22 years
1816	December	14	Ann Maud Prince, of the Green Court. Age 59 years
1817	February	19	Hannah Jager, of the Precincts. Age 55 years
1817	May	25	Charles Hammond, of All Saints. Age 56 years
1817	September	8	Margaret Johnson, from Cogan's House, St Peter's Parish. Age 64 years
1817	December	31	Thomas Gilbert, of the Precincts. Age 63 years
1818	April	24	Charlotte Wright, of the Precincts. Infant
1819	March	26	Ann Le Grand, of St Margaret's, died March 15th. Age 83 years
1819	August	16	Mary Clothro, of the Union Workhouse. Age 86 years
1819	August	25	Ruth Simmonds, of St George ye Martyr, Canterbury. Age 70 years
1819	September	13	The Honble William Boyle, of St Lawrence in the Isle of Thanet, 3rd Son of the Earl of Glasgow. Age 16 years. Died Sep. 7th
1819	November	24	Mary Wright, died Novr 17, of the Precincts. Age 39 years
1819	December	22	Dorothy Ford, of the Precincts. Age 73 years
1820	January	19	John Radcliffe, M.A., of the Precincts, Minor Canon of this Cathedral. Age 49 years
1820	March	27	George Simmonds, of the Precincts. Age 39 years
1820	May	15	George Steady, of the Precincts. Age 23 years
1820	October	13	Stephen Simmonds, of Northgate. Age 45 years
1821	February	5	Thomas Sewell, of the Precincts. Age 66 years
†	March	19	William Willis, of St Margaret's, Canterbury. Age 91 years
†	August	28	Thomas Parnell, of the Precincts. Age 76 years
†	September	1	Edward Phillips Birt, of the Precincts. Age 1 month
†	October	18	Eleanora Johnson, of St George's, Canterbury. Age 72 years
†	October	24	Powys Starr, of Charter House School, London. Age 13 Years
†	December	8	Elizabeth Parker, of the Precincts. Age 67 years
1823	January	9	Sarah Dunn, of the Precincts. Age 76 years
1823	May	6	John Ifield Scott, of the Precincts. Age 15 months
1823	November	6	Col^{l} George Lyon, Age 54 years. in the Cloisters
1823	December	3	Henry Adams, of the Precincts. Age 50 years
1824	January	12	James Ford, A.B., of the Precincts, 46 years a Minor Canon of this Cathedral. Age 73 years
1824	April	2	Angelina Ann Beamish, of the Precincts, Age 3 yrs. 5 mos.
1824	April	13	Sarah Wright, of the Precincts. Age 12 years
1824	July	31	Elizabeth Salmon, of the Precincts. Age 87 years
1824	November	29	Thomas Bennett, of the Precincts, one of the Minor Canons of this Cathedral. Age 54 years

* There is no date in the original.

† In the original no year is written against these entries; the page is headed thus, "1821-2-3." The first entry doubtless belongs to 1821, but the five latter may be 1821 or 1822.

Year.	Month.	Day.	Names.
1825	January	31	Gerrardine Baker, of the Precincts. Age 5 months
1825	February	21	Charlotte Croft, of the Precincts, Wife of the Revd James Croft, Prebend of this Church. Age 37 years
1825	March	1	Mary Waters, of the Precincts. Age 46 years
1825	June	12	Richard Reynolds Frend, of St George's, Canterbury. Age 5 months
1825	August	7	Lawrence Desborough, of the Precincts of the Arch Bishop's Palace, Age 67 years
1825	November	22	William Howell, of the Precincts. Age 59 years
1825	December	28	Thomas Dashwood, of St Mary Bredin, Canterbury. Age 75 years
1826	May	11	Jemima Marriott, of the Precincts. Age 14 months
1826	October	19	Lieut.-General W. Bentham, of St Mary Bredin, Canterbury. Age 65 years
1826	December	16	Catharine Hayes, of the Precincts. Age 24 years
1827	February	13	George Nixon Ramsay, Captain in H. M. Reg^{t} 6th or Enniskillen Dragoons, died at Gunnersbury, Middlesex. Age 24 years
1828	January	3	John Whitehurst, of the Precincts. Age 45 years
1828	October	25	Harvey Wood, of St George the Martyr, Canterbury. Age 26 years
1828	December	27	Sarah Cross, of the Precincts. Age 53 years
1829	March	10	Frances Sayer, of the Precincts. Age 69 years
1829	March	11	Elizabeth Jeffery, of the Precincts. Age 62 years
1829	April	6	Mary Sayer, of the Precincts. Age 74 years
1829	September	19	Robert Page, of Russell Square, London. Age 55 years
1829	December	24	Frederick Warren, Workhouse, Archb^{ps} Palace. Age 71 years
1830	June	3	William Anderson, Veterinary Surgeon of the 7th Dragoon Guards, died at the Barracks, Canterbury. Age 58 years
1830	October	31	John Springall, of the Precincts. Age 81 years
1831	March	19	Anna Maria Legeyt, of St George's, Canterbury. Age 90 Years
1831	March	29	Robert Croft, Clerk, of the Precincts, Canon Residentiary of York. Age 76 Years
1831	April	12	George Frend, an Alderman of the City of Canterbury, of St Andrew's, Canterbury. Age 39 years
1831	November	30	Catharine Curteis Frend, of St Andrew's, Canterbury. Age 11 weeks
1832	February	7	Hester Elizabeth Saffery, of the combined Workhouse in Archbishop's Palace. Age 77 years
1832	May	4	Harriot Wright, of the Precincts. Age 24 years
1832	May	29	Sarah Royce, of St Alphage, Canterbury. Age 88 years
1833	February	8	William Welfitt, D.D., of the Precincts, 46 years a Prebendary of this Cathedral. Age 88 years
1833	March	26	Hugh Boscawen, of the Precincts. Age 11 weeks
1833	September	7	Augustus Frederic Peel Marriott, of the Precincts. Age 11 months
1833	November	30	Mary Ann Cook, of the Precincts. Age 4 years, nine months
1834	September	15	George Ramsay, General R.A., of the Whitefriars. Age 71 years
1835	July	14	Eleanor Thomasine Southey, of the Precincts. Age 18 years
1835	November	12	William Tench Sutton, of the Precincts. Age 49 years
1835	December	7	Lt General Sir William Inglis, K.C.B., of Ramsgate, Colonel of the 57th Reg^{t}. Age 71 years

Year.	Month.	Day.	Names.
1836	March	30	Mary Elizabeth, Wife of the Revd George Bridges Moore, of Tunstall, P. curate of Iwade. Age 22 years.
1836	May	31	Jane Hover, of Canterbury. Age 80 years
1837	February	6	Elizabeth Welfitt, of Burgate in Canterbury, Widow of the late Dr Welfitt, Prebendary of this Church. Age 92 years
1837	October	21	Harriet Starr, of the Precincts. Age 32 years
1837	November	2	Margaret Freeman, of the Mint Yard. Age 93 years
1837	November	17	Ann Lee, of the Precincts. Age 62 years
1837	December	13	Lady Margaret Marianne Inglis, of Blackheath in the parish of Lee, in Kent
1838	January	18	Charlotte Louisa Dashwood, of St Mary Bredin's, Canterbury. Age 80 years
1838	March	2	Charles Tylden Chisholm, of the Precincts. Age 12 years
1838	June	2	Henry Boswell Bonnett, Lieut. 45th Regiment, killed on the 31st ultimo, in Blean Wood, in a conflict between the military and certain insurgents. Age 29 years
1839	January	20	John Baynes, of the Precincts. Age 69 years
1839	March	29	John Silcock, of the Precincts. An Infant
1840	January	1	George Henry Lee-Warner, of the Dane John. Age 37 years
1840	January	18	Sarah Salmon, of the Precincts. Age 78 years
1840	January	25	The Revd Jean Francois Mieville, of Watling Street. Age 79 years
1840	March	26	Thomas Starr, of the Precincts. Age 71 years
1840	August	27	William Hards Renwick, of Burgate. Age 44 years
1840	September	5	Sarah Allen, of Burgate. Age 62 years
1841	March	5	William Culling, of the Precincts. Age 20 years
1841	June	3	Mary Harnett, of St George's, Canterbury. Age 32 years
1841	July	3	George Austin, of Northgate. Age 85 years
1841	December	3	Charlotte Stephens, of the Precincts. Age 72 years
1842	August	19	Edward Deedes, of the Precincts. An infant 3 days old
1842	August	22	Henry Deedes, of the Precincts. An infant 6 days old
1842	December	12	Harry Finn, of the Precincts. Age 3 years, 6 months
1843	June	4	Elizabeth Walton, of the Precincts. Age 72 years
1843	December	10	Mary Ann Russell, of the Precincts. Died 5th. Age 25 years
1844	February	8	Emily Frances Wallace, of the Precincts. Age 2 yrs. 7 months
1845	January	8	William Wallace, of the Precincts. An Infant
1845	January	8	Archdale Todd Wallace, of the Precincts. An Infant
1845	January	12	Thomas Walton, of the Precincts. Age 79 years
1845	January	24	Elizabeth Gilbert, of the Precincts. Age 85 years
1845	February	24	Lucy Ann Finn, of Burgate. Age 4 years
1845	March	21	John Barber Culling, of the Archbishop's Palace. Age 14 years
1845	April	10	Joanna Beatson, of the Mint Yard. Age 77 years
1845	July	6	Harriet Kennett, of Palace Street. Age 23 years
1845	August	27	Louis Martinet, of the Mint Yard. Age 7 months
1845	October	19	Hopkins Francis, of the Precincts. Age 43 years
1846	March	24	Sarah Clayson Culling, of the Archbishop's Palace. Age 28 years
1846	March	26	Emanuel Hill, of the Precincts. Age 23 years
1846	May	18	Richard Frend, Esq. of St Peter's, Canterbury. Age 84 years
1847	January	2	Sophia Ann Weldon, of the Precincts. Age 73 years
1847	February	26	Catherine Mary Finn, of St Alphage. Age 7 months

Year.	Month.	Day.	Names.
1847	March	8	George Gipps, Knt., of St Martin's, Canterbury. Age 56 years
1847	May	1	William Williams, Paymaster of the 16th Lancers, of the Precinct of the Archbishop's Palace. Age 71 years
1847	July	9	Richard Marsh, of St Stephen's. Age 88 years
1848	January	6	Catherine Parnell, of Butchery Lane. Age 87 years
1848	January	8	Mary Austin, of Northgate. Age 89 years
1848	April	22	Dells Starr, of the Precincts. Age 80 years
1848	November	2	George Austin, of the Palace Precincts. Age 62 years
1848	December	4	Mary Wells, of the Precincts. Age one day
1849	September	1	Mary Ellen Austin, of the Precincts. Age 21 years
1849	November	22	Elizabeth Ramsay, of Whitefriars, Canterbury. Age 81 years
1850	May	22	Thomas James Russell, of the Precincts. Age 3 months
1850	June	18	Henry Linom Cullen, of Palace Street. Age 22 years
1850	July	17	Mary Anne Carter, of the Precincts, for 16 years a faithful servant in the family of the Rev. W. S. H. Braham, M. Canon. Age 32 years
1850	December	20	Thomas Chaney, of the Precincts. Age 74 years
1851	May	1	Elizabeth Brampton, of the Precincts. Age 16 years
1851	July	5	Frederick Vernon Lockwood, of the Precincts, Canon of this Cathedral. Age 47 years
1852	July	2	Thomas Wright, of the Precincts. Age 83 years
1852	October	15	Elizabeth Gonham, of the Precincts. Age 18 months
1852	October	30	Francis Dawson, of the Precincts, Canon of this Cathedral. Age 64 years
1852	December	7	Mary Foord, of St Peter's Street. Age 70 years
1853	February	26	William Grant Broughton, of Chester Street, Grosvenor Place, London, Bishop of Sydney. Age 64 years
1853	March	25	Jane Culling, of Palace Street. Age 42 years
1854	June	26	Charlotte Julian Bennett, of the Precincts. Age 71 years
1854	November	6	Maria Charlotte Hart, of Canterbury. Age 78 years
1854	November	18	John Hume Spry, D.D., of the Precincts, Canon of this Cathedral. Age 77 years
1855	February	6	Charles Rouch, of the Precincts. Age 27 years

Burials ceased for all but privileged persons.

Year.	Month.	Day.	Names.
1874	July	16	Elizabeth Gipps, of 11 Chester Street, Grosvenor Place, London. Age 77 years.

Since the printing of the Christenings, the following entries have been made in the Register:—

CHRISTENINGS.

Year.	Month.	Day.	Names. Residence and Profession of Father.
1878	August	27	Agatha, Daughter of James & Georgiana Mangan, of St Mildred's Rectory, Canterbury, Clerk in Holy Orders
1878	September	18	Mabel Lilian, Daughter of John & Ann Elisabeth Hartley, of the Ville of the Archbishop's Palace, Poulterer & Fishmonger
1878	September	29	Margaret Roper, Daughter of Allen Page & Eliza Harriet Moor, of St Clement's, Truro, Clerk

INDEX OF NAMES.

C.

D.

E.

H.

K

M

O.

P.

Q.

R.

S.

T.

U.

V.

Y.

ERRATA.

Page 38.	1788	November	13	For "Anna," read "Ann."
,, 38.	1790	January	1	For "Henry, son of Henry Humphry Sandys," read "Henry, son of Edwin Humphry Sandys."
,, 43.	1808	December	11	For "Pursey," read "Pursey."
,, 51.	1861	December	6	For "December 6," read "December 26."
,, 52.	1870	June	24	For "Forward," read "Forwood."
,, 53.	1872	June	7	For "Hannan" read "Hannah."

Mitchell and Hughes, Printers, 24 Wardour Street, W.